First published in Great Britain in 1998 by Virgin Books
an imprint of Virgin Publishing Ltd.
332 Ladbroke Grove
London W10 5AH

A catalogue record for this book is available from the British Library.

ISBN 0 7535 0260 7

Printed and bound by Jarrold Book Printing Ltd., Norfolk

Credit: Spectrum and Boy's Own flyers designed by Dave Little, Shoom flyer by Steve Reid

Once in a
lifetime

The **Crazy Days** of **Acid House** and **Afterwards**

Jane Bussmann

'Something's happening, Reg! Something's finally happening!'
Monty Python's Life of Brian

Virgin

PARADISE
PRODUCTIONS

'The key, the secret to the whole thing, is fun. People have never had so much fun.'
Paul Oakenfold, **NME,** *1988*

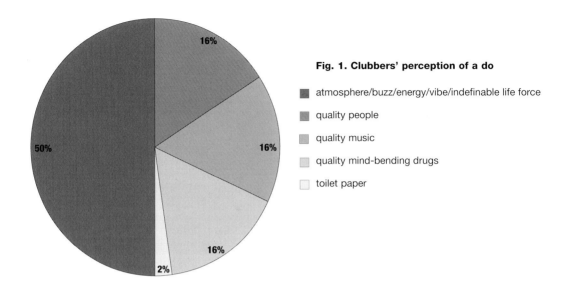

Fig. 1. Clubbers' perception of a do

- atmosphere/buzz/energy/vibe/indefinable life force
- quality people
- quality music
- quality mind-bending drugs
- toilet paper

16%

16%

50%

16%

2%

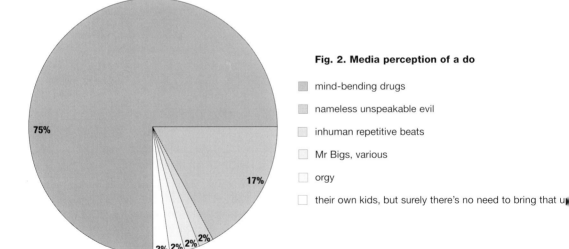

Fig. 2. Media perception of a do

- mind-bending drugs
- nameless unspeakable evil
- inhuman repetitive beats
- Mr Bigs, various
- orgy
- their own kids, but surely there's no need to bring that up

75%

17%

2% 2% 2% 2%

Prologue
IT'S 1987 AND I WISH I WAS DEAD

Before the eighties, if a British teenager woke up in the doorway of Woolworth's it was the result of a heroic night on the sauce. The speed with which society came crashing round our ears in the eighties was dizzying; health care, education and the North of England were seen as the result of some perverted trend that the government was trying to wipe out. School careers advisers simply showed you a picture of a supermarket and laughed. These days the nuclear threat is a quaint faded sticker on old camper vans. In the eighties most of us were scared witless by *Threads* and *When The Wind Blows*, the government was stocking up on nuclear weapons like they were Buy Two Get Three at Superdrug and people thought we could go up any minute. Resistance was futile, and often pathetic. Katherine Hamnett went to meet Mrs Thatcher in a T-shirt saying 58% DON'T WANT PERSHING. 'I think you're in the wrong party, dear,' said Mrs Thatcher witheringly, 'we have Cruise, not Pershing.' How could Katherine Hamnett answer back? She hadn't brought a change of clothes.

The 'happening' London scene consisted of ten people dressed like the Bisto Kids standing in the Wag Club pretending they liked James Brown. Meanwhile, the rest of the South-East was sponging Slimfast off its shellsuit and wondering when someone was going to invent car-boot sales so that it could get rid of the four thousand Ronco Rollermeasures it had been conned into buying in the seventies. In Scotland, pubs served draught heroin and the rest of the country spent its days picking soot out of its mullet haircut. There was no scene, only style. Style meant sports cars, bachelor flats and cocaine: single-seater cars, single-seater flats, single-seater drugs. Nearly fifty years after World War II, sixteen-year-olds were buying Brylcreem. Something had to give.

'I opened the doors and I couldn't believe it. There were hundreds of people out there. It was like everything was ready to go. From the off the vibe was out there: it was a matter of just lighting a match. Everyone was waiting for something, it was like putting a light to a tinder.'
Lu Vukovic, co-founder, RIP club at Clink Street

DISCLAIMER
All dates, locations, fashions, medical and musical information
contained within this book are 8% to 80% inaccurate.

January
Margaret Thatcher becomes the longest-serving PM this century.
February
Lesbians abseil into the chamber of the House of Commons to protest at the anti-gay Clause 28 of the Local Finance Bill.
March
MP Ron Brown picks up the mace and throws it on to the ground after a sitting on the Community Charge Bill; he is suspended.
May
The Wag Club makes an Easter Sunday trip to Amsterdam.
The Face reports people 'dancing to acid house when it wasn't even on the turntable'.
June
Salman Rushdie is condemned to death by the Ayatollah Khomeini, who is then killed by old age and shame in the same month.
July
The Piper Alpha oil rig in the North Sea explodes, killing 167 men.
September
i-D predicts Latin as the dancefloor theme of the next summer.
Liverpool fans have a new terrace chant: ACIEEED!
October
The *Sun*'s Bizarre column advertises 'a groovy and cool acid house T-shirt for £5.50'.
Shadow chancellor John Smith survives a heart attack.
Liverpool player Jan Molby is jailed for three months for reckless driving, inspiring the terrace chant: 'He's fat, he's round, his car is in the pound, Jan Molby.'
November
Titchy sports minister Colin Moynihan announces that ID cards will be compulsory for football spectators in England and Wales from 1990.
21-year-old Janet Mayes dies after taking two tablets of ecstasy at a disco in the Jolly Boatman pub in Hampton Court, Surrey. The Mecca entertainment group ban acid house discos from their forty nightclubs.
Ex-boxer and ex-con Pat McCann, 37, is named by the *Sun* as the Mr Big of acid parties, employing teenage 'runner-boys' to guide fans to parties and setting aside special rooms for drug dealing. McCann phoned the *Sun* to threaten their reporter, saying, 'If he comes to my house, I'll hurt him, I'll hurt him real bad. If he comes mob-handed, he'll still be seen to.'
The *Sun* begins its Say No To Drugs campaign with a special badge. 'It's bright yellow (like the smiley badge) but with a frown and a sad mouth,' the *Sun* says.
The stars come out against drugs. Freddie Starr, Lofty from *EastEnders*, Mark Moore, Tim Westwood, Jimmy Saville, talking-testicle Dave Stewart, Frank Bruno, Boy George, Bros, Philip Schofield, Keren from Bananarama and Lulu all warn against taking drugs. Fuck me – if that didn't put a stop to it, what could?
And the *Sun* withdrew its acid house T-shirt offer. Garry Bushell said, 'Sadly, events have tarnished acid house's reputation. We detest the drugs on the fringes of this scene.'
The *Sun* reports that *EastEnders*' Ian Beale, wearing a smiley T-shirt, bandana and flared jeans, is to try to jump off a bridge after taking acid. He is saved by an old woman with a dog.
Midweek free magazine runs an unfunny piece by The Men Who Know about ecstasy. 'Makes you buy Grolsch lager,' they claim. No it doesn't.
December
'If my mum could see me now, she'd have a fit. I'm wasted!' says seventeen-year-old Asha, who had gone to Amsterdam for a 'three-day drugs binge'.
In 'Dodgy Roger The Acid House King', the *People* exposes Roger Goodman as the evil drug baron behind the acid house craze. 'This man is an utter menace,' storms the *People*, poshly.
As BSE turns cows' brains to soup, their unsteady weaving and bopping is blamed on acid house.
A Pan Am jumbo jet is blown up by a terrorist bomb and crashes into the Scottish town of Lockerbie. 276 people die, including seventeen in the town itself.

Chapter One
1988: FOR FUCK'S SAKE DON'T TELL ANYONE ABOUT THIS

'I wouldn't do it again but I don't regret it. Not at all.'
'Maybe it's just me, but no one I know has regrets.'
'Regret it? I'd do it again tomorrow. Now, in fact.'

What could have inspired such fierce loyalty?

THE BEGINNING OF ACID HOUSE

Call it the second psychedelic awakening or just some excellent drugs, one thing was clear to everybody: when the door to this new phenomenon opened, something extraordinary happened.

'I just think we were a nation thoroughly pissed off, let down. We were told we would go to college and that there'd be this wonderful life for us, and it wasn't happening. Acid house was a chance to make it happen for ourselves – this was how we could make our futures. Our clubs were support groups, a society. A lot of people's hopes were in it – a job, a life – and we were writing it as we went along.'
Nicky Trax, co-founder, Confusion club

Unbeknown to the general public, by the end of 1987 there were some young Britons who had made the getaway and were about to take the rest of us with them.

Question 1. Acid house: who started it?

a)

Radio One's 'Woo' Gary Davies

b)

*Paul Oakenfold, DJ,
early Ibiza dance pioneer*

c)

*Osho,
formerly Bhagwan Shree Rajneesh*

Answer: Contrary to his own theories, it wasn't Gary Davies.

Since the sixties, followers of the late Guru Osho, formerly the Bhagwan Shree Rajneesh – yes, *that* Bhagwan Shree Rajneesh – had had a base on Ibiza where he advocated the use of ecstasy for social understanding, personal development and dancing a lot. The followers, or Sanjasin, were trance dancing and practising free-love culture decades before it made that most unexpected transition to the bleak British inner cities. Clubbers were impressed by what they saw.

This is what happened next …

THE ORIGINAL IBIZA TRIPS

Ibiza has always been a party island. Legends include the Roman army tradition of rewarding soldiers who'd done well in battle by packing them off to Ibiza with a galleyful of women and wine for a fortnight – the original Club 18–30 fortnight. There is a rock off the coast of Ibiza that is supposed to have been where the sirens tried to lure Ulysses. Freddie Mercury's parties on Ibiza are where the rumours about goldfish bowls full of cocaine started. In the sixties the jet set moored their yachts there and some earnest hedonism began. By the eighties it was attracting a very high calibre of punter: Roman Polanski, Jack Nicholson, Aristotle Onassis. They were joined by the most influential ex-pats in the history of the island: a gang of teenage British scally thieves.

IBIZA FACTS AND FICTIONS

Wham's 'Club Tropicana' was filmed at Pykes Hotel.
Spandau Ballet, Sade, and Animal Nightlife were regulars.

'My brother has a photo of [AN EXTREMELY FAMOUS EIGHTIES POP STAR] being carried out of Amnesia very much the worse for wear, dribbling. A lot of very famous people used to go there to get off their heads without being seen. [EVEN MORE INSANELY FAMOUS SINGER] was running round there off her head on E. My friend sat in her limo.'
Boy George, cultural icon, DJ

'In Ku, you'd see men with cow-print fur chaps with no pants – they'd turn round and they'd be about forty.'
Phil Perry, DJ

'Me and my cousin went to Freddie Mercury's birthday party. There were platters of cocaine on the tables – everyone was helping themselves. I, of course, took a pocketful …'
Trevor Fung, DJ

There were now two distinct types of British tourist in Ibiza: the sun, sea and sangria foot soldiers; and the sun, sea and vast quantities of mind-expanding class As space cadets.

18–30S: A DISGRACEFUL AFFAIR

'The level of humour among these package-tour teds is appallingly low, with their trump card being when the fattest slob in the party drops his kecks … The knobs even walk around the airport with only a pair of shorts and sandals on, mistaking the bright airport lights for the currant bun …'
The End, *Liverpool fanzine*

While the 18–30s drank Heineken out of each other's front bottoms, a far more revitalising holiday was being had behind their backs but they never found out. Firstly, Ku and Amnesia were out of the way and, if you weren't looking for them, you were unlikely to reach them in your two-week break. Secondly, in 1987 it was ecstasy that was refreshing Ku and Amnesia, the places beer drinkers couldn't reach. Even if you did find these clubs, for the cost of one night in Ku you could enjoy fourteen days of out-of-date Heineken and banana-boat action. This is still the case, but young Britons have made some enlightened lifestyle choices. An influential club promoter from the South was about to join them.

In summer 87 the suave, venturesome Ian St Paul and his cousin DJ Trevor Fung landed on the island. Ian took over a bar, called it the Project Bar after his own club night in South London, and the adventure had begun.

'I was sorted: I had the bar, a jeep, money, I had Trevor DJing and by the time the end of July came I had hooked up with the main dudes. They were young, they were scallies from places like Sheffield and Manchester, and they were going round Europe on Interrail cards robbing. We called them the Boccy Boys, because they used to sit outside the Café Del Mar living off bocadillo sandwiches because they had no money. Bocadillos cost 400 pesetas at the Café Del Mar, so they'd buy them at the supermarket round the corner for 200 and eat them at the café and really piss off the café owner.

'I gave up the bar and started hanging out with these scallywags. It was very exciting – they were only nineteen, twenty, twenty-one. I found myself driving my jeep as their getaway car while they were robbing hotel safes and petrol stations. They never got caught; they were professionals.'
Ian St Paul

EXCURSIONS ABROAD

I was walking around town the other day
When I saw three scallies walking my way
Training shoes and neat combed hair,
Schoolies follow them everywhere.
As they walked past, I heard them say
That 'Soon they would be going away'
Germany and Switzerland too,
There's lots of things to rob and do ...
Poem in Liverpool fanzine The End

But life was considerably more than burglary and sandwiches. Their minds were about to be permanently expanded.

'We instigated acid house. This was the starting point. The first time me and Trevor took ecstasy we didn't know what to expect; the Project Bar had a spiral staircase, and our legs were going in different directions. The whole day became about going to Amnesia. Life was getting up at night, stealing a few things to eat from the local supermarket, wheeling and dealing and going to the club. I'll always remember sitting in the jeep as we were driving along that road to Amnesia – you'd come over the hill and it would be "Yeah! I can see it!". You couldn't relax until you had that first pill in your mouth. Everyone had their own spot that they danced in ... If someone danced in your spot you weren't comfortable till you could push them back out again.

'Alfredo played European pop dance, anything from Cyndi Lauper to Michael Jackson. After Amnesia, we'd go on to Glory's, which was open till lunchtime, playing hard Belgian New Beat. Then, in August 87, Nicky Holloway turned up with everyone else for Oakenfold's birthday ... It wasn't just the English clubbing over there, I met some wicked Spanish people that summer. Little Gaultier gays from Valencia and Madrid, bringing over mescalin capsules – we was flying off our heads on those ones. Then in August Paul came over for his birthday. He brought Nicky Holloway ...'
Ian St Paul

'... and Danny Rampling and Johnny Walker. I hired a villa for my birthday and we all flew out. It was completely different to anything I'd seen in London: the mix of people, the freedom of expression, the mix of music. What Alfredo was doing was changing all our attitudes. We thought, Yes, I'll have some of that!'
Paul Oakenfold

'At Amnesia all the top ICF faces were on the dancefloor with a load of trans-vestites and gay people. I thought, This is fucking strange. I saw a guy called Nino, an old guy with the beard who looked like Poppa Smurf, dancing away to "I Still Haven't Found What I'm Looking For" by U2. It was like your granddad was on the dancefloor and all I could think was, Yeaahh.'
Nicky Holloway

Popular opinion has it that the British ruined Ibiza, but in the beginning Ian's new scally acquaintances were a positive blessing. On the floors of Ku and Amnesia the Spanish might have done some dancing, the Italians had rhythm and the French occasionally twitched if they heard music, but only the British were going mental. The club owners started laying on the odd freebie to hang on to their new British cheerleaders for the Ibizan experience. That was just as well because, unlike most dropouts, their money didn't come from trust funds and the more money they needed, the more they were likely to steal anything they could stuff down their baggy trousers.

By the end of the summer the damage was done: these young innocents had been infected with a sick lust for drug-fuelled dance orgies. Coming home, they went straight into withdrawal.

STARTING THE CLUB FUTURE

'In November 87 we came back to London. It was awful; we couldn't give up what had started in Ibiza. Three weeks went by and everyone's dying for a party. I didn't know what to do, so I called Paul Oakenfold – meanwhile he's buying up every record that was played in Amnesia. He's already got more than Alfredo. Paul's found his niche and he's ready.'
Ian St Paul (left)

Paul had contacts at one of London's oldest and best nightclubs, Heaven. Heaven was perfect: bang in the middle of town, down a tantalising back alley, with staggering special effects – and completely unaffordable. In a matter of months Ian and Paul would take over Heaven with Spectrum, the best night in its history, but in the meantime they made do with the Sound Shaft, the little disco joined to the back of the bigger club, theirs on a Thursday night for £300. Everybody was ready. All they had to do was light the touchpaper …

'On the first night Future didn't even have its own entrance. Security would have been an extra hundred quid, so instead we had everyone meet outside Heaven itself. We collected their fivers off them and then all of us, the whole hundred people and the DJs with their record boxes, walked through Heaven through all these other clubbers, through the connecting door into the Sound Shaft. We couldn't wait; we ran in, put the music on as fast as we could and, by the time the management of Heaven came down to check on us, people were standing on the speakers, hanging off the walls, climbing up every available surface. They couldn't be high enough. The management couldn't believe their eyes.'
Ian St Paul

Meanwhile, Danny Rampling was setting up his own version of the Ibiza experience, Shoom in south-east London, and Paul Oakenfold had bigger plans for the Project.

'The Project was open from ten till two. One night we flew in Alfredo from Ibiza to play an after-hours party from two till six. I invited down *Boy's Own* from the Wag Club. They turned up in their big floppy rare-groove hats, and I said, "No, no, no: that's not it any more…"'
Paul Oakenfold

Britain was about to have its eyes opened for ever.

WHY BRITAIN GAVE UP THE DAY JOB

'It's as if music is translating our lives, rewriting our genes'
Louise Gray, The Observer

Something was happening.

'If you walked into the club three or four hours after it opened you'd actually feel something going on. You'd literally feel the energy coming off people. You'd sense it. I used to wonder what that would look like if you had extrasensory perception. There were people who didn't take drugs who definitely got off on the buzz. That third party; an incredible energy coming from people. You felt if it was harnessed it would go through a brick wall.'
Kym Kennedy, market trader

Something was happening: something with a life of its own. Suddenly you could go out and have a private revolution in your head while a public revolution was going on among hundreds of others. Acid House gave a new perspective, a perspective that made nine-to-five jobs look very unimportant indeed. The result of this new optimism was low-level anarchy; people jacking in mundane jobs to do their own thing.

Danny Rampling was a painter and decorator, Terry Farley was a gas fitter, John Kelly worked in a foundry and Shaun Ryder was a thief. Before acid house, self-expression was for art students from St Martin's. Now you'd see fifteen-stone roofers walking down the street in multicoloured ponchos, electricians voguing in the middle of fields. Something was happening and it gave people huge motivation. Grand beliefs poked their heads out like daffodil shoots. Everyone felt a wave of confidence: you could design T-shirts, make clothes, set up a shop to sell them ('and it could have a café with someone playing records and we could do parties in it and …'). Everyone who had harboured a secret talent could get it out via this thing.

'It was an interesting time. It seemed there were lots of people wanting to do things, making things, reading you things they'd written …'
Kym Kennedy

'Nobody laughed if you said you were going to make a record – they encouraged you.'
Martyn Passey

'Charlie Chester dragged me up on the club stage to sing "Promised Land" a cappella – and there was a totally epiphanous moment where the crowd went from wondering, "Who is this crank just standing there?" to having me bring them right up. A bit of ego therapy! Afterwards people came up to me with that childlike wonder you used to get, that celebratory thing.'
Ben McKnight

Handmade Shoom necklaces, hand-printed op-art T-shirts, hand-drawn fanzines – if you could make it, someone would buy it. Acid house expressionism might have spawned some astonishing crap, but it beat working in an office.

'People used to get out of bed, drive down to Charing Cross just to stand outside Spectrum at two or three in the morning to get some flyers and see what was going on.'
Anon

Chill out room at Spectrum, 1988: Danny Rampling (centre)

THE SECOND SUMMER OF LOVE – BETTER THAN THE FIRST?

John Hopkins (Hoppy) was at the forefront of the British sixties psychedelic movement. He opened the legendary London club UFO, after a couple of parties he'd put on featuring the then-unknown Pink Floyd 'went rather well'.

'In those days it was a very alternative thing. People used to say things to you like "Rock music makes men and women infertile". The scene nowadays has considerably more freedom. I love it! The people are so nice! [John's Tottenham Court Road club was the prototype acid house party, although with slower bpm.] We started having lightshows, coloured oils mixing together and projected on to the walls. We had the first fluorescent artwork. Because it was in the West End and it went on all night, people used to just drop by. The Beatles and Jimi Hendrix used to come. It was more of a happening than a nightclub, in the sense that anything could happen.'

Was acid house the second Age of Aquarius? Or simply a pleasant way to systematically fight the world MDMA surplus? Opinion was divided …

1. The hardcore-hippie angle
The venerable psychedelic journal, *Encyclopaedia Psychedelica,* made a significant discovery in its winter 1988 edition:
'The sudden popularity this summer of acid house music marks the historical beginning of the Second Psychedelic Wave. Our predictions that this will be a hundred times bigger and more "successful" than the first wave are born out by the fact that a "secret" underground movement has been joined by a million new young fanatics in just three months … DANCE TILL YOUR SOUL SPLATTERS ALL OVER THE FLOOR. THEN DANCE ON THAT.'

2. The hard-man angle
'Just pills an' a laugh, innit. [Pause] I love you.'

LIFESTYLE

FUN

'People would literally jump and scream. You could almost see the relief on people's faces. This is where I have one strong visual memory from some place in Battersea; they had this raised platform in the middle of the floor with people sitting up on it, and all of a sudden people started skipping round it. Grown men spontaneously holding hands and skipping, almost morris dancing. I mean, girls, fair enough, they can do what they like – but grown men, skipping in circles! Hooligans with bells on!'
Anonymous 'committed raver'

In 1988, 'fun' meant yuppie pursuits like skiing and wife-swapping. Fun had to have a purpose, usually sexual or sporting. Having fun for its own sake was perverted. If simply pratting about on your own was social deviance, it was incomprehensible to the authorities that people could break into a warehouse for the sole purpose of having a good time. There had to be something behind it, and that something was usually A Nameless Unspeakable Evil.

Apart from huge quantities of mood-altering drugs, what could have caused this spontaneous outbreak of fun? The music: cool and silly at the same time, acid house was fun because it was full of ridiculous noises like giggling, squelching and bleeps – records like Bam Bam's 'Give It To Me' were mischief anthems for cartoon baddies. Feeling like a baddie was the best part of it. Suddenly everyone was breaking the law in a variety of new ways. A lot of the venues were illegal; during the First World War, the government introduced licensing laws to prevent people taking their minds off carving up the enemy and 'forgot' to repeal the new laws when the war was over, rather like the 'temporary' VAT on fuel. Seventy years later, to hold an all-night party you usually had to break the law. And people preferred illegal venues. The mission was to take over disused, secret addresses where you could create your own private anarchy, to take this *thing* rampaging across London.

«LOVE»

Love at The Wag. Friday night in Soho: people 'turning up in carpet slippers'

'People were very anti-club – people would go and break the toilets just to flood the club. Venues would change all the time. At Clink Street it would be a different room every time.'
Nicky Trax

And all sorts of people – many of them social pillars – were finding themselves outlaws. People felt awake. You could change your life, change your crowd, get to know almost anyone you liked. You were no longer on a treadmill; suddenly your options were thrown wide open. You were travelling to places you'd never have stumbled across. You were forming friendships with the kind of people who'd never have spoken to you before.

'I used to love driving around at about four or five in the mornings. Everything was very peaceful, very still. The streetlights would be on and everything would be quite bright – the colours would be sharper. It was very mellow – you'd drive with the windows open. You're more tactile, your senses are more alive – you'd really feel a cool breeze on your skin. It was quite an incredible feeling.'
Kym Kennedy

'It was beautiful. I was young and not very sure of myself but acid house meant I could go up and talk to anybody. The blokes didn't look at you like "Who the fuck's this cunt?" and the girls didn't look like they was worried that you was going to chat them up. There was some huge big guy, really rough looking. I crashed into him and knocked him over. I was like "Oh shit!". I was waiting to get beaten up. But he's grabbing my arm and saying, "It's fine, mate," like I'd done him some kind of favour! One night after Spectrum we walked all the way home from Charing Cross to West London through Hyde Park, saying, "It can't be no good for you, but it's fucking great!" It did seem very pure and right.'
    Chris, who was not a hippie but a strapping great geezer working a fruit and veg stall

'You'd find yourself with totally different groups all the time. You'd spend the whole weekend with people you'd only just met. One of the blokes I'd started going round with at Legends said to me, "Can I tell you something?" I said of course, and he said, "Sometimes when I'm on E I put on my girlfriend's tights and wank myself off with a bottle of amyl under my nose." That was the point when I realised I had no idea about half the people I was mixing with.'
    Janet

MFI at Legends. Earliest recorded incident of the phrase Mad For It. Spike and Neville and Judge Jules in London's fabulous Mayfair

If you sat down for more than five minutes by a dancefloor in 1988 you would hear one of the following:

It's brilliant in here, isn't it?

I can really talk to you.

I had a terrible childhood.

Are you on one?

Sorry, I thought you were a chair.

WE ARE FAMILY

One phenomenon that happened spontaneously was the acid house family. It was the same story up and down the country: everyone had a new family which was often better value than the old one, and certainly more affectionate.

'The one thing people loved about Solaris was that they really felt part of a family – they had their membership card, they knew everyone, they were the Solaris family. It really mattered to them. Eight years later I met a man who said he knew me but he couldn't remember where from. When we finally realised it was Solaris he was amazed. He really perked up, saying, "Thank you! Thank you! It was such a major part of my life!"'
Ian Pendleton, Solaris

'We got T-shirts made saying Belfast Posse. It sounds naff but at the time it was natural. We even went on holiday together because we couldn't bear to be parted – a group of forty people all off to Greece.'
Mandy Cavanagh, Sugar Sweet

'At Confusion people would arrive early just to talk to each other. People would come to Confusion with facepaints and go round painting everybody. Everybody wanted to give something to the scene. There were other people that would bring sweets. All sorts of stuff were being shared.'
Nicky Trax, Confusion

SECRET

'House music had been around for a while, but it hadn't really broken. I remember asking a DJ, "What's happened to this house thing?" and he said, "Oh, it's nearly died out. It's only on at this one little club …"'
Leigh Marling, Blue Source

Why had nobody rumbled this? Because the only signs were some people wearing unusually bright colours and unusually big smiles at unusual times of day. Once you'd tried it, you were part of a secret, an underground thing that made the uncool people hip and the cool hopelessly dated. The class weirdo would pop up at a rave. You'd see one person from your area who was into it and suddenly you had a major bond with that person:

'It was like a magnet: if you heard house music or you saw someone who looked like they were into it, you'd naturally go over to them. In those days you could tell if someone was into house: they had an air about them. You might even go over and talk to someone because they were wearing a brightly coloured T-shirt.'
Nicky Trax

'All those people who had spent all those years grooming their career at *The Face* were surplus to requirements, out on their ear, in favour of some scally football-hooligan types that had good drugs and knew where to get cool records. You could sit down and have a chat with people who were your heroes.

Every weekend was a journey. Every weekend had a different shape. You split up into different groups and reunited like a blob of mercury. More importantly, it was a journey inside your skull that could take you to entirely undiscovered parts of your personality.

TOP THREE WORST WAYS TO GET HOME FROM A DO

1. On the train

Big mistake. You've spent your last cab money on a pill that's turned into white pulp in your pocket lining. You think you're holding it together in front of the office people, despite that moody woman opposite, when you suddenly realise you're at the end of the line, the train's empty and you've been pumping your arm to imaginary music with your eyes shut.

2. With those mad people you met on the podium

They're great fun on the dancefloor, their catch phrase is 'you wanna meet my mate' (beware: this is not a question), and your mates have all fucked off. Nothing else for it you are going to have to get a lift with the Mad People. First you find out they haven't got a car at all: they've got an old Escort van between the six of them. Then you find the back of the van is a lake of oil and it's ruined your jacket. Lastly, you're wedged up on the lap of a brickie on his first E who gets just a bit *too* matey.

'Aw, you're smashin, you are.'

'Cheers.'

'No, you're really smashing. Gis a kiss.'

The oil never comes out. The brickie does.

3 With the bloke you had a really deep conversation with

You say you can't believe you've told each other so much. Two hours later the pills have worn off and you *really* can't believe it.

'They'd just introduced Hoppa buses and I noticed that the destinations all had a letter E after them. I thought it was a London Transport employee in the know.'
Anon

Six months before they'd have been behind the velvet rope in the VIP room. The first time I met Martin Fry from ABC – I loved ABC – there he was trancing out at Shoom.'
Steve Hall

'The only thing that it was similar to was the early days of punk. I saw the Sex Pistols and followed Adam Ant and nothing ever lived up to it. Then, with the house scene, I felt that energy again: *this is now.* And I knew from being in the punk scene how special that feeling is and how rare, how it only happens every ten to fifteen years. When punk happened we all thought it would go on for ever, so now I knew house wouldn't last for ever, you had to just experience it and *fuck* everything else. House was healthier than punk because punk was very destructive. Enjoyable, but destructive. House gave you this wild optimism. I never felt comfortable in the eighties. I was in a council flat and all my friends were getting mortgages. That's why there was this insane optimism – because there was this feeling that it was really going to change things.'

Fiona Cartledge (above right) who, in 1988, gave up her job at the BBC to do this

BRITS JUST WANT TO GO MENTAL
On the sly, the British are the most hedonistic race of all.

'1976: When Joey [Ramone] came back, you could see in his eyes that something had happened. Joey kept saying, "Legs, you wouldn't believe it! You wouldn't believe it! They love it!"'
Legs McNeil in Please Kill Me: An Oral History of Punk

'I couldn't believe it. They were jackin' the house like I'd never seen before. I was shocked … The clubs have died back home.'
Kevin Saunderson in Sky *magazine, 1988*

No one loves it like the British. Just as the Ramones were staggered at what the UK had done with their very minor art-movement punk, so Inner City's Kevin Saunderson was knocked sideways by the reaction to house. The national craving for hedonism took a minority music, developed it into an entire lifestyle and sold it back to America.

'I went to Nevada on a shoot. Out in the middle of a desert we went to this little student café and there were all these eighteen year olds in dungarees with little teddy bears and all the accoutrements like we used to wear at Shoom, and it's mad to think it all came from those few little clubs.'
Leigh Marling

Des Penny, band manager, was a young blade from the notorious Regents Park council estate. After a few seminal weeks at Spectrum, he saw a striking change:

'The next summer I went back to Tenerife and whereas at Christmas it had been narky – no one wanted to talk to you – this time you met *everybody.* And it weren't "This is Des: he's from Camden, he supports Tottenham". It was "This is Des: he's from Spectrum and Future", "This is so and so: he's from Shoom". And they were proud of which club they came from the way they used to be proud of their football team. Punk was too busy trying to make a statement, be political. That was the beauty of acid house: it just got on with it.'

'I remember acid house started in a bar in Manchester called Stuffed Olives. It went from funky hip-hop to house. It was definitely noticeable that people were on ecstasy. People of great notoriety like Bez and Shaun Ryder were there dancing around off their heads in a virtually empty club.'
Gary Maclarnan, Potential Development

'My first clubbing experiences were at the Hacienda. I was living in North Wales and I'd been a couple of times around the "Jack" time … I went back a few months later and it was full-on smiley T-shirts and trance dancing. That was what got me into it. The first six months I went completely drug free and alcohol free and I just totally got off on the vibe.'
Sasha, DJ

FASHION

HONEST, THEY'RE WEARING SHORTS IN THERE

'In 1988 the dress code went to the toilet.'
Nicky Trax

Unlike punk and New Romantic, the acid house look didn't come from copying pop stars. Bizarrely, while Britain was stripped down to its sopping jeans and T-shirt, the people making the records were dressed up to the nines in leather jackets with shoulder pads, sculpted hair and lace, looking like *Battlestar Galactica*'s gay infantry. Imagine Michael Jackson in 'Billy Jean'. Like that, only worse. And, as for the European musicians making Balearic anthems, we all know what continental pop stars look like: they look like Spandau Ballet *thought* they looked. The acid house look came from Ibiza, as legend has it, but even that wasn't purely a fashion thing.

'The fashion (so called) that has already made its presence felt in London of baggy clothes and hippie insignia was really forced on the "refugee" due to heat, lack of money *and* lack of clothes.'
Balearic Beats FFRR press release, 1988

The phone lines to Ibiza were pretty primitive so a lot of people got their bright new Chevignon wardrobe with stolen credit cards. The acid house look couldn't have been cooked up in Britain: the country is fundamentally too cold. While urban trendies were buttoning up their sterile black and white suits and the rest of Britain was laminating its feather cut with hairspray to stop heat escaping through the top of their heads, that handful of ex-pats arrived home, still wearing their holiday clothes.

In 1988 baggy jeans and psychedelic T-shirts were as resolutely anti-fashion as tight jeans and slashed T-shirts were in 1976. What was the opposite of an urban trendy? A rural peasant. Spurning the Gaultier, the cognoscenti could be spotted in straw farmer's-boy hats and Mexican peasant ponchos. What was the opposite of cold, dressed-up fashion? Beachwear. In 1988 it seemed like everybody was going acid surfing. Surfwear is the original trendy-dropout kit: Gotcha, Quicksilver, Hot Tuna and, later, Stussy summed up a lot of people's new permanent holiday vibe. Then there was the ethnic wave: rich textured skullcaps, Peruvian woolly hats with ear flaps. Big warm Aran jumpers with spliff burns in the cuffs nobbed the stark, 'Dallasty' designer look right off. You might have looked like Banjo Boy off *Deliverance*, but you knew exactly what you were doing. Terry Farley makes an important point:

'Now you can go down your high street and buy an outfit for a club. In those days you had to make an effort to get the gear. I hear people say that it didn't matter what you wore in those days – that's absolute bollocks. You might have been wearing dungarees, but it had to be the right dungarees, and you knew what they were.'

BEGINNINGS OF ODDBALL

Acid house was accused of breeding a nation of fashion sheep but, if the merchandise in clubwear shops like World in London was anything to go by, acid house was far more the age of the individual than the yuppie era. World was a small shop run by Michael and Gerlinda Costa – the people behind Kinky Gerlinky – who used to turn up at Shoom in full Tibetan national dress.

I HEARD THE ROZZERS ARE USING 2CVS NOW: BEING FOLLOWED

You knew acid house was well and truly out of your system when you no longer got that twitchy cold feeling if the car behind wouldn't overtake. Even if prior to 1988 the most illegal thing you'd ever done was wear a batwing sweater, suddenly you were very much on the wrong side of the law.

Five points to remember when you think you're being followed:

1. You're not
2. Well, you might be
3. If it's a blue Vauxhall containing two men in brand-new sportswear, this ups the chances
4. But it probably isn't
5. Do not, repeat, do *not* pull over, get out the car, hand over all your drugs and collapse sobbing unless you actually *are* pulled

KICKERS

'Kickers were these big square-fronted things with a thick sole which you could get in all these mad colours. They came with this little leather tag in the shape of a tree and we used to rip the tags off loads of different pairs and wear them all down the side of one shoe. That was a South London hardcore thing.'
Oz

ACCESSORIES

Strawberry smoke, no relation to strawberries
Strobes. Wow! Slow motion!
Light-up yo-yos
Clockwork Orange noses (Andy Weatherall)
Kush balls: fluorescent balls with rubber tendrils
Teddy bears
Five-inch-long mouth ulcer running round your gums

LONG-SLEEVED T-SHIRTS

To this day no one's invented something as perfect for dancing in as the white long-sleeved T-shirt. Long sleeves to pull down over your hands overcome initial embarrassment at foolish dancefloor cavorting; white cuffs will not expose scummy bits-o'-spit collection; delightful yards of cotton billow in the fan and absorb gallons. Plus, stupid patterns on the front were good for visuals.

Lofty with tambourine

DUNGAREES

It was a truly liberating sensation to be strolling around the town's hippest nightspots in a vast denim balloon looking like a cross between Babapapa and a dancing Schmoo.
'In our lot, if you were a bloke you had to wear them with the top down. The girls bought boys' ones and they were always really long. I remember going to the secondhand store and suddenly, where it had been full of dungarees, there were only about four pairs left, the shit ones that were cut off at the bottom.'
Jayne

BANDANAS

These cannot be easily explained. We were pirates.

BLOKES WITH BOBS

The coveted acid house hair: the been-in-it-for-years bob. Wildly attractive to women of all ages. Not feminine at all and much missed. Any longer and you look like you fancy yourself; any shorter and you've probably just done your first E. But at that certain length … Reach out and touch somebody's hair.
'I remember when I went out the second time I desperately scraped all my hair into this pathetic, tiny little ponytail on top of my head because I was really agitated about having that relaxed look.'
Russell, record-label boss
'Ponytails wherever possible – you'd see huge geezers with little spikes of hair in hairbands coming out at ridiculous angles.'
Committed raver
'Brrr! I copped off with some horrible div on a roof at a party. He had the really long hair, a real Balearic Brian.'
Alison, teacher

Rubber polo shirts, sequined mobcaps … People wanted *new* things, the weirder the better. Glitter shorts, lunatic Andy Pandy suits – if you had the bottle, you went for it.

'Eric Barker who used to dance with 808 State was probably responsible for skullcaps. He would dance on a podium at the Hacienda wearing a cape, a stick, and a skullcap, pretending to be a wizard.'
Gary Maclarnan

NO FASHION AT ALL

For a lot of people, particularly women, it was about stripping fashion, make-up and hairstyles away, bringing it down to just you and the music. With people's lives being reprogrammed left right and centre, a plain white T-shirt and jeans was the way to set your mind free.

'I'd go out with my money and nothing else. Just a pair of track pants and a big jacket.'
Nicky Trax

'I'd been in America where everyone was disgustingly naff and into Guns 'n' Roses, so when I got back I made a real effort to look *au fait*, to show I was still fashionable. I'd only been gone about six weeks but my friends stared at me and said, "Well, you're a bit overdressed." I thought, Overdressed? The cheek. This is a minimalist Katherine Hamnett suit.'
Anon

Richard and Steve at The Hacienda: Blokes with bobs

Bandanas and 'Ponytails wherever possible'

DRUGS

There are a lot of people who shouldn't and don't take drugs. This is a good thing as it means there are more left for the people who do. Drugs are a short cut to a state people simply don't have time to meditate their way to. They are not an ideal short cut as you don't always get what you pay for, and even if you do they are not the health equivalent of a wheatgrass pie. Nonetheless …

ECSTASY: THE FAST-ACTING ANTIDOTE TO BOREDOM

In the seventies, MDMA was used quite legally by thousands of US psychotherapists. Even though it is now illegal, there is still some underground therapeutic use. From 1988 to 1993, the Swiss government allowed some psychotherapists to use MDMA with their clients. It was found – anecdotally – to be effective. Psychotherapists have reported numerous positive effects from MDMA, such as improved mood changes, attitudes and relationships, diminished use of other substances and ability to break through internal 'blocks' and open up on a deeper level. Hence the endless 'I had a terrible childhood' conversations by the cloakrooms.

ECSTASY'S EARLY OUTINGS

'In the mid-eighties a friend of mine went to a party at *[FAMOUS CLUB]* in London. It was £20 to get in and that included an E. She said it was unbelievable: people who normally wouldn't talk to each other were snogging in corners, all night people were disappearing on to the roof to have sex.'
Andy Carroll

'You used to get a leaflet with them saying, "Remember the quality of this experience because you can't do it all the time." Oh, the irony! Personally, I'm allergic to ecstasy.'
Patrick Lilley

'My first ecstasy was in Amsterdam. We went to this café and I ate about five slices of hash cake and was fucked out of my mind. I remember sitting in a toilet in a hotel that seemed like the smallest room I had ever been in. It was actually quite big … I came out squeezing myself through the door. I had to ask people if I was talking to them because I wasn't sure if I was imagining it. Then I did half an ecstasy, so I was being pulled all ways. I wasn't euphoric or rushing and my face wasn't going all over the place; I just felt really happy and positive. The first few times I took ecstasy I wanted to tell everybody. It was a real evangelical drug.'
Justin Robertson

'It wasn't long before we spotted the bright-orange Next carrier bag under the dining table. "I want to marry that bag," I said, and was only half-joking … In the end we decided to make it the centrepiece of a Next shrine in the middle of a Habitat unit …'
Journalist 'Thomas Quincy', Midweek, November 1988

Bar the odd spliff, in 1988 most people had never taken drugs. Got valiantly drunk perhaps when the occasion required it, but not crossed that line. Drugs, as everyone knew, were serious, plunging you into a monochrome world of depravity, friendlessness and greasy hair. But people who'd tried ecstasy were coming back with all the wrong answers: 'I knew what I was doing', 'My teeth didn't fall out or anything', 'It's definitely not addictive' and 'Have you met my 600 new friends?'. Campaigns against drugs overlooked one minor detail: they were great. In the end it was a very eighties philosophy which made people break absolutely every moral code hammered into them – *Just Do It.*

'People like drugs. They're not stupid, they know drugs aren't good for them, but they like them. Ecstasy has actually got *less* harmful in the public consciousness. Nowadays, we know it causes depression. In 1988 we really thought it would give us Parkinson's disease, but *we still did it* because that's what people are like. Having said that, most people don't do it any more because the pills are crap.'
Anon

E didn't seem like a drug. There was no scrabbling around with bits of Rizla, no rubbing down sticky, slimy surfaces to sniff it, and certainly no poking around in your arm with a needle. E was a sneaky little fellow you could knock back in the car on your way into town. It was more of a magic potion, straight out of an *Asterix* book: just swallow and wait for dramatic effects. Boom, you were through the happy door. Ecstasy was a chemical adolescence. You went in one side a sulky product of the eighties and came out the other an unselfconscious, confident communicator.

'Whether you're cynical or whether you're soul-searching, drugs are a path to spiritual experience. People are searching for a spiritual connection. Ecstasy gave you a connection, the same thing as a spiritual connection but it connected you to people. The last time I came across that ambience was in the dance tents of Glastonbury. There was an incredible feeling of connection: there was this really heavy trancy beat and absolutely everybody was moving to it.'
Anon

Taking E had a much deeper effect on most people than making them dance. Gradually, day-to-day existence seemed to be fresh and new. E wiped the mud off everything. Miserable bastards suddenly found they weren't. After years of being stuck with the way their minds worked, overnight people were able to take a step back and re-evaluate their whole personality. You seemed to see things for the first time. You'd see exactly how silly a cartoon face on a bottle of bubble bath is. The fact that he was called Matey was too funny for words. Life was fun again.

'In the bathroom we had a bottle of Matey with a sticker saying GET ON ONE stuck on his hat. That amused us for weeks.'
Anon

'If you look at a young kid, they are very much alive, very much aware. As we grow up these senses, this enjoyment of life gets lost: there's something that dulls it. This drug definitely gave people a sense of what life could be like. I really miss feeling more alive. Not a lot of us get a chance to live that kind of expanded life. Some people never needed to take the drugs; they were totally relaxed people and could tap into the energy.'
Kate

'It was so nice to be that emotional. I remember going and telling my mother, "I really love you."'
Mandy Cavanagh

Apart from the individuals that, like Obelix, seemed to have fallen in the E cauldron when they were a baby, most house fans were buying Es and using their tonsils for target practice. Accidentally nudge a DJ, promoter or clubber in 1988 and they automatically blurted, 'It's got nothing to do with drugs!' Ten years on and no longer facing prosecution, most people admit that they were off their faces at every opportunity. But they are also very clear on one thing: what drugs did was release something that was already in people, lying dormant. In most periods in history we could have grown old and died without ever knowing we had it in us but, by some staggering act of generosity on the part of fate, ecstasy coincided with Great Britain and house.

'It couldn't have been just drugs because there were plenty of people who didn't take it – because it was twenty quid a lot of the time and they couldn't afford it, or because it didn't agree with them – or who used to take it but stopped and carried on going out.'
Sue

GET BACK YOU ACID BASTARD – OUR TEMPERAMENTAL PSYCHEDELIC FRIEND
'We were all running about like lunatics. Stomping round like Mr and Mrs Happy, tripping our tits off. We found a small forest and ended up running through the trees, among swirling volcanoes. You'd say, "Look at that: that tree's winking!" and everyone would look and see the tree winking. We thought it was a magical forest full of fluorescent blobs and fairies. A few days later we went past where we'd been and I realised I'd been

tripping my bollocks off and skipping round a couple of trees in a lay-by. That night we got home and it just didn't fuck off, did it? Phil's got quite a hairy chest and I'm lying there running my fingers through it going, "Animal Man! Animal Man!" I dread to think how long I was doing it: probably about an hour and a half. It was only when Phil said, "Vegetable Man!" that I came to. I could see all these red welts on his chest where I'd been doing it for hours.'
Fiona Crawford

Then there was acid. This heavy-duty cerebral skillet underwent a massive revival for one main reason: at £2–£5, compared to £15–£25, it was cheaper than E. Looking back, now that most people are a little bit better off, it seems alarming that you would regularly put your brains in a blender to save twenty quid. Until house, acid was traditionally pampered with sunny outdoor locations and small groups of friends. One of the reasons some people lost it during acid house was that, unlike the sixties with their analyses of psychedelia, by the eighties people had to look tough. It was harder to admit the messy contents of your head. People doing battle with the massed legions of Saturn's death baboons in an orange peel space suit would just mutter, 'Phew! I went right off on one there.'

'Everyone had a few nights when they wished they were back in bed. I distinctly remember older people saying to me that they couldn't believe that young kids were going to warehouses full of thousands of people they didn't know and doing acid. They wondered if the acid was weaker these days. In their day, the bravest thing they'd do was sit in their living rooms with a Yes album, and even then they'd shit themselves.'
Committed raver from Hertfordshire

'I was one of those people who gravitated towards drugs long before acid house, but you think it through: you do a bit of research, know a few people, check it out. I've got really mixed feelings about the acid house drug thing. I started meeting people who weren't emotionally old enough to cope. I know this really young girl who started taking trips like they were sweets. She started keeping this very mad diary. Her mother found it, realised she'd been taking drugs, and freaked.'
Nicky Trax

However, for the majority who didn't lose it, taking acid was a whole new brain. You could take a step back and understand your personality. Your mind seemed to be working so fast you could catch that moment between noticing something and whatever your normal emotional reaction to it would be. If you were used to feeling depressed by the weather, between your eyes seeing the rain and feeling depressed you'd have the perspective to realise it was just rain. And then feel depressed.

Get back you acid bastard

SPREAD LOVE – WHY GETTING YOUR NAN ON ONE IS A BAD IDEA

'We were completely convinced that, within the year, everybody of every age would be doing E. It was just so fucking good we wanted to get our families on one. At Christmas 88 we seriously worked out how we were going to do it. We bought six mince pies, scooped out the middle, crushed up the Es and put it back inside. We had them ready for Christmas dinner.'
Anon

There are several reasons why getting your nan on one is a bad idea. You want to spread the love. No, you don't. You'll end up sitting on the sofa with your nan cackling knowingly when a dumpy Goth student on *Blockbusters* tells Mr Holness she'll 'have an E, please, Bob'. Do not teach the world to sing. They'll only start singing. And those are just the long-term problems. You don't know this yet, but old people don't say much because their life is a constant battle to keep gallons of saliva *inside* their mouths. Half a pill and the floodgates would open. By the next morning your nan would have gnawed her false teeth down to the pink horseshoe.

'I would like to say that we gave up on the mince-pie experiment for scientific reasons, but in the end we went out on Christmas Eve and caned the lot.'
Anon

WHY GETTING YOUR MUM ON ONE IS A GOOD IDEA

'Me parents had got to the stage where the kids were off their hands and, as far as they were concerned, they could have fun. It all started when I woke up one morning pilled up, tooted up and battered to find the top had come off a bottle of amyl nitrate in my room. So I'm amyled off me nut as well, when me mum came in to find me trying to open the windows. She's asking all these questions and in the end I'm like, "This is amyl, this is speed, this is charlie – next time you're doing the fucking hoovering have a sniff of that and you'll do it quicker." She's done it, she's hoovered like mad, she's told the old man and that was it. So now we've got my mum and dad and my uncle and me, all having a board meeting with all our drugs round the kitchen table on a Friday night: everyone trying everyone else's, then go out. I used to pay the housekeeping in coke. She used to say, "Oh, give us a gramme instead." It got to the point where I'd get to the Café de Paris and the bouncer would say, "Splurge! Your mum and dad's in there!" They'd do about ten pills each! One Sunday we were all up Haven Stables and my dad's done a trip. Only there were three stuck together. We found him sitting in the middle of Ealing Common five hours later with just his jeans on. No shoes. Completely gone. Imagine a 55 year old with three blotters in him. My mum was a brilliant dancer – we'd give her a parcel and she'd sniff up and get on the dancefloor. Her favourite record was "City Lights". I tell you what, they were the best days of my life and it was so nice to have your mum and dad there.'
Splurge, friend of Dee and very loving son

MUSIC

Acid house: take a pill, get the joke. Take enough pills, remember the joke.

Long before hardbag, handbag, and a million other genres, there were two main

sounds: acid house and Balearic Beat. There were also Belgian New Beat and hip-hop and soul but life is with us only fleetingly. To objective, sensible people acid house and Balearic Beat may seem like two kinds of dance music that got played in 1988, but what do they know? At the time it was East and West Germany.

House was straightforward: it was elating, soulful, American electronic dance if you were British; perverted nigger faggot music if you were American. Balearic Beat had no such clean musical definition as the name described the feeling of the music rather than the records themselves. Born under the stars in Ibiza, Balearic Beat was Alfredo's baby. Paul Oakenfold and Danny Rampling kidnapped it and raised it indoors in cold, grey London. Any bloody tune from hearty Mediterranean pop like Enzo Avitabile's 'Blackout' to sleeve-tugging indie like 'Driving Away From Home' by It's Immaterial was Balearic. Balearic Beat was a smudgy description of a whole shower of oddball records that had that elusive, naughty, outlaw, stomping, sunny, happy something. People made valiant efforts to find tunes that had that elusive something.

'Steve Proctor's attempts to break 'Black Betty' are applauded at *Boy's Own* mansions'
DJ Terry Farley writing in Boy's Own

And a whole lot of tunes didn't have it. Some frankly diabolical tunes snuck in under the Balearic curtain.

Original 1988 insult: 'It shows how many people were on drugs that they danced to Cyndi Lauper/Mandy Smith/U2, etc., etc.'

Naturally, many house records were also Balearic. Confused? It gets better: the meaning of Balearic changed and the first factions started. The difference between Balearic and acid house became desperately important to the original clubbers. The 'Come As You Are' of the original Balearic vibe became 'Don't Bother Coming As You Are Unless You're One Of Us Already And Wearing A Nice Shirt', in a powerful mix of passion and snobbery aimed at keeping it private.

Meanwhile, acid house was blowing the roof off. Rude, silly and as cool as the strange kid that doesn't care what anybody thinks, acid house and the British were made for each other. But they didn't hit it off at first.

'I was at a club where Simon Goff was playing. He stuck on a house record and all the black guys on the dancefloor stood there with their arms folded. Then someone passed a note to Simon. He showed it to me. It said, "Why are you playing this homo shit? Fuck off."'
Johnny Walker

DJs playing house even had bottles thrown at them. Why, it was almost as if there was something missing.

16

'The rhythm and the spaciness of acid house, the warmth of acid house, the slightly scary side of acid house seemed to clock in with ecstasy. It was more that link between the drug and the music that defined the scene.'
Dave Haslam, DJ

For a latent musician, a nation wanting to dance was a dream come true.

'I didn't get out much in 87. I was working at McDonalds, who were just about to sack me because I worked too much. I'd do a double shift every day, 6 a.m. to 4 in the morning, to get the money to buy my equipment. I was earning more than the managers. 808 State got wind of this somehow and said, "Why don't we do a house group as well as a hip-hop group?" We used to give demo tapes to Jon Dasilva to play down the Hacienda. It was a good feeling getting "Voodoo Ray" played for the first time in the Hac, and watching people go nuts.'
A Guy Called Gerald – Gerald Simpson

Acid house: crazy name; crazy music. Take your pick from:
a) Acid because it sounds caustic: it burns your ears.
b) Acid because 'acid burning' is an American DJ term for mixing.
c) Acid because Marshall Jefferson allegedly said, 'I discovered if I turned my 303 up all the way it makes a funny sound, like the sounds you hear when you're on acid.'

Drugs aside, it was the sheer power of the music itself which delivered hippie values for hard people, because without it there would have been no dancing. It was the tough rhythms that made the intensely spiritual lyrics palatable. Regardless of how many punters were drugged up to the eyeballs, it was a startling achievement by the musicians involved to get some of the most cynical people dancing to some of the most altruistic songs in years. E-MIX was MC at some of the pivotal acid house clubs, including Confusion and Clink Street. Here he tells a true story from the Clink:

'Those times for me were beautiful. It was when people started communicating … Really and truly you could almost say it was biblical. There was one night we got everyone to sit down and basically pray. The sun was rising, beaming through a hole in the wall. It was bright and early on a Sunday morning. For me that may be the essence of it: you're in this room just before we all left and we're winding down. I think "It's Alright" or "Someday" was playing, or "Promised Land". We started saying, "Everybody raise your hands!" and they raised their hands. We said, "Put them together!" Everyone put them together. After that it was "Kneel down" and everyone kneeled down. And so we just started praying. Everyone said what they wanted to say and I'm up there saying what I was feeling. I've played this back so many times in my head and it happened … It was the turning of the tide. It will take another twenty years for an arising like that.'

To get the full impact of this story you have to have some idea of the songs this mix of ordinary bods and violent villains were kneeling to. Here are the lyrics to Joe Smooth's 'The Promised Land':

'Brothers, sisters / One day we will be free / From fighting, violence / People crying in the street When the angels from above / Fall down and spread their wings like doves / As we walk hand in hand Sisters, brothers, we'll make it to the promised land'

An all-time favourite record of people whose preferred recreational activity, prior to acid house, was fighting, violence and people crying in the street.

DEAR EMMA, I'M DANCING LIKE A TREE

'Dear Emma,
Sod the job, you've got to come back to England. Clubs are the best they've been since 1980. I'm dancing like a tree ...'
Letter received by ex-pat, July 1988

Officially, dancing is a means of touching the opposite sex without having to take them to a Harrison Ford film first. Unofficially, it is the most essential social activity after eating and complaining. For as long as there have been communities, people have had a basic need to get together in groups, dress up in ridiculous clothes, consume whatever hallucinogens are to hand – be it coca leaves, Martini or something that dropped off the lucky village cat – and dance until they feel better. In 1988, Britain was coming out the arse-end of the longest danceless period since Queen Victoria's day, when any young woman who danced was lashed to the mast of a bounty ship and sailed out to serve as a jig-a-jig girl in a men-only colonial fort. Disco was an embarrassing memory, soul and jazz funk were minority sports and Five Star didn't count.

It had got to the point where most people *didn't dance,* and didn't think they ever would. Dancing was for the terminally flash, people who left a pheromone slick behind them. Furthermore, the dances were all too hard. Look at the speed with which breakdancing and bodypopping caught on – enormous fun, but you had to be a twelve-year-old boy with your clothes on back to front, and if you tried it for more than twenty minutes your spine would shatter and you'd have to be carried round on a spade.

None of the musical cults could get everybody on the floor. Rare groove was by definition for the few. There were the New Romantics, but they didn't so much dance as lurch like shop dummies in an earthquake. Rap and hip-hop weren't exactly a hedonistic laugh riot. When they weren't posing in old Ford Zephyrs that smelled of snails, rockabillies with names like Jez and Tab got to throw each other round the room in an earthy jump jive, but there were only ten of them, their names were really Jeremy and Tabitha, and as soon as they got their paws on that hand-me-down GTI the Zeph was going in the canal. Psychobillies certainly let it all out, but it was more an illegal boxing match than a pleasant social interaction: headbutting your partner with your ten-inch steely quiff. Psychobillies didn't brush their hair out at night; they just bent it to one side.

'I was out there and I wasn't an idiot. I was dancing – bloody dancing! I'd never had the confidence to dance. For fuck's sake, I'd never danced in my life!'
Stuart Powles, photographer

Hello, Mr Acid hands-in-the-air House: get out there and don't worry if you make a prat of yourself. In fact, go out there and make a prat of yourself. No rhythm? Here, have this one. Woo! Funny patterns in the strobes! Before house, speakers were something you avoided, thanks to that eighties obsession with everyone being deaf by thirty from pop's crazy beat. Once you'd experienced the all-body surround sound of house, speakers were for drilling your head into.

EVENTS PARTIES, CLUBS, DOS, WITLESS FARRAGOS

SLAM, GLASGOW • HOT, HACIENDA, MANCHESTER • NUDE, HACIENDA, MANCHESTER • HEDONISM, HANGAR LANE, LONDON • DESTINATION MOON, WAREHOUSE, WEST LONDON • COOOZ, NORTH LONDON • JIVE TURKEY, CITY HALL BALLROOM, SHEFFIELD • THE STEAMER, LEADMILL, SHEFFIELD • SHOCK, WAREHOUSES, LONDON • THE GARAGE, NOTTINGHAM • SOUL II SOUL, WAREHOUSES, LONDON • QUEENS, QUEEN MOTHER RESERVOIR, SLOUGH • GENESIS, WAREHOUSES, LONDON SUNRISE I, EQUESTRIAN CENTRE • RAGE, HEAVEN, LONDON • MFI (MAD FOR IT), LEGENDS, LONDON

Unreliable Memories From These And Other Events

HEDONISM, HANGAR LANE, LONDON: GROWN ADULTS DOING THE *HAWAII FIVE O*

Hedonism was among the first acid house warehouse parties, and was completely against everything clubland stood for.

'My memory of London before 1988 is clubs that closed at three that black people couldn't get into … There was a flyer that was going round: it was really big and it had little diagrams and it said, "Free drugs! Free Party!" And it was all night – wow! It was the flyer for Hedonism. It was like nothing I'd ever seen. There was knock-your-socks-off bass – you just didn't get that in clubs. People were taking Es and speed and smoking spliff, but what struck me was that it was much more open – before people used to go to the toilet to do them. There wasn't that embarrassment: "Oh, I use drugs." In Hedonism they were telling people they were on drugs or were sharing them. They had the first chill-out room I'd ever seen – just loads of cushions. But, most of all, people were all talking to each other. I've never met so many people as I met in 1988. They didn't look at you like, "Don't ask me a question! I don't know you!"'
Nicky Trax

'Hedonism was the idea of a Canadian guy who had to go back to Canada, but before he went back he wanted to do a free party, being in the spirit of the age. He got a big warehouse at Hangar Lane and booked brilliant DJs like John Green. Hang on – who's John Green? I don't remember any more. This keeps happening! All the people who were so important have disappeared off the face of the earth. Soul II Soul came on in the middle of the night, put on the theme to Hawaii Five O, and the place went mental. There were these big metal frames lying around near the dancefloor and people dragged them out, sat in them on the floor like they were canoes and started paddling to Hawaii Five O.
'At one point I remember there were no refreshments left so a group of people went out to a garage. They bought every single drink in the place: every Coke, every Evian, all the sweets, the lot. The guy working there that night had no idea what was going on over the road. Then they came back to the party and handed it all out for free. That's what it was like.'
Ashley Beedle, DJ and Ballistic Brother

'They were moving the sound system from one end of the room to the other and they had to shut down. There was no music and everybody decided, "OK, we'll make it ourselves." They took up cans and whatever they could find and started banging them on the wall. Chanting, singing, for half an hour. That was the first time I went to a club and saw everybody in pure unison, in my eyes. Everyone jumped on one rhythm, banging in time, chanting in time and still dancing.'
E-Mix

THE THIN GREEN LINE

Nicky Trax describes a typical Laurel and Hardy raid at her Sunday-evening club, Confusion:

'It was the end of the night. We'd packed up and we were up the ladders taking down the last of the curtains, when suddenly the doors opened and about forty police ran in. Dunno where they got their info from: we'd been closed for an hour. It must have cost them a fortune – seven vans full in the middle of a Sunday night. They looked so embarrassed; they were only there about five minutes, desperately looking for any telltale signs of naughtiness. Then this very young copper picked up a bottle of amyl, said, "What's this?" and took a huge sniff. He went bright red in the face and we laughed so much we nearly fell off the ladders.'

'I used to fly back from Ibiza with Es in my pocket. I just told customs they were headache pills.'
Extremely famous DJ

'They had a dance. Danny used to lead the dance'
Patrick Lilley

SHOOM, LONDON

Shoom coined the phrase 'Happy Happy Happy', and from the beginning in a cold, uptight 1987 Shoom wore its heart on its sleeve. Future opened at the same time and the Project was already going, but according to lore, Shoom was *the* acid house club.

As Danny puts it, 'a club is its host', and by winter 1987 Danny Rampling was a host with a message.

'In a naive way we considered that a new age was starting, the Age of Aquarius, and we were at the core of it. We were spreading the message of unity. It was a unique, magical time. The best three years of my life, unforgettable. I hadn't heard of Ken Kesey and the Merry Pranksters until a couple of years ago, and when I read it, it brought it all back. The positive energy between the people on the dancefloor was incredible. Was it real love? I'd say eighty per cent of it was.'

RUSHTASTIC: Oop, hang on – here it comes...

In exam terms, that's not a B+, it's a distinction. Danny's affection for his own band of Merry Pranksters is still obvious. Without even having read about Ken Kesey, Danny Rampling's new troupe were painting themselves day-glo, staring into strobes, riding the crest of a wave of social change.

'When Danny Rampling approached me for PR, I knew he had a youth cult in him. Visually he had something: he had this very skinny look and wore baggy clothes, he had a slang – "on one", etcetera – and they had a drug, but most of all, they had a dance. Danny used to lead the dance. The dance made the biggest impression: everyone noticed them. One night at Westworld in the Brixton Academy, I'll never forget the look of horror on the face of the rare groove lot that a new dance was happening and they weren't doing it.'
Patrick Lilley

Before all the dramas of months to come anything was possible. People recall nights there being phenomenal psychic journeys, and 'the early days of Shoom' became a club cliché. Shoomer Chris describes a trip to a soul weekender at Broadstairs, when the soul crowd – a rather serious bunch of trainspotters – made the mistake of inviting Shoom to come down: 'The place is full of straight soul and jazz bods. We've come in sword-fighting with plastic swords, wearing flower garlands round our necks. Danny's marched straight up and put two strobe lights on the deck, there's one of us lying down while we pour Smarties on her and there's Jimmy Jewel, who used to paint himself day-glo all over. I've gone over to the bar and said, "Can I have an orange lolly?" One of the punters said, "Fucking drink beer when you're in here." And we've said, "We don't want beer! We've got these!" and showed him a bag of Es ...'
Chris

...Ooh blimey!

Outbreaks of love, peace and smiling led on to hippie behaviour of the first order.

'Your whole week would revolve around the Shoom. You'd go home and talk about what you could go dressed up as next week. We had a serious discussion about arriving on spacehoppers with orange deely boppers.'
Ben McKnight

'We had a flower party. Me and my friend made cardboard petals, stuck them on a headband to wear round our faces, and made little crepe-paper skirts and got the bus down there dressed like that.' Once they got there, things got even Shoomier. 'One of our friends from Shoom arrived naked. He'd given away his clothes...'
Shoomer

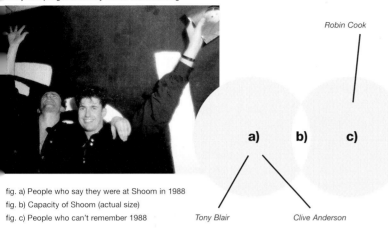

Danny Rampling and Johnny Walker are shooming

Robin Cook

a) b) c)

Tony Blair Clive Anderson

fig. a) People who say they were at Shoom in 1988
fig. b) Capacity of Shoom (actual size)
fig. c) People who can't remember 1988

The Naked Shoomer later explained that he'd got on this thing where he believed everyone who went to Shoom was part of some secret society that couldn't be seen by anyone else. He thought they were invisible to normal people: therefore, it was fine to walk around naked.

At first, the locals couldn't quite get their heads around Shoom.

'One night Shoom had so much steam coming out the windows some passer-by thought it was on fire and called the fire brigade.'
Chris

'The Fitness Centre was a real gym during the day and I think the barmen at Shoom were bodybuilders from the gym. They couldn't believe their eyes – they'd never seen people behave like us. You'd go to the bar and say, "I'd like five Perriers, please!" and you'd line them up on the bar and pour them over your head, going, "Woo-oo-oo-oo!"'
Wade

'My boyfriend worked for one of the biggest law firms in London, and he ended up off work wearing a catheter after he ruptured his willy vaulting a bollard in Amsterdam. We still went to Shoom. I have a strong image of him dancing in the smoke at Shoom with his catheter hanging out of his shorts.'
Anonymous Shoomer

'Saturday afternoon, I'd get literally nauseous with anticipation. We used to have these rituals to get us through the day till nine o'clock. We'd have a baked potato in the afternoon, something light, so we'd have an empty stomach by the time we got there, then we'd go to the pub and play pool, trying not to look at our watches. Finally it would get to eight o'clock, and thank God! We could leave to go to Shoom!'
Russell

'I used to take the other people presents every week. I really wanted to give them something. I wanted them to like me. For that matter, I wanted everyone to like me.'
Shoomer

Word of Shoom spread like a forest fire. The best warehouse parties Britain had ever known were sparking up in illegal venues up and down the country, but to have a regular night uninterrupted by idiots or police was a tricky balancing act.

Membership was a huge drama, particularly at Shoom. By autumn the backlash had started. Faced with the whole of London trying to get in, the frankly terrifying Jenni Rampling's behaviour on the door was pissing people off, and there was a rumour that membership was less than egalitarian.

'Future never got the respect it deserved. It wasn't trendy like Shoom so no trendies were interested in it. Shoom was a Saturday-night club for trendies. We were running Spectrum on Mondays and Future on Thursdays. You had to be committed to come on those nights. Future was the workers' club. One Saturday Ian St Paul organised a coach trip to Gravesend that would go to Shoom on the way back, and when we got to Shoom Jenni wouldn't let us in. That was it. We stopped going after that.'
Paul Oakenfold

'Of course there was a fucking A team. I don't know why people even deny it, it was so fucking obvious. The A team was only about 150 people. It seemed to us Jenni realised the potential of the thing, because Jenni wanted to be part of the inner circle ofLondon trendies. It seemed to us Danny was like, "I'm really happy: all my mates are having an absolute scream," and she was like, "We could have the best club in the world – let's ship in Bananarama."'
Russell

'People were saying, "That's Bananarama, that's Paul Rutherford," which just shows you how egalitarian it all was – not.'
Ben McKnight

He called it Acieed. Gary Haisman (left),
the man that coined the catchphrase for a generation

'I think Danny and Jenni were just desperately worried about letting people in, in case they didn't get it.I remember one night this man wasn't enjoying himself and Danny was saying, "Oh dear, do you think I should give him his money back?"'
Roger Beard

'It wasn't elitist, not at all. It was that there was only room for 200 people. The management were threatening to close us down if there were more people than that, all the time ... All credit to Jenni for how she ran things. No one else could have done that door: it was a really hard job, the abuse she used to take. I only went up to the door two times, and got my fingers severely burnt! We're both from London, we know what rough people are. On the first Shoom flyers we put "No Ruffians", and we meant it! I'd had years of ruffians. The people we ended up with in Shoom were wonderful people. It could be perceived as a unity thing, and we just couldn't have done with a bigger number of people, because we weren't experienced ... We could have made a fortune! An absolute fortune! What's more, we disagreed with the huge entrance fees being charged, people capitalising on something that was a very geuine statement.'
Danny Rampling

But what about the A team?

'I have absolutely no idea what people are talking about.'
Danny Rampling

'That queue – I saw girlfriends separated from boyfriends...'
Fiona Cartledge

Jenni Rampling

'We were Danny's old friends, we'd known him from when Kiss was still a pirate station, but Jenni wouldn't let us in. We told her to fuck it.'
Clubber

But Shoom was still the Holy Grail and if Jenni had turned round and said to anyone, 'Come in! Join the A team!' they'd have dropped their oldest friends and sailed to the front of that astonishing queue.

MANCHESTER

Andrew Barker, member of seminal Manchester house group 808 State, describes the early Manchester house scene:

'The Thunderdome [in north Manchester] used to play Glenn Miller to the crowd outside when the club was full. We DJed there until we got told by people who knew people not to play there any more. We went to the Soundgarden on Saturday nights, about the time we were doing the Sunset radio show. There were a lot of baggy jeans at the club, and a lot of lads. There wasn't a lot of trouble, but I do remember seeing someone being chased out of the club with a spade.'

Ben McKnight, Gretchen and Tommy.
The last night of Shoom at The Fitness Centre

'Once we did a party in these arches. They were being renovated, so we got in and set up. It carried on all night, and into the morning, when all these people started turning up for work in their overalls. I imagine that was quite a mad sight. It was eight in the morning and everybody had been dancing all night, with strange-looking eyes, sweat everywhere. I think everyone looked quite shocking, y'know. There was a lot of LSD, and a lot of ecstasy, but it was £25 a go. Quite a lot of money, so people used to go halves. There'd be a lot of people pilled up, oracting like they were. There were a lot of people who went silly for it, but I don't know anyone who went really mad. I don't know anyone who got sectioned, but I know a lot of people who, say, went to Ibiza and stayed. I don't think anyone thought about the health side of it. People'd just go out dancing and wouldn't think about the down side.'
Andrew Barker, 808 State

'Manchester? I used to go out every day! I bumped into Shaun Ryder the other day and he reminded me of this club we used to go in Gorton called the Arches. I used to really like the Kitchen [after-hours drinking club in Hulme]. The Kitchen just reminds me of people being off it. I had a squat in Hulme, and there was a rock concert one night, in the middle of the Crescents [part of the old Hulme estate]. I remember looking out thinking, Fuck, there's I don't know how many people living round here, and no one even minds the noise: they're all having it! It was like a mad community, travellers, lines going into the flats to get electric off people.
Gerald Simpson, AKA A Guy Called Gerald

Outside The Hacienda after Nude

In 1988, Paul Roberts of k-Klass was working for British Telecom. One night he was persuaded to go to Nude at the Hacienda.

'I was dumbfounded by what I saw ... there was no attitude, no tension between the gangs. Even the dealers were nice people. I spent the week ranting on about it, and saved every penny so I could do the same thing again. Even if I had no money I'd hitchhike up there from Chester. There were all sorts of nutters: one bloke used to stand on the stage and throw his voice, do weird vocal tricks and sound louder than the music. On man who was an accountant by day used to never talk to anyone, just turn up and dance all night. I went back two years ago: he was still there, dancing.

23

The notorious doormen at The Hacienda having a rather good evening

'After the Hacienda you'd go to an illegal after-hours club called the Kitchen on one of the Crescent housing estates in Hulme. The biggest death trap waiting to happen in terms of fire hazards, but if you're talking about the true underground scene, that's where it started in Manchester. One night we were there, the police were trying to get up the stairwell and people were throwing sofas and chairs at them – all good-humoured stuff to keep the party going. The rest of the band and I went, week in, week out. So much so that I ended up losing my job at British Telecom. The only people that I see now that were part of that scene are either involved in the music business, in prison or in hospital.'

By 1989 Paul was a pop star with k-Klass's 'Rhythm Is A Mystery' at number three in the UK charts. Paul shows no signs of returning to British Telecom.

THE STATE, LIVERPOOL
DJ Andy Carroll describes early acid house days at the State:

'The State Ballroom is a very sumptuous palace with a marble floor, plaster frescos and stained-glass windows. It was Liverpool's own Balearic scene, although it had nothing to do with Ibiza. In 1986 we started to mix some house stuff in with the New Order dubs, Talking Heads, Simple Minds etc. Promotions men used to come up from London. They couldn't believe what we were getting away with.

'Then acid house started taking off and people couldn't get enough. It had hit London, Liverpool, Manchester, Birmingham and Glasgow. I was trying to do a mellow evening on a Tuesday night at Kirklands in Liverpool, but no one would have any of it: they wanted acid house every night. In the end I gave in. The police had no idea what was going on. The clubs had gone ballistic and all they knew was that acid house and ecstacy were the reasons … I was followed, stopped and searched all the time. Finally I had my phone tapped. I could hear the clicking and tape whirring. I used to put a microphone next to the receiver making a piercing high-frequency sound and shout, "Get some of this, mate!"'

THE TRIP, LONDON
When Nicky Holloway, the club promoter behind the Special Branch parties, got back from Ibiza he waited till June and then opened the Trip. In the huge West End rock venue, the Astoria. Shoom, Spectrum (see below) and Future were ticking away nicely but when Nicky opened the Trip the whole thing went off like a firework up a cat's arse.

'I'm absolutely knocked out by this. I've done some promoting of gigs over the years but this is THE BUSINESS!'
Nicky Holloway after the first Trip, Update, *1988*

'This gig was like ten to midnight on New Year's Eve, only better.'
John Cecchini, DMC, Update, *1988*

'We've lit a fuse here tonight – stand by for a lot of explosions!'
Paul Oakenfold, Update, *1988*

Fran Davies was twenty and had just come down to London from Bristol to live with her boyfriend. She first went out in June 1988 to the Trip at the Astoria in London. Now she has a little boy and lives in Bristol working as a teacher.

'I couldn't understand why the queuing was madder than anything I'd ever experienced. People were pushing and shoving, desperate to go in. I remember the security were nasty, really big guys using Rottweilers. The poor sodding dogs had obviously been starved because someone dropped a beefburger on the ground and a dog really lunged for it like it hadn't seen food for days, but this big black bouncer hauled it back. You'd be shoved up towards the entrance then, when you finally got there, you just forced yourself through.

'Inside it was like a heat wave, *so* hot! The first thing I noticed was that *everyone* was dancing *everywhere,* on the stairs, at the sides, at the bar, in the toilets. It was this enormous old building but the whole crowd was moving. The management must have known what was going on because even then they were charging huge amounts for water. I was looking around, going, "Why are they all paying two pounds for a bottle of water?" People were offering you sweets, for God's sake! Then I came up on the E and instantly I was dancing, too.

'When it finished no one wanted to leave the club. I remember just walking out into a sea of people in Tottenham Court Road. People were dancing on the pavement; some people had brought their cars round and they were sitting on the roofs waving their arms, even dancing on the car roofs. Then the police pulled up, because there was obviously something happening. The police got out of their cars and were staring at us. I remember them looking at each other, looking at the scene, and standing there stunned. They knew we weren't going to cause any trouble: it was just people having a fucking good time.

'My boyfriend Stuart said to me, "Fran, this is the start of something completely new. I can feel it." Those were the best times. Just after that he went out and bought this bright-purple top with a big yellow smiley the size of a plate. No one had anything in those sorts of colours then, and we'd walk through the park and these odd pockets of people would recognise it. I remember this big bloke walked by and, as he passed us, he patted Stuart on the shoulder and just said, "Yeahh!"'

STREET PARTY! THE YMCA CAR PARK

The Trip spawned perhaps the most famous incident of acid house:

'The spontaneous street parties have been continuing wherever three acid house fans get together, especially after club one-nighters. They've partied till 5 a.m. in Trafalgar Square, 8 a.m. in an undisclosed London Bridge car park, and blocked Tottenham Court Road for the fourth week in succession after the final night of the Trip club … hundreds of happy acid fans swaying yelling "Street party! Street party!" in unison. The police were less than amused but stayed cool under pressure, but the traffic-jammed car drivers were totally mystified … With habitual shrieks of "Acciiiieeed!" and "Ec-stasseeeee!" the mob stormed the bowels of the YMCA, there to harangue a set of hapless stranded Porsche drivers with the inane "Can You Party?!"…'
Time Out, *August 10 1988*

'I was at Trip at the Astoria, and when it finished Nicky Holloway got on the PA and said, "It's the last one – everyone go down to the YMCA car park and turn your stereos up!"'
Vicky

'We got a big van, a generator and a set of decks and left it parked in the car park, ready for after. It was jumping! We only got to use it for twenty minutes before we were stopped but it was worth it.'
Nicky Holloway

That stage at The Hacienda

'The car-park party after the Trip was one of my best memories. We came out the club, and in those days you didn't really have a lot of after-parties, so everyone was saying, "What are we going to do?" So we went down to the car park and I was in Pigbag and Esgache's car. The boot went up, the music went on and it was D:Mob – acciieeed! The car next to us turned on their stereo and they had the same song – double ammunition. The police left us alone because they had no concept of why these people were being so friendly.'
Timmi Magic

'I couldn't get my car through the lights because people were dancing in the street. Baggy people in Indian tops, big baggy jumpers. I saw people going in the fountain, dancing on the side of the fountain. More and more people were pulling up their cars, opening the doors and playing music.'
Kym Kennedy

JOY: SHOOM AT SAMURAI STUDIOS, LONDON
'There was no oxygen. We were lighting our lighters and the flames were going out.The bloke I was with puked all over someone who was sat in a corner. The bloke he'd puked on smiled and waved back at him.'
Emma

SPECTRUM, LONDON
'By the sixth week we were £12,000 in debt, and we just didn't have the money to pay the management back. But I believed. Then all of a sudden …'
Paul Oakenfold

'I don't care what anyone says, Spectrum was better than Shoom.'
Vicky, clubber

'When 'Jibaro' came on the whole club would explode and start dancing, wherever they were – on the balcony, at the bar – it really was a tribal dance at Spectrum.'
Anon

The best acid house club ever? If a night in Ian St Paul and Paul Oakenfold's staggering Theartre of Madness didn't blow you away you were already dead. Spectrum was in Heaven, Richard Branson's purpose-built club, and it made the most of it. Spectrum was a huge, dark, underground playground of acid house, with clothes stalls, startling lasers, weird stage shows involving the Statue of Liberty, a giant spider and castles.You might come one night and find the place flooded with fake snow.

'I spent the whole of Christmas and New Year covered in little bits of polystyrene from a night at Heaven. They had a snowstorm in the VIP bar and I lay there all night up to my neck in it.'
Johnny Rocca

'You'd have the strangest encounters at Heaven. I wandered into the upstairs bar one night and found two naked girls painting themselves as ringmasters. I looked again and one of them was my next-door neighbour. She was only about seventeen, quite posh, and I didn't even know she went out. I said, "Lizzy!" and she turned round and went, "Oh fuck."'
Spectrum fan

'The only clubs I went to before acid house were illegal drinking clubs, right dirty places where you'd meet your mates after they'd done a job. It'd be all champagne, double smart. Then a girl told me about Future, but I didn't want to go because I didn't think I'd get in. But after standing in the queue I knew that it was different: the faces were right, the clothes were right – it was people I'd want to talk to. We started going to Spectrum, too. Upstairs it was like 1967, full of hippies listening to "Sympathy for the Devil" and the Thrashing Doves, "Jesus on the Payroll". Downstairs it was Vietnam: full-on acid house.'
Des Penny, manager, Flowered Up

'It was like walking into this wonderland. You were at the beginning of a revolution but you didn't know it. We just thought it was like this everywhere.'
Andy Carroll, DJ

SUNRISE AT THE EQUESTRIAN CENTRE

The first of the monster dos, Sunrise was the labour-intensive creation of university lecturer's son Tony Colston-Hayter, who took on responsibility for the good time of thousands, right down to coaches, bouncy castles and flares lighting the way along country lanes.

'I was selling tickets for Tony Colston-Hayter, so I had my own coach of people, and Brandon Block had another. We arrived and it was like nothing we'd ever seen – it was my first bouncy castle. We all ran and jumped on to it: RAARRH! They had these lasers that made tunnels in the air. You'd be dancing in square green tunnels and round pink tunnels. They had disco balls, everything.

'Tony had told the woman who owned the equestrian centre he was making a film for *World In Action* and when she came down and saw what was going on, thousands of nutters in big baggy jumpers going mental to Reese and Santiano, "Rock To The Beat" – "say rooooock to the beat, say rooooock to the beat" – *she* went mental.

'That night Tony's people found this guy lying face down in the mud, not moving. He told them, "I was really tripping and I thought at the party I'd gone to heaven, then when I came outside it was all cold and muddy so I thought I'd gone to hell. Seeing as I was in hell I thought I'd better throw myself on the ground and keep quiet."'
Vicky from Notting Hill

'Someone gave me a little bit of gear to skin up. I got the Rizla out and my mate said, "Hang on: that's sheep shit." I went storming back to the bloke that gave it to me and was having a go when Ben Volpierre-Croissant [eighties twat from Curiosity Killed The Cat] took it, skinned up with it and said it was fine.'
Trevor Fung

SUNRISE AT GREENWICH

A huge and chaotic night of scrambling over wasteground and a brilliant, unforgettable off with the police.

'When the police are laying siege to a party, there's a half-hour period where, if you can get enough people inside, the police have got a public-order offence on their hands if they try to stop it. When we arrived at Sunrise at the gasworks, the police had set up a blockade and they were saying, "It's off. It's all been stopped." But we could see lights from across the wasteground, and suddenly someone yelled, "There's a hole in the fence! Come on!" Seventy people have legged it through the fence. It felt like a wartime escape from a camp: a half-mile dash over all sorts of obstacles, what seemed like bits of tank and craters ...'
Anton Le Pirate

'Sunrise at Greenwich was the best party I ever went to. We looked across and suddenly there was a wall of police on the other side of the dancefloor. Until that moment I'd never actually seen a thin blue line. The DJ booth was up on the wall and Steve Proctor was in it when they turned the sound off. It was off for ages and we wouldn't accept that we were going home ...'
Vicky

'Then we beat the police with sheer numbers. They had to let it go on. Just that feeling when they left and the sound system came back on. I looked across at the crowd and Steve Proctor dropped Kraze, "The Party" – *Let's Get This Party Started Right* – that has to be the most well-chosen record of all time.'
Dale

RUSH, SLOUGH

'It was called Rush [hysterical laughter]. At the end of it Weatherall was standing there, going, "I am Jim Morrison!" The police were outside for the whole thing but all they knew was that there something very strange going on inside. They were saying, "Are you selling alcohol?" And we said, "No, we're raffling it." Because you could get away with that scam in those days. They said, "You know it's illegal to sell alcohol?" We said, "People are buying raffle tickets, and they're winning drinks. Everyone's a winner!"'
Phil Perry and Fiona Crawford

The Slough Centre: Weatherall, a very skinny Rocky and Phil Perry to the right

CARWASH, WAREHOUSE, SOUTH LONDON

'It was madness in there. There were between three and five thousand people a night. People were jumping in and out of diplomatic cars, having sex in the side rooms, dancing in the car park. The layout of the building was really lucky: there was a big room right at the back – this was the main club – and it meant that the police could come and I'd show them the back bar and they'd go away again.'
Tank

CONFUSION AT BILL STICKERS, SOHO, LONDON

'Because Bill Stickers was a really hideous Hollywood-style restaurant with no dancefloor, people danced on the seats, on the tables, everywhere. We used to put poppers in the smoke machine. We set up the Acid Curtain for people to go and dance behind. We had an illegal extra room at the back we called the oddbod room. People could do what they want in there, even spray the walls. There was a guy called Greg who used to turn up with a staff, a black capé and a skull T-shirt and a hat and shades.'
Nicky Trax, co-founder, Confusion

FIRST PERSON

GET RIGHT ON ONE MATEY! ORIGINAL CLINK STREET DJS REMINISCE

RIP at Clink Street, run by Lu Vucovic and Paul Stone, was London proper: a dark, cobbled backstreet down by the river. The magic was happening in a rough-and-ready recording studio on the site of an old prison – hence 'the Clink'. Going there felt like the opposite of West End tack: it was dark, Dickensian and really, really exciting.

In 1988 Ashley Beedle was a young lad from Wembley working in a timber yard and DJing with the Shock sound system.

'That spring I never slept all weekend. I spent the whole weekend in Clink Street, apart from Saturday morning when we'd walk out the club mullahed and go to the pub in Smithfield Market. There'd be two sets of people in the pub: meat people getting pissed, and kids flying off their heads. We'd get pissed and then go straight back to Clink in the afternoon and crank up the music again. I got sacked three times during the Clink Street days. My friend Cecil worked in the Nat West. God knows what went on in his Nat West on Monday morning.

'It was a real scene. We'd all walk the same and look the same – we'd be in the uniform: dungarees and Converse flack baseball boots. If I remember one lyric from all the records we played, it would be "A-a-a-cid, man!". We did the back room with the camouflage netting at Clink Street. The weekend I remember the most was when my mate Shakespeare was tripping. He grabbed the microphone and told everyone to pull the camouflage net down. The whole lot came down on top of them – it was hundreds of people wriggling around under the netting. What did Shakespeare do? He got out a guitar and plugged it into the system and started to play along like Jimi Hendrix. He blew the speakers playing along to a pile of people.

'Meanwhile Vince was also on acid, and he got this idea to start digging through the walls to release something. He was digging away at the walls with a screwdriver. He went through one layer of plasterboard and just kept going. Finally he got to bricks but they were so old and fucked he got straight through them. Next thing we knew he'd disappeared into the hole: he'd made a tunnel through to the outside wall and dug through

Clubland meets the Jet Set at Amnesia: Jeremy Healy and Boy George are enthralled by Dynasty star Tracy Scoggins

that. We looked through and we could see Vince at the other end about six feet away in a silhouette with the sky behind him. The barman did acid that night and gave away the drinks – the promoter was not happy.'

'I was chatting to this very hard-looking black bloke and my mind wandered and he finally said, "What are you looking at?" I said, "I'm sorry, I've got to tell you that you've got a purple face and mauve hair." He said, "Oh yeah? And why's that?" I told him I'd done acid. He said, "That's bad shit, man. You don't want to be doing that." And pulls a huge flick knife on me. I nearly shat myself. Then he pulls a big block of coke out the other pocket, cuts a bit off, chops it up on the bar, scoops it up on the knife and says, "Get that up your nose and sort yourself out!"'
Chris

'The people that used to come to Clink Street were the most extraordinarily diverse range of people. Serious fucking football villains from different teams – out there, there'd be big wartime business going on, but as soon as they walked through the door it was peace. The first time I saw one of them I thought he was Old Bill, this big villain surrounded by all these dollybirds. Then you had every variety of street people, then millions of shades in between … Posh people used to go: Philip Glass, Nigel Kennedy, Lofty from *EastEnders* – people that I considered from another class. So many people passed through it, but everyone was equal for that moment. It was a brief moment of freedom. Where for the first time a group of people crossed over in their consciousness, a transition point – a fucking Age of Aquarius, whatever you want to call it. Then it all went pear-shaped. But for a moment it just *worked*.'
Lu Vucovic

'One particular night I was at Clink in my ecstasy wizard outfit, a big purple cape thing, 1500 soaking-wet quid in one pocket, a big bag of Es in the other, tripping my nuts off. They had this big ceramic sink and I filled it with water and climbed in. I was sat in it pouring water over my head with a pint glass. I had to be reprimanded.'
Anon

'He's sat in the sink with his wizard's outfit and Boy George has walked in. I shouted, "Look out! He's had a whole sheet of trips!" and Boy George scarpered.'
Johnny Walker

NEWSPAPERS ON DRUGS – 1988 IN THE PAPERS

'Ecstasy is said to have the power to make people trust one another, to banish jealousy and break down the kind of barrier existing between parents and children and also lovers,' the *Daily Telegraph* reported, before acid house. It was claimed that a New York writer who tried it had compared it to 'a year of therapy in two hours', while Brother David Steindl-Rast, a Benedictine monk in Big Sur, California, said, 'A monk spends his whole life cultivating the same awakened attitude it gives you.' In 1985, *Newsweek* declared, incisively, that ecstasy 'is not a party drug.'

On 5 September 1988 the *Sun* first mentioned 'London's weirdo acid house craze', saying, 'Trendies are wearing massive crucifixes and religious brooches along with their Dayglo clobber and fluorescent-green shoes.' And, even when on 16 September Richard Branson banned acid house from his London club Heaven after the *Sun* revealed that dealers were selling LSD to 'hippie-style kids' at the venue, no *direct* connection between the music and drugs was made.

THE CRAZY DAYS OF DRUG NONSENSE

'Someone briefly had the notion that if you crunched it up it would work quicker. Luckily, that was only a phase.'

'Making mobile-phone calls at eleven o'clock at night to say, "Fifteen T-shirts, please."'

SUMMER 1988:
Making sure you only took the smallest bit.

WINTER 1988:
Making sure you always got the biggest bit.

By SUE EVISON and PETER WILLIS
THE designer drug Ecstasy has become the sinister sideline for evil dealers cashing in on the teenage Acid House music craze that's sweeping Britain.

The popular cry of "Are you on one, matey?" echoed on Acid House dance floors from Cornwall to Caithness is really asking if youngsters have popped a lethal white pill.

And while it may just be a trendy, meaningless chant to some young people, the answer is increasingly "Yes" among vast numbers of teenage victims on the lookout for fast thrills.

Ecstasy is the street name for the illegal drug Methylendioxy Methamphetamine, known at MDMA. It was developed by American psychiatrists to help ... severely ...

Danger drug that is sweeping discos and ruining lives

In fact, on 3 October, the *Sun* ran a top-ten-hit list 'for acid boppers', including 'We Call It Acieed' by D-Mob and 'Burn It Up/Acid Burns' by the Beatmasters, and advertised its splendid acid house t-shirt, which made the wearer look like they had vomited on themselves. There was something in the air. On 6 October, under the headline 'Love Drug Stampede', the *Sun* announced: 'Sun readers rushed yesterday to snap up a new love drug. We exclusively revealed details of the love potion Eldepryl – developed by a Hungarian boffin – which increases rats' appetites for sex ten times, and makes them live longer. Tests are now planned on humans. Thousand of readers flooded Britannia Pharmaceuticals with calls volunteering to be guinea pigs or asking how much of the drug they could buy.' Less than a fortnight later, the *Sun* mysteriously lost all interest in selling love drugs and published a story headlined 'Evil Of Ecstasy: Danger Of Drug That Is Sweeping Discos And Ruining Lives'. Dr Vernon Coleman, the *Sun* doctor, tried to put the shits up the nation by saying, 'The pushers who sell ecstasy claim the drug offers excitement without danger. They are lying.' He carried on in a brown froth: 'You will hallucinate. For example, if you don't like spiders, you start seeing giant ones … There's a good chance you'll end up in a mental hospital for life.' Finally, for readers not scared of spiders or insanity he lustily asserted, 'If you're young enough, there's a good chance you'll be sexually assaulted while under the influence. You may not even know until a few days or even weeks later.' In the *Observer*, Kate Ellerton wrote one of the (unintentionally) funniest 'I took drugs' articles of all time. '"Mmmmm … I'm a cat," I said, entwining my hand through someone else's hair.' Later, she gets the urge to dance. '"I'm a rocking cat," I declared, so full of delight I couldn't stop.' She then asks a woman to leave the room because her earrings are spoiling the perfection of the room.

The *Sun*'s anti-acid house stance was influential in a typically crap British way. After D-Mob appeared on *Top Of The Pops*, producer Brian Whitehouse banned all records with the word 'acid' in the title or the lyrics. 'I've been forced to make this decision,' said TV's Lord of the Trends, 'because reaction to last week's show was so strong.' Top Shop and Top Man banned the sale of smiley T-shirts on the orders of Burtons' boss Sir Ralph Halpern. (Sir Ralph, who had recently had an affair with five-times-a-night Fiona Wright, was then criticised by lost hero of acid house, DJ Captain Acid – Captain Cash's wayward brother – who said, 'How can someone with his lack of morals lecture kids?')

In November 1988 the *Sun* cut the crap. 'Shoot These Evil Acid House Barons,' it concluded calmly. Finally, the quality rock journalists caught up and, with insight as sharp as their lightning recognition skills, declared that acid house was rubbish. 'Clearly, you aren't supposed to listen to acid house at all,' said Robert Sandall, a music journalist who smells of patchouli. 'It aspires to an absence of content just as its devotees do to freeing themselves of studied snobbery. Which is carrying pop's distinguished tradition of symbolic naivety a bit too far for me.' Tosser.

THE END OF THE YEAR

The miracle discovery of acid house made for internal conflict: you wanted to keep it a secret but you also wanted to get the whole planet on one. In the end you were very careful and only told your few close friends. And so did two million other people.

DON'T BE A SUCKER

By Vernon Coleman

THE SUN DOCTOR

THE pushers who sell Ecstasy claim the drug offers excitement without danger.

They are lying. And anyone who believes them is a sucker.

Ecstasy is so dangerous that if you take the drug and don't suffer any damaging effects, the pusher has probably sold you a watered-down version.

Here are the medically-proven effects caused by taking Ecstasy:

● Nausea, sweating, dizziness, tremors and headaches. You'll shake, your heart will beat faster and your breathing rate will increase.

● Colours will seem brighter and small sounds will become loud.

● You will hallucinate. For example, if you don't like spiders you'll start seeing giant ones.

● Hallucinations can last for up to 12 hours. So effects that seem pleasant and fun when you're with friends in a club can turn into a nightmare soon after you get home. This can be terrifying if you are alone.

● The quality of hallucinations is unpredictable and will vary according to where the drug was made. Street Ecstasy is concocted in illegal kitchen laboratories by crooked and incompetent chemists.

● Panic attacks are common—sometimes lasting for two days. You'll be physically and mentally terrified and unable to do anything about the way you feel.

● Bad memories will come flooding back—and you

may become depressed a violent.

● Most Ecstasy users ... flashbacks—and they ... happen up to six mont ... later. If you get one in ... wrong place, you could k ... yourself. For example, y ... may try to stop cars ... standing in the road.

● There's a good chan ... you'll end up in a men ... hospital for life.

● ... you're young enou ... there's a good chan ... you'll be sexually assault ... while under the influence ... You may not even kno ... until a few days or eve ... weeks later.

● Ecstasy is also known ... E, XTC, Adam and T ... Love Drug.

Chapter Two
1989: FOR FUCK'S SAKE WHO TOLD EVERYONE?

'*Boy's Own* – the only fanzine that gets right on one, matey!'
Boy's Own *issue five*

'The only fanzine that wishes it hadn't claimed to be "the only fanzine that gets right on one" a few months back – oo-er, madam.'
Boy's Own *issue six*

January

An independent enquiry clears Thames TV of criticisms levelled against *Death On The Rock*. Thatcher gets rid of Thames TV anyway and replaces it with the quality television company, Carlton.

The Face's tips for 1989: P-Funk, Prince, real soul, freestyle, heavy reggae raves and Miami bass.

February

The Union Carbide Corporation agrees to pay $470 million compensation to the people it poisoned in Bhopal, India. Investigations reveal clown cars with higher safety standards than Union Carbide.

March

The tanker Exxon Valdez spills eleven million gallons of crude oil in Alaska.

April

MP David Alton writes to sports minister Colin Moynihan expressing concern about ticket allocations for the Liverpool v Sheffield Wednesday match at Hillsborough. He is told it is a matter for the football authorities. No action is taken.

15 April: 95 die at Hillsborough. Using as evidence the claims of Tory MP Irvine Patnick, himself acting as a mouthpiece for the South Yorkshire Police, that friend of the working man the *Sun* reports 'Some Fans Picked Pockets Of Victims. Some Fans Urinated On The Brave Cops. Some Fans Beat Up PC Giving Kiss Of Life.' The *Sun*'s sales collapsed on Merseyside.

June

Mr Bigs of 1989 include Tony Colston-Hayter and Jarvis Sandy. Police tell Mr Small to watch it.

'Of course young people are harmed by drugs. But if they weren't taking them at acid houses they would be taking them somewhere else,' writes Peter McLie in the *Evening Standard*.

Essex-girl jokes are all the rage.

The Earl of Errol, 42, Lord High Constable of Scotland denies rumours that he has held an acid house party but adds, 'It sounds a very good idea. They make a lot of money, don't they? It's better than computers.'

August

The *Marchioness* pleasure boat sinks on the Thames after being hit by the dredger *Bowbelle*. 57 people are killed.

In Club Aire in Madrid T-shirts are for sale with the slogan '¿Donde esta la fiesta acid?'.

For some reason, the inflatable banana becomes a *de rigueur* terrace accessory.

September

In Risley, Cheshire, ravers drive a forklift truck at riot police.

Graeme Park and Mike Pickering record an acid house version of 'Wimoweh'. It is never heard of again.

American dancer Digger starts a swingbeat club called Bounced for people 'who are tired of the monotonous house beat'. 'If it ain't got that swing,' advises *The Face*, 'you can't do the Reebok.'

Canny marketing men realise that, after a year on the drug slash, young folk are getting hyponchondriacal enough to pay nearly two quid for anything claiming to be restorative. Aqua Libra claims to be an ancient Swiss remedy, although being mysteriously vague about what exactly it's remedying. 'Restorative' drink Purdey's is launched, inspiring a whole slew of drinks that taste like old widdle.

October

Brookside is slammed after Barry Grant sets up an acid house party. Several people claim to have been to it.

The acid house police squad is formed at Gravesend, Kent.

Guns and knives are found after a police raid on an acid house party in Essex. Inspector Roy Clarke says, 'A pump-action shotgun isn't the sort of thing you take to a party.'

November

The Berlin Wall comes down.

An acid house party in Bere Regis, Dorset, with 1200 revellers present, is stopped by police and the A35 closed because of 'the dangerous way revellers had parked their cars'.

December

Leaflets are circulated warning of acid-impregnated stick-on tattoos. The aim, says Dr Edward Mucklow of St Mary's Hospital, Isle of Wight, in a letter to the *Lancet*, is to cause dependency and new customers for Europe's drug trade.

Democratic US troops invade Panama to depose drug-trafficker and pineapple-faced dictator General Noriega by playing horrible rock music all day until he gives himself up.

Question 2. Acid house: for fuck's sake who told everyone?

a)

Radio One's 'Woo' Gary Davies

b)

The Sun

c)

You

All right, so a few friends told a few friends, and Radio One's Gary Davies definitely showed a couple of ladies the bright lights of Ibiza, but the press told everybody else. In autumn 1988, the tabloids announced a drugs for drugs' sake free-for-all: just turn up and pop a pill. Prompt and keen as only the young can be, a million British kids did what they were told and trooped out to take drugs in the places where they were told they could get them. As Rik off *The Young Ones* would have said, had he been into acid house and not a fictional character, the real Mr Big of acid house was Rupert Murdoch.

DO THE GOVERNMENT AND THE MEDIA *REALLY* HATE RAVE CULTURE?

'It's the closest thing to mass, organised zombieism and I really don't think it should go any further.'
Peter Powell, Radio One DJ

God had his revenge: for years, Peter Powell *loved* Anthea Turner.

Great headlines of punk, no. 1: 'Must We Fling This Filth At Our Pop Kids?'

The media loved acid house. For the press, acid house wasn't a brave new force for social change or a wave of world-changing love, but a new reason to write an old story. And, in a week when journalists are lucky to get a story about a breakfast TV presenter caught having a dull dinner-and-a-bunk-up with a dumpy researcher, a story about thousands of young folk going mental at huge parties is a dream come true. Even better: although trends and cults have always been the subject of blind, slavering tabloid rage frenzy, most of them have rarely warranted the amount of coverage they got. Mod, skinhead and even punk were never as popular with young Britain as the tabloids claimed (or, rather, hoped). For the first time, acid house really *was* as massive as the *Sun* said it was.

The papers, geared since the days of the teddy boys to covering bad youth excess, were ready. With immense skill, fat old hacks managed to get into the early raves, unnoticed except by everyone. In June 1989, after attending the giant Sunrise party outside White Waltham in Berkshire, the *Daily Mail* ran the definitive acid house outrage piece. It contained all the classic phrases of Old Whisky Buffer Moral Panic. Attending 'the biggest acid house party yet held in Britain' were '11,000 youngsters, some as young as fourteen'. These teenagers became even younger a few words later when the drug dealers turned up, 'happy to ply their trade to the children'. Fortunately, no one enjoyed their drugs, which were apparently taken to 'degrading effect'.

The agony of the ecstasy, wrote the papers; the frown behind the smiley. In fact, behind the smiley was another smiley. The government and the media hate young people in groups. Why?

Theory One: Jealousy – We Didn't Have Any Fun In My Day

True. They are incapable of describing the 'mob' as a 'group of friends' and the 'mindless frenzy of dancing' as 'fun' because it would make them too depressed. Tony Parsons hasn't smiled since 1979 when his wife fell downstairs.

Theory Two: Fear – Groups Are Dangerous

Government and media attitudes to people in groups are based around the idea that the population is innately thick as pig shit. If you are in a mass, you're being conned (or a zombie) because people don't like each other. A sense of community is extremely inconvenient for authorities hoping to run countries for economic benefit. Britain might still be paying poll tax if a large group of people hadn't made its feelings known in 1990. As it was, the government was just bowing to pressure from freshly looted electrical retailers. Some countries have even more to lose: the Israeli government sent a jumbo jet to forcibly bring back its young citizens from Goa, and even jailed trance musicians Total Eclipse and Juno Reactor when they arrived to play a party in Israel. Israel has military service, and if you've done the Goa rounds you are unlikely to want to strap on an AK47 and shoot people, unless you'd been to some spectacularly awful parties.

Theory Three: Concern – They're Worried About Our Health

An old adage. If at any stage in the last fifty years an elected government had shown a genuine interest in banning tobacco, this argument would hold water.

According to the *Mail* it was a horrible night. Teenagers 'headed for danger' (apparently it's got a brilliant sound system). Local residents in their 'beautiful houses, neat gardens, stables' were 'confused and terrified' by their arrival. Many of the drug-using, body-twitching disco ravers also seemed to be confused, one passing a 'rolled-up "tab" or pill of LSD to his friend' as they 'puffed on a marijuana cigarette, their voices becoming ever more hysterical as the drugs' cocktail took effect'.

Despite the easy availability of ecstasy (known by the unbreakable codeword 'E') everyone in the *Mail* article was drunk. 'No alcohol was served. Really, there was no need. Many of the dancers had arrived worse for drink from pubs and nightclubs.' It was a night of unfettered evil. 'In one dark corner of the hangar, underneath an overhead walkway, was a parents' nightmare. Youngsters lay on the concrete floor, their stoned eyes staring vacantly around them … Littered around them were young couples in various forms of intimacy. No decent parent could have been anything but revolted and afraid for the children there.'

With the promise of stoned intimacy and overhead-walkway rumpo, tickets for the rave were going to be hard to come by. The *Mail* had to meet a 'small, middle-aged Liverpudlian' called Bob in a car park to get tickets, while the actual ravers – tiny little children, some no bigger than a man's thumb, pissed and shagging – virtually had to join the mafia to get them. Because 'Sunrise members prefer to stay out of the limelight, meeting privately in the "right" places, among them West End clubs, where they recruit new members.' Presumably with a ritual where palms are cut and the blood mixed with E.

The *Mail* did not say what happened to the punters: they may still be there, smoking acid roll-ups and twitching. But we do know that, knackered from recruiting new members in the right places and terrifying people in their beautiful homes, the Sunrise organisers all went on holiday because they were

exhausted. More to the point, however, 'the people of White Waltham were also exhausted. And furious'.

The *Mail*'s version sounded rather depressing, which is probably why the *Sun* took a different tack. In search of teenagers having sick-rude-drug-fun, the *Sun* went to Longwick, Buckinghamshire, and made taking drugs and dancing all night sound great. 'Worst Ever!' the *Sun* said ecstatically. '15,000 at acid bash! Drug pushers galore! Kids of twelve go wild!' It was clearly the party of a lifetime as '20,000 youngsters, many stoned on drugs, went wild at Britain's biggest ever acid house party at the weekend' and 'dozens of evil drug pushers preyed on thrill-seeking teenagers'. The kids, who admittedly were now only 'looking as young as twelve', took E (now being advertised by the *Sun* as 'the mind-bending, yuppie drug ecstasy') and happily told reporters, '"We've had a great time. The party was absolutely mental,"' confirming this as they 'screamed the acid house chant "Mental!"'.

More seriously, the article ended with reports of arrests at parties in Oxfordshire and Essex and the fact that Tony Colston-Hayter (the 'yuppie whizzkid') would be appearing in court charged with not having a public entertainments licence for the June party. There was also an editorial that asked the unusual question 'Who cares about evil drug men?'. Referring to the Buckinghamshire party, it said, 'Our reporters saw drugs openly on sale. They saw youngsters barely into their teens stoned out of their minds. The police presence was described as low profile. It was so low that it did not appear to exist at all. Don't the police care any more about enforcing the law of the land? Are they not troubled about what is happening to our young people? Just when will they decide to smash the evil drug pushers in our midst? Only when the drug habit has spread to all of Britain? When the party stretches from shore to shore?' It was baiting like this that bullied the police into action.

From now on, the police would be in the spotlight every time they failed to stop a rave or arrest hundreds of wild kids of twelve, their stoned eyes staring vacantly around them. As the summer ended and the new craze didn't – for the second winter in a row – the police, under pressure from the embattled middle classes and the press, adopted heavier tactics. In October 1989 the Acid House Police Squad was formed in Kent. Throughout November and onwards, mass arrests took place and, in the North, partygoers began to complain about police violence, while police pointed to arson and violence against their officers. From now on, acid house wasn't a funny youth trend like Hula-Hoops or Gonks; it was a major social issue.

OLD BILL, OLD BILL!

Whatever their motivation, the authorities took shutting down raves very seriously. By summer 1989 the police were using savage and often illegal methods – according to testimony: batons, police dogs, raids, roadblocks, confiscation of equipment – making every night a liability. Since most raids happened in the middle of the night and required enormous police manpower, the overtime costs to the taxpayer were horrendous, for very small beans.

'In a way it was more threatening than punk because it was on a large scale and it had an identifiable drug. It's an anarchic situation. If there's 10,000 people on drugs, that's a threat.'
Jack Barron, journalist

The irony of it was – as everyone who went out knew – give or take the odd gastric accident in a forecourt, pilled-up dancers were the most harmless bunch of people ever: 'puppies', as Boy George put it.

Theory Four: Tightness – It's Costing Them A Fortune
Take an E; drink less beer. The breweries killed acid house – it's a delicious theory, but will it ever be proved? 1990: Pub visits by young people had fallen by eleven per cent since 1986.
The Entertainments (Increased Penalties) Bill of 1990 – the one with the £20,000 fines and six-month prison sentences for party organisers.

– was put up by Graham Bright, MP for Luton South
– Whitbread plc is based in Luton
– which doesn't necessarily mean anything
– according to the *Observer*, 20.10.96, 'in 1993... Whitbread was paying Mr. Greer's firm more than £30,000 a year as a lobbyist.'
– Ian Greer is the Mr. Fixit that fell from grace in the cash-for-questions scandal
– who admitted, according to a report in the *Guardian*, 12.5.94, that he broke parliamentary rules to get questions tabled for clients
– Ian Greer Associates' MD Jeremy Sweeney then went one further, running off a list of MPs he claimed to have connections with
– which included Graham Bright as 'somebody I can pick up the phone to and just run things past on a totally off-the-record basis.'
– Graham Bright was himself implicated in a questions-for-cash scandal. In a letter leaked to the *Guardian*, 26.6.96 he invited a businessman to put his political views forward before asking, "Are you happy for this viewpoint to be passed on to the Number 10 policy unit (the Prime Minister's office)?", then "Would you consider making a contribution (to the Conservative party)?"

All in all a set of unrelated circumstances and bold speculations that should in no way be allowed to cast a shadow on Graham Bright's selfless commitment to 'protecting young people'.

Theory Five: Arrogance – People Can't Look After Themselves
In fact, most people are whey-faced invertebrate lily-livers when it comes to drugs – they don't overdo it. No one gets duped into taking drugs. Drug takers are not innocent victims of evil pusher Fagins; they are fans of an illegal intoxicant. People on drugs are not 'mindless': taking drugs is hard work. If you knew how hard their brains were working, you'd be stood there with your gob open, too.

Theory Six: Testosterone – It Gets Them Hard
Acid house is a bogeyman, and we need bogeymen to feel good about ourselves. There are only two types of people in society: people like us and scum.

LIFESTYLE

'You're going out Monday, Tuesday, Wednesday, Thursday. Friday you'd *have* to go out; Saturday was a definite. Sunday you might chill until something happened Sunday night, but you'd have to go out Monday to tell everyone what you'd been through.'
Jarvis Sandy, Biology

ANTICS

By 1989, Britain was in the grip of a national silliness. No one had thought it would still be going by Christmas, let alone by the next summer. Liberated by drugs and dancing, people from their teens to their forties found themselves in the throes of a second childhood. And they were making the most of it: silly clothes, silly dancing and doing a whole range of very silly things indeed …

'In the early part of 89 I was taking such large quantities of ecstasy and acid I was convinced I could talk to animals and that they could understand me. I was living in Chelsea and, when I'd been out, I would come home and go into the garden and talk to whatever animals were available – a lot of birds and the odd dog. There was this black cat that I was convinced was in psychic collusion with my ex-girlfriend, spying on me.'
Jack Barron, journalist

'Nonstop naughties: it was like being back at school. You couldn't even go to the service station without a party. The back door would burst open, the music's blaring, people are dancing around the cars. Yahoo! In the middle of Sunday afternoon. I always wonder what the bloke in the garage made of it.'
Raver

'You'd wake up in the morning and the room would be full of things that people had made, like mobiles made out of bananas. Fimo necklaces. Everyone had to wear beads in our gang. One of us got sacked for losing it sitting at her desk with a selection of toys. Who was the black guy that dressed as a bishop?'
Helen, administrator

'We were sat on Brighton beach tripping, winding up the tourists. One of our mates had his arm in a huge plastercast and halfway through the day he said, "Fucking hell, for a minute there I thought I had a broken arm." I said, "You cunt! You fucking cunt!"'
Des Penny, manager, Flowered Up

'… all of us walking round this very posh area wearing newspaper hats. We found a load of dead-bird feathers and stuck them in and carried on …'
Janet, nurse

'I got banned from driving because we got caught racing Porsches. Racing them backwards. We did anything we could think of. Bungee jumping tripping … everything in those days had to be done tripping. Go to the Epping Forest, tripping; go to haunted houses, tripping …'
Wayne Anthony, promoter, Genesis

'We were very into going home and watching children's programmes. One night we got it into our heads that we had to go to Toys R Us. As soon as we reckoned Toys R Us would be open, we headed out for it. We never got there – I think we just forgot. Instead we ended up in this boating shed in the middle of this field in Totteridge, watching the ducks. Another night I was running round the club doing Les Dawson impressions, burrowing my head into the DJ's back while he's trying to mix, flapping my arms like a seagull and going, "I'm not saying my wife's fat, I'm not saying my wife's fat …"'
Ben McKnight, public-relations manager

Ben McKnight reflects on his excursion to Toys R Us

'I was living with my friend and her mum in a big posh house on Kingston Hill. We were rolling in the sandpit and painted the interior of this beautiful house all mad colours and wrote "Acid love children" in fluorescent colours on the wall. Her mum banned her from seeing me.'
Vicky, mortuary attendant

'One of the strangest things that happened to me was a guy who knocked on the DJ-booth door with a gun and asked for my records. It all appeared so surreal that I just closed the door and carried on playing.'
Dave Haslam, DJ *magazine*

SOD MONDAY – A CELEBRATION OF SUNDAYS OUT

You can go out all week, but no day feels like Sunday for sheer hedonism. By six o'clock on a Sunday evening any sensible person has gone home to watch something sponsored by bad lager with Helen Mirren in it. You, however, are standing on the grass verge of a B-road waiting for some loopy teenage girls you've just met to remember not just *where* they left their car, but *if* they had a car in the first place.

Having a nine-to-five job didn't seem to make the slightest difference: in 1989 Tuesday was the new Monday. People stayed out as long as humanly possible and, where sterling drugs allowed, longer. If the three-day week had happened in the late eighties, it could have killed half a million people.

No one wanted to break the journey. By Sunday people were going deeper and deeper into the sensation, the connection getting more and more intense: at some points people could communicate just by looks. With the music rolling on and on wherever you went, weekends were a never-ending musical voyage with tapes in the car, tapes back at the house, pirate radio crackling away in the background like a Geiger counter, music for cups of tea, ashtrays and sweaters. It could feel like you'd been in a battle, an historic event. The trick was not to go home…

SUNDAY CLUBS – WE WILL REMEMBER THEM

Stawberry Sundae
Sherbert
Haven Stables
Shave Yer Tongue
Passion At Valbonnes
Solaris
Eclipse

Swimming pool action on Sunday nights: could things get any messier?

Sunday Club – Solaris

Solaris was a much-missed, high-energy, Sunday-night club, run by fashion designer Nick Coleman, Dave Manders and Roscoe. Ian Pendleton worked there:

'Solaris was a weird place to have a club – it was in the basement of a city wine bar in Grays Inn, and the whole area was completely dead on Sunday night. Inside it had a low ceiling and it was all about dancing. There wasn't really any way to talk: people would arrive and go straight on to the dancefloor and dance for six hours solidly. Solaris was such a happy club: everybody seemed to be having a brilliant time and throwing their arms round each other. There were people of different ages, even one old guy who must have been about sixty, totally into it. He'd always have a hat with dangly beads he'd bought in Thailand, and he'd spend the whole evening from six o'clock to one in the morning on the dancefloor. By the end of it some people looked a complete mess – you'd get these guys coming up to you on their way out covered head to toe in sweat, throwing their arms round you: "Thank you, thank you, it's the best place on earth." The only horrible sight was at the end of the evening when they had to empty the air conditioning. They opened a series of taps in the ceiling and put a bottle under each tap. The liquid would just pour out and there would be six buckets full of sweat, literally brimful of horrible human sweat.'

GREAT LOST SENSATIONS OF ACID HOUSE – GOLDFISH-MEMORY SYNDROME

'You were in mid flow – you just go completely blank. And everyone who'd been intently looking at you, hanging on your every word, just looks at you and they can't remember a thing either. It's "You said this, then I said that and … Oh! Nearly had it then". Fuck! I've lost the plot. Call the police and have me arrested.'
Fiona Crawford

GREAT LOST SENSATIONS OF ACID HOUSE – SPASMS

'One Monday morning I was at my desk typing and my head started to drop and I had a huge spasm: one hand knocked over the tea, my foot kicked out and the bin went over. I probably went "MMMUHHH!" as well.'
Anonymous girl

GREAT LOST SENSATIONS OF ACID HOUSE – TWITCHING

'Twitching! I used to shout out and twitch. When I'd really been at it there'd be no gaps between twitches.'
Another anonymous girl

GREAT LOST SENSATIONS OF ACID HOUSE – SHOPPING

'Trolling round a supermarket at seven in the morning, all the products are all the same label. Everything had gone Repo Man.'
Beautiful Ben

GREAT LOST SENSATIONS OF ACID HOUSE – SPATIAL-AWARENESS PROBLEMS OR 'OW BIG?

'I knew I'd overdone it when I was driving a little car, a Suzuki Whizzkid, and, when we got to the width restrictions at Hammersmith Bridge, even though the car was tiny I had to get out and push the car through.'
Vicky from Notting Hill

Embarrassing Day Jobs – The Grange Hill Gang: One of the girls from the 'Just Say No' anti-drugs song was out all the time.

Mysteriously, few vouchers were ever used

Queens Night Club

This ticket entitles you to £1.00 off your meal

Solaris Sharons: massive white trainers, long-sleeved white T-shirts, white baseball caps, and shorts with shiny black tights. And, as for the men …
'Solaris had a real look: there were the Nick Coleman T-shirts with long sleeves with a slight American baseball influence – maybe orange sleeves with white cuffs or coloured panels. Massive hightop trainers – Nike Air, Travel Fox – and a rucksack on their backs. And a stupid hat. There were a lot of all-white, American shellsuits – they were quite a new thing then. Stripes down the sleeve or down the leg. Roscoe had a particularly horrible one in silver and red – he wore that every week.'
Solaris clubber

'Hats were *de rigueur* at Solaris. One night I remember the dancefloor looking more like a Lapland deer herders' convention than a nightclub.'
Mick Robinson, Duffer Of St George

'Solaris started on Sunday evening and people had already been raving all weekend. They'd have been out in the countryside somewhere, got back in the afternoon, gone back to someone's for a spliff and a bowl of cornflakes, then come straight to Solaris to start dancing again. I noticed people starting to bring a clubbing kitbag: a rucksack with a change of clothes, even a plant-sprayer full of water. Halfway through the evening they'd hide near the cloakroom to change and get straight back on the floor.'
Ian, Solaris worker

Sunday club – Queens

Queens was the country club of the house scene. Phil Perry and Fiona Crawford took over a dodgy disco pub over the Queen Mother Reservoir near Slough and turned it into the definitive out-of-town Sunday experience. You parked the car, climbed up the hill, said hello to the people on the trestle tables on the balcony, briefly stared at the barbecue in disbelief, and headed for the dancefloor. It was a perfect picture: the misty turrets of Windsor Castle above you, the beautiful people cruising slowly on their boats below and, in the middle, hundreds of dishevelled weekend-warriors going berserk.

Martyn Passey and friends on the terrace at Queens

'I remember running up that hill – can't wait to get in – panting. We used to have this thing that we'd drop our Es at Heston Services. Then we knew we'd be up when we got there, and it would be straight on the dancefloor …'
Wayne Shires, promoter

All the tensions of Saturday night would be over. Everyone had a chance to relax in the ecstasy afterglow, ready for a soothing pint or five to calm nerves frazzled by pharmaceuticals.

'There's always been a club this side of town on Sundays for about seventeen years. It used to be the Belvedere, run by Chris Brown. Everybody used to congregate there, in the days when pubs used to open till three o'clock. People used to come from all over the place, even as far as Brighton and Oxford. When the Belvedere finished, there was a gap with nowhere to go, so we started Queens in March 1988 on that same tip.'
Phil Perry

Queens posse: Phil Perry, Ali, Wayne Shires, Max, Paulo

'When people found out there was this little club over by the airport, that was it. It all took off one Sunday after one of the Sunrises. We looked round and thought, Christ! There's seven hundred people in here: where did this lot come from? What I remember most is the faces walking through the door. Somebody had found this little secret.'
Fiona Crawford

'Me and Kate used to go to Queens in her old Talbot with the hole in the roof. Kate had to be up early on Monday because she worked in an office, but we still stayed out every Sunday. We'd always come back after Saturday night but only to have a cup of tea and go straight back out again. We used to read the Sunday papers – they were baffling.

'We used to stand on the terrace at Queens looking down the hill to see who'd turn up. You could tell where people had been the night before from the state of their clothes: people would turn up at Queens covered in mud if they'd been to some do in a barn, or if they'd been to a film studio they'd have paint up their legs. No one gave a shit.

'In those days the only people that looked smart were the Arsenal boys, the brothers who always wore things like camel coats. People didn't mind being filthy: it was part of it. I didn't want to wash my hair until the weekend was over. I liked the feeling of my clothes loose from dancing all night, with a flat stomach from shitting my brains out, my hair gone wild and smelling of fags and wherever we'd been. All I wanted was clean hands – washing your hands was a thrill! I think the day people started dressing up to go to Queens was the day the whole scene went down the pan.'
Emma, member of Queens

Boy's Own *East Grinstead*

BOY'S OWN

'I was DJing and this punter comes up to me, and he says, "*Boy's Own*? *Boy's Own*!" and gives me this nod. Like it was a secret society!'
Ashley Beedle, DJ

Boy's Own defined the Balearic movement with a fanzine with everything from vivid social comment to book reviews, running a *Boy's Own* film day and parties that feature in sociology books about the era. The people behind it, Terry Farley, Andy Weatherall, Cymon Eckel and Steve Mayse, were highly influential, using *Clockwork Orange* imagery while everyone else was a fluffy love muppet (Shoomer, 1989: 'There aren't enough bunny rabbits in the world.'). At a time when the style press had its head so far up its arse it could mouthfart Yohji Yamamoto interviews (fact: no one ever bought a Yamamoto garment, ever), *Boy's Own* was writing about the perils of E versus lager. Vicious, funny, passionately left-wing and passionately anti-rave, their fanzine was on the money and wrote about what people cared about.

DRIVING AROUND IN THE MIDDLE OF NOWHERE

'... in the middle of the countryside, it's pitch-black and you realise the address you've got for the party is just that little bit wrong enough for you not to be able to find it – then you see a police car parked in a side road. You carry on past it, of course, and an hour later when you still can't find the party you go past it again and it's still there doing nothing. You know that if it's sat there it's probably because the party's down the side road – but how long will it take you to get the bottle to turn down that road and drive past it?'
Anon

GOD, WE LOOK NICE

'When you were on E you'd look at yourself in the mirrors in the toilets and you'd look incredible: your skin, your big soft eyes ... There was a halo around people: they were just special and nice. I think it's because they looked innocent. They *were* innocent. They looked beautiful because you were looking at their innocent souls. I used to fancy people I'd never quite fancied, but it only lasted a couple of hours.'
Kym Kennedy

LARGE EDDIE – GOD'S GIFT

Combinations of ecstasy and cocaine created a kind of hyper-geezer.
Meet Large Eddie, a man who, despite the huge weight of looks and style God had asked him to bear, bravely struggled on with the task of sharing his greatness. Below are just three items from Eddie's *Phrasebook of Large*:
1. 'I'm digital.'
2. 'I've got a rocket in my pocket.'
3. 'You should have seen me last night. I was large. Not as large as I could have been, but large.'

Life with Eddie was full of peril:
'I was in the back of the car and Eddie was driving. We were coming up to the traffic lights and he was looking at himself in the rear-view mirror. He said, "I'm looking pretty good, aren't I?" and Bang! We shunted into three cars.'

DANCING TO THE SILENT BEAT

'One night after Confusion, I remember two kids dancing to the inaudible beat in a doorway and the police walking by and not stopping them.'

'You could see people walking through Kings Cross in bandanas, in silence, dancing with their arms.'

'Some of our lot were in a back room at Turnmills, chatting and smoking and listening to the music. After a while the cleaners came in and told them they'd been locked in for hours and they realised they could still hear the music in their heads.'

How They Met

'Andrew and Cymon were from Windsor and me and Steve were from Slough. It was the posh and the scum! The local kids used to go over the river to Eton to beat up the kids from the private school. That's what the Jam song 'Eton Rifles' was about. The thing was: if the Eton kids fought back they'd be expelled, so you'd get these horrible little oiks from our way going to beat up great sixteen-year-old rugby players knowing they couldn't fight back.'

Terry Farley

Since the early eighties, Liverpudlian Peter Hooton and some football hooligans had been writing a very funny, opinionated left-wing fanzine about dole casuals called *The End* (below left), inspiring a Chelsea fan called Terry . An excellent writer, Terry picked up the sartorial baton and soon *Boy's Own* was laying down the style laws for southerners.

From a small self-published fanzine, *Boy's Own* grew into a party organisation, a record label and, today, their splinter record label, Junior Boy's Own, originally a collaboration between Terry Farley and label manager Steve Hall, is one of the most influential independent record labels in the country. It launched the Chemical Brothers, Underworld, X-Press 2 and half of Beth Orton and recently did a deal with Richard Branson's label V2 for an awful lot of money.

In August 1989 they put on the *Boy's Own* East Grinstead party, a night widely agreed to be the best do of the whole movement in the South, on a par with the early Blackburn raves. By 1990 *Boy's Own* wrote about things being 'far from rosy in our garden', and for a few more months Andrew Weatherall bravely struggled on with the burden of being the living Christ, but the love horse had bolted.

The End, 1983: Scouse v Cockney

Boy's Own Party Highlights

'The first one we did was probably the first outdoor party in Britain, in an old barn in Guildford. It was in a barn in the garden of this guy's farm – in spring, 1988. Danny Rampling didn't do that one because he wouldn't close Shoom for the night. It was the early ecstasy thing, and it was a little bit too much for everyone. There'd be a lot of collapsed bodies lying about. The police didn't have a clue what was going on. They hadn't even heard of ecstasy. There were all these people smiling, going up to the police and chatting, offering them Lucozade. One of the policemen looked around and said, "I think we can leave this lot: they're a silly old bunch of cunts, aren't they?" and left.'

Steve Hall, Junior Boy's Own

HEAD TOWARDS CROYDON OUT OF LONDON DOWN THE A23.

ONCE THRU NORBURY TAKE THE A22 DOWN PURLEY WAY.

FOLLOW THIS ALL THE WAY TOWARDS EAST GRINSTEAD.

'Best party? I have to say *Boy's Own* at East Grinstead, simply because it was such a nightmare to put on, because those things were illegal then. You could pay someone to use their land, but it was still illegal because no one had a licence to play music, or sell drinks! Then on the actual night there was one of those big tacky raves about ten miles away from where we were having ours, so the police stayed there all night, because there was all these nutcases running round the local village.'

Terry Farley

JUST BEFORE YOU ENTER EAST GRINSTEAD,

THERE IS A SET OF TRAFFIC LIGHTS MARKED A264 (GATWICK) and EAST GRINSTEAD STRAIGHT ON.

GO THRU THESE LIGHTS FOR 300 YARDS TO THE NEXT SET AND THEN TURN RIGHT DOWN IMBERHORNE LANE.

'The thing where people say "I was there" always goes on. It's like "I went to Shoom", "I saw the Sex Pistols in 77". Our parties became one of those things.'

Steve Hall

DRIVE DOWN THE LANE, STRAIGHT ACROSS THE CROSSROADS.

NEXT JUNCTION VEER RIGHT, CONTINUE ALONG LANE.

YOU WILL THEN SEE ENTRANCE AFTER STEEP HILL.

'It wasn't till ten in the morning the police turned up. They were really angry. The place was full of drug paraphernalia, and it was time to pack up. But by then we'd had the night. At the time there were really a lot of people who were very creative, making things, and they were all there. It was really hot and we were sitting back watching the swans flying over the lake at dawn. It was the feeling that it would never be this good again – and it wasn't.'

Terry Farley PLEASE DRIVE CAREFULLY – THESE LANES ARE DANGEROUS.

'I always see a load of pictures from that one, these great images of acid house – people lying about on haystacks, dancing around as the sun came up. A hippie vibe still prevailed, rather than techno till you drop. It was a bit more "love and peace".'
Steve Hall

Boy's Own Top 5 Moody DJ Names
1. Darren and the Get Mental Crew
2. Reg E Reg
3. Mad Axe
4. Rodge the Dodge
5. Jim the Music Man

Dave Little

Boy's Own At Butlins: Mike Reid, Boy George and Brandon Block In Glamorous Granny Contest

'We did this weekend thing in Butlins in Bognor in about 1990. We were putting the sound system up and one of the Butlins staff kept looking over and smiling. Eventually he came over and said, "I know what you lot are up to: you're having a rave, aren't you? It's OK. Come and find me later and I'll sort you out drinks." Later, he came over and said to us, "Oh, this is great, I've done a trip," so as the evening progressed he got worse and worse, and eventually we lost sight of him, until we saw security pushing through everyone, and there he was, in his Butlins red coat jacking, and trancing out. Security had to pull him out. I checked later and he'd got the sack, poor bloke, but he was having fucking great time.

'That same weekend there was an *EastEnders* function going on. Everyone was shitfaced, and we'd worked out that we could infiltrate the other halls. Boy George, Brandon Block and a couple of other assorted people entered the Glamorous Granny Competition, compered by Mike Reid and Ma Fowler. It was surreal – people off their heads shouting at Frank Butcher.'

Lovable Club Speak
1. 'I'll do biscuits for a cockle, and Archie Moore for the capsules'
2. 'Stick me on the G.L. and I'll nose up the doorman'
3. 'Order me a sherbet, this gaff's jank'
4. 'Alright Babes, join me for some dom'
5. 'Listen geezer I'm doing a rave over south'!!!
Boy's Own

Where Are They Now?
Terry Farley is a successful producer and remixer and records with Pete Heller as Fire Island. Andy Weatherall set up the record label Sabres of Paradise, and records under the same name. Cymon Eckel co-owns the excellent London bar Riki Tiks, named after the sixties venue of the same name, does vast club nights and invented the colour combination of orange with navy blue. Meanwhile, from his Covent Garden HQ, Steve Mayes is fighting a one-man land war against all the evil in the world ever.

MANAGING THE DAY JOB
'One weekend, we had this big project and had to get all this documentation out to France, but I went to Queens and still managed to get into the office on Sunday night. I've no idea how. By that time alcohol had re-entered full pelt into my pharmacopoeia. I was wearing a Vivienne Westwood bondage suit as well, so I must have looked a bit mental. I had to use a hole-puncher, and serrated every single document, screwed them up and went and hid under a desk and phoned my boyfriend.'
Beautiful Ben

TOUGH-GUY SECURITY
'There's no way you're going to have an event and have eighty thousand pounds go through your turnstiles and no one try and take it. And you're out in a field in the middle of nowhere, and not a bobby in sight. It's a lot of money. Think what people will go through to rob a post office, and it doesn't matter if there's an old lady or an old man behind the till: they'd get a clump, too. And me? A brown guy in the middle of a field?'
Jarvis Sandy, Biology

OUR YELLOW VAN
'It was such a refreshing change to be going out in big groups – such an adventure every night. Every weekend was a mission. That summer I bought a car just for going round in – an old Post Office van sprayed yellow, almost smiley yellow – and I used to pick everyone up on the way into London. It was the most illegal vehicle possible. One night we started off near Borehamwood and went down through north-west London and, by the time we got to some warehouse or other in East London, 24 people jumped out. We counted them: it was either 24 or 26, that's the truth. Towards the end of the summer people had to stand up in the back of the van because there was no room to sit. We decorated the inside with posters, and started to get people to bring their own blankets and duvets and that's how my smiley van ended up being the first mobile chill-out room.'
Raver, Borehamwood

DRUG OF THE YEAR – DENNIS THE MENACES

Roguish little red and black capsules that looked like cartoon insects. Powerful chaps, they turned your legs heavy and made you want to sit on the floor. Gurning epidemic in clubland.

'We had the first Dennis The Menaces as testers. We took them to Kaos and this bloke came up to me and said, "It's not working, give us another." We forcefully advised him against it but he wouldn't be told. He came back after a while and said, "These are crap." By this point he was propped up against the wall. As he took the third one, the first one hit him and he was on the floor.'
Anonymous house DJ

CHARLIE THE HAT'S EAR INFECTION

'Charlie is older than your average raver. He was involved in some fracas in a pub and the police got called. He got taken to the police station and they found two red and black capsules on him. But the thing is: the police know about drugs but if they haven't got their rave hat on they aren't looking for it. And Charlie was pulled in a pub, and he looked comparatively old. They said, "What are these, then?" And Charlie said, "Oh, I've got a really bad ear infection: I have to take one in the morning and one in the evening."

'He spent the night in the cells and the next day he gets woken up by one of the police. They said, "How's the ear infection?" And Charlie said, "Er, it's pretty bad." And the police gave him the capsule and a cup of water and said, "You'd better take this, then."'
Paulo

ETHER – FAXING THE FIRE BRIGADE

'I had a huge litre bottle of ether in my bathroom. I bashed my knee in France and they gave me it to clean the massive scab. We came in very pissed one night having had some ropey Es and I mentioned the ether was in the bathroom. My friend went downstairs to investigate, then his girlfriend stomped after him.

'After a while they ran back upstairs, grabbed a load of teacups, filled them with water and disappeared. We ignored this. Then they came running upstairs and said, "There's a fucking huge fire in your bathroom!"
'The whole bathroom was glowing orange. There was a fireball in the bath and the shower curtain had evaporated completely. He'd been down there sniffing the ether; she'd snatched it and tipped it down the bog – then thrown her fag down the bog after it. The whole toilet went up. They were so off it they tried to fax the fire brigade. I put the fire out but I singed all the hair on my face. I had a bristly forehead. They couldn't even remember if the ether was any good.'

WHAT ARE *YOU?* WEIRD PILLS 1

'From one tiny grey and white capsule, I had a four-dayer, from Monday night to Thursday. It was very nice, no comedown, no depression. My pupils got bigger and smaller as the day went on. I was walking round Tesco's in dark glasses looking at the colours, all these pinks and reds. I remember following anyone because they were wearing a red coat.'
Anon

UPPERS
Having a mob of soldier ants as pets

DOWNERS
Seeing your pet ants 'thugging it' at the match on TV (wait till them little sods get home)

Sometimes hedonism requires you to go out on a limb, to throw caution to the wind, to join the paramilitary wing in the battle for the good time. It is just such fierce manoeuvres that lead to …

Extremely Embarrassing Moments
If You're Going To Do It, Do It With Style

'I walked around a *Boy's Own* party all night with vomit all over my shirt. I didn't care at all. I had a straw hat on and this really nice black silk shirt with a streak of sick down it. The worst thing is I threw up all over myself in front of Bobby Gillespie. I used to throw up quite a lot. Another time I remember being at a party in Southern Ireland on my hands and knees in front of a group of about ten people apologising for Oliver Cromwell. I was feeling full of remorse saying, "It's terrible what he did to Southern Ireland."'
Justin Robertson
Author's note: Justin Robertson is the coolest man in the world

'I passed out and my friends took my glasses off, wrapped them in sellotape with two bits of cucumber on the lenses, and put them back on my face.'
Colin Hudd

'Colin woke up, looked round at all of us, and said, "I don't think I've ever been this off it before in my life."'
Colin's friend

'I was staying on Gordon Mac's settee and I used to watch all his dirty videos. While he was in the next room I'd be sitting there bashing one out and coughing to cover the noise of the freezeframe. But what I didn't know was he had a window that swung out, and him and his girlfriend used to sit there watching me. I didn't find out till he got up and told the story in front of everybody at a Kiss Christmas dinner.'
Nicky Holloway

FIRST PERSON

RUDE BIRDS: THE LADIES OF ACID HOUSE

'The first time time I met Karon she was sitting in a puddle, shouting, "Fucking come on, then. Let's have it."'
Janet

'... police were surprised by the large number of girls who had to be searched and questioned ...'
Daily Mail, *1989*

According to the tabloids, acid house turned women into helpless flopsies, certain to be raped at one of the inevitable orgies that came with every acid house party. 'You'd be powerless to resist,' panted the *Sun*, its eyes bulging. Girls were innocents who only took drugs if men (usually evil, foreign men) spiked their drinks, like page-three Tracey ('the worst thing was hallucinating about those ants,' Tracey gasped).

In fact, the opposite was true. Most women agreed with the following:

'One of the great things about acid house was that I was able to go out on my own as a woman. I felt totally free.'
Kym Kennedy

'Acid house started the travelling around the country. Blokes used to go up and down the country for football matches but it never happened for clubs, so no women got to travel. Venus, the Hacienda, Scotland ... That had never happened before.'
Karon Dunn

Acid house was probably the most liberating invention since the pill. As anyone who lasted the night knew, acid house bred a legion of spectacularly intrepid, red-blooded young ladies. House fans were not dippy pictures of feminity, washing their hair in waterfalls. While the official British female was at home comparing whites and being grateful for the right to make gravy for her ugly bald husband and fat vegetarian daughter, the ladies of acid house were climbing on the roof of a car doing ninety. And, when they got going, they were worse than the men. One committed raver suddenly found his group was half girls:

'I noticed with rave that girls went from being the first to go back home to being really up for it. They'd be out all weekend. They weren't worried at all about going round with blokes. Without wanting to sound patronising, a lot of them were quite reasonably educated, but at the weekend it was off with the court shoes on with the Reeboks, and off they went. It was as though they seemed to be saying, "If only our parents could see us now." These girls mixed well with the narcotics, too.'

'I've got to behave myself today. After last time my boyfriend made me have bottom sex as punishment.'
Anonymous Rude Bird, following a display of lion-hearted vulgarity

'My definition of messy is trying to get a cab to Space. Standing outside Space.'
Dale

'The best fun I ever had was at First Tribal Gathering at Oxford, so fucked we were rolling around in the mud singing "Piggy Eat My Poo".'
Janet

Hold Me Coat – I'm Making A Mess

Some of the most memorable affrays of the house scene were started by girls.

1. The Doughnut Fight, after Respect at Bray.
'Suddenly the whole car park was doughnut rain. We saw off Anton the Pirate. I never saw him again after that.'

2. The Orange Fight, Deja Vu Magical Mystery Tour
'Whack! An orange! Bosh! Hundreds of them! The biggest fight I ever saw, oranges flying across this field ...'

3. McDonalds, Slough
'An excellent food fight, great, tremendous. It got a bit out of hand – suddenly a pot plant landed right in someone's burger box ...'

You're Fucking Nicked, Young Lady

'I was caught dealing acid. I was off my head and when they dragged me outside the club there were all these other plain-clothes with long hair in smiley T-shirts, which made it worse – I couldn't stop laughing. I was going "Ha! You've got it wrong: you've got your T-shirts tucked in your jeans!" At the station they couldn't get any sense out of me so they put me in the cell and I thought I'd better sleep, but the bed had this blue fluffy blanket and bits kept coming off it. You know when you're on acid, I thought all the bits of fluff were getting in my mouth – so I couldn't sleep.

'Then I thought, what can I do? I know: I'll sing to cheer myself up. So I started singing "Girl I'll House You" by the Jungle Brothers. I was dancing round the cell singing, "When – you're – in – my – house ..." Then I hear singing, coming from the next cell, and it's some young bloke joining in. We both ended up singing 'Dance With The Devil' in our separate cells, doing all the bells together – "Da da daaa! Da da daaa!" – and jumping around the room.'
Anon

Vicky, 28, used to go to Shoom, Sunrise and Spectrum and now goes everywhere.

'I used to work in the anatomy department of [major city-centre hospital], embalming dead bodies for the students. I used to take trips to go to work, which was to shave the bodies, cut their legs open and put two formaldehyde pumps in the main artery. I had to inject the fingers and then I had to drill a hole in their heads and do their brains with a syringe. All this, tripping. I used to dance around with the skeletons singing "Can You Feel It?". My behaviour got so strange they sent me for a brain scan.

'The corpses were mostly old people who had donated their bodies to science I used to give them mohicans with an electric razor. I thought it was really funny – vrrrh! I used to sniff the ether for a buzz. They had chloroform there, but I thought, No, don't – chloroform's bad. One day I came to work and said, "Right, I'm going to do the choloroform." I had a big sniff and thought, This doesn't do nothing. They had these big stone steps there and I started to walk up them, then straightaway flopped right back down. They thought I'd fainted and gave me the day off. Wahey!

'The day I knew I'd lost it was when I went in tripping and got all the hand-towels, wet them and built statues out of handtowels in the sink. They came to find me, but by then I was hiding in the toilet and I'd made loads of ammunition. I had balls made out of wet handtowels and I started pelting them. They stood staring at me and I was laughing my head off.'

Revenge!

'Our mate was going out with this promoter and he'd been a real cunt to her, getting off with other women. So we went to his club one night and, while he was talking to someone at the bar, we went downstairs and found his office. We needed to go to the loo and I bent down and had a wee on his carpet. Then I opened his desk drawer and had a poo in it. It was a real Mr Whippy one as well. My friend couldn't believe I'd done it. We laughed so hard my friend knocked the first-aid cabinet off the wall. The best bit was that we knew he'd probably take some bird back to his office and, sure enough, later we saw him through the window in there talking to this bird. She was sitting on his desk and we knew it was just a matter of time before she said, "What's that smell?"'
Ann

BIOLOGY – MR BIG REVEALS ALL!

At six foot four, Jarvis Sandy will always be Mr Big. Stalking into a Chelsea wine bar in an extremely flattering sweater, he leaves a trail of ladies' glances, waiters' nods and Jaguar salesmen rubbing their hands with glee.

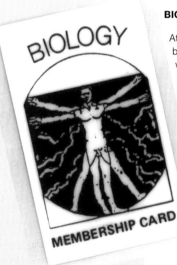

'People say, "Jarvis, you flash bastard," because I wore nice clothes. We'd arrive at someone else's rave by limo, ten-handed, with a couple of cases of champagne. I'd hired Bros's limosine. It had a televison; it was lowered...

'At first my mum thought I was mad. My friends are telling their mums what we're up to; their mums are reading the papers and ringing up my mum. [In a West Indian falsetto] "Jocelyne! Do you realise what your son's doing?" As far as she saw, it was drugs etc., etc. I had to put it on the table to her: "Mum, I've done worse things to obtain money. I wasn't selling drugs. I had people coming to me after my dance saying, "Boy, if only you knew how much I earned at your party tonight!" They'd tell me what they'd earned: they'd earned more than me! Forty grand, fifty grand profit.'

The 40,000 People Rave That Never Came Off: £170,000 Down

'I was trying to illustrate that it was about dance music, so I flew to NY to arrange to bring in Public Enemy and EPMD as well as all our house acts like Richie Rich. The venue was an equestrian centre and the people that owned it were two, shall we say, very rich ex-gangsters, so the police going to them, "You know you're going to have drugs in here, blah blah blah," wouldn't phase them. I knew they wouldn't budge. The police served an injunction on me. It was the first time I'd ever had to cancel an event and I went back to my office and I sat in my chair and cried. I wish I'd said, "Fuck the Old Bill!" and gone ahead with it.'

FASHION
I CAN'T BELIEVE I USED TO GO OUT IN A SUIT

'We used to walk up and down the King's Road looking like luminescent Belisha beacons: pinks, oranges, mauves … We used to call it going out to scare the public.'
Anton Le Pirate

There was a point in 1989 where it seemed like people would never wear tailored clothes again. If it wasn't rainbow-coloured and cut like a rhino's birthday suit, it didn't get worn. By the second summer of the second summer of love, fashion shops had caught up with ravers and you could easily buy clothes that looked the way you felt. Now there were casual lines like Naf Naf coming into their own, and the hardest, most muscly ravers were proudly stepping out in the most unlikely colour of the spectrum – lilac.

This could be the Maddest party you've been to. (well, in a club anyway).
Don't fear – no ~~Ruffians~~ will get in!
'Lilac clad casuals!
Try to get Thursday off of work (if you can!).
R.I.P. SHOOM! CPS. Try to bring your nen cards!)
Love + Respect. The RAMPLINGS. ☺ ☺

HOW MARTYN PASSEY BECAME THE PEOPLE'S POET

It gives you some indication of the kind of scene it was that from time to time the DJ could interrupt the evening, leaving thousands of clubbers stood there in mid-dance, while someone read poems. Nelson Mandela, Hillsborough, the death of a clubber – Martyn Passey was your rhyming Balearic Gazzette.

Martyn is unusually sanguine for a poet. 'It's now hip to be a poet, with Murray Lachlan Young and that. But when I was doing it, ten years ago, it wasn't. I admit I wrote some terrible poems, but it doesn't have to be clever or rhyme; it just has to come from your heart. You can become very introverted but, if one person comes up to you and says they're into what you're doing, you are no longer isolated.'

Literary snobbery aside, there's no denying it took some bottle to get up and get poetic in front of some of clubland's most horrible people, 'and get away with it'. Until he took a wrong turning on a narcotic expedition, Martyn had never picked up a quill:

'I took a purple ohm, and it just went the wrong way. I ended up in West Middlesex hospital, where they stripped me naked, put me on a stretcher in a corridor where all the accident victims came in and left me there all night. This sister leant over me and her face was a massive caricature, really distorted, and she said to me, "Are you the man that's taken acid? Serves you right!" I remember asking a doctor, "Am I going to die?" and he looked at me and said, "That's not for me to say, is it?" which really freaked me out. When it was over I felt so good to be alive, because I thought I was going to be dead or mad, that I went home and started writing this poem. This freaked me out because I'd never written poetry before. I had no interest in poetry, but from that moment I couldn't stop doing it.'

SIGN OF THE TIMES
SUMMERS PAST
this place was here before us
LIKE the trees that stand so tall,
But these memories that it holds for us
WE'LL never lose though trees may fall,
For these people, and their music
& their smiles that shine so bright,
and those friendships that we've made here
that fill these dark dark days with Light,
So when your peering through the twilight
Of these years you've yet to come,
Just Remember this was special
& the times we had were fun!
MP 89
1st floor, Kensington Market,
Kensington High St. London, W8
TEL:- 376 0762

'You'd see people dressed head to toe in paisley. A mate of mine came to Love at the Wag straight from the building site, and it didn't matter – the bloody Wag club! I remember a friend of mine turned up at the Wag in a pair of slippers. This was not a fashion statement, but purely because he desperately wanted to party that night against his girlfriend's wishes. He told her he was popping to the shop to buy some fags and came via the Wag. The shoes changed the fastest. I remember being out one night and noticing that overnight absolutely everyone was wearing Kickers. Timberlands I always thought were a very strange phenomenon as they're the most uncomfortable to dance in – they kill your feet for at least two months and cost an arm and a leg, only to be completely ruined on a warehouse floor. A warehouse floor that produced a mysterious dark mush that was impossible to get off your shoes. A mush that came in different colours, for some reason. If you met someone during the week you could tell that they had been to the same party because their shoes had the same colour mush.'
Mick Robinson, fashion chap at Duffer of St George, and the man who brought you the Cheeky Half parties

FLARES
AARGH! IT'S HAPPENING AGAIN

Photo: Joe Bloggs

'You knew him by his dress … his hair was plastered down upon his forehead; he wore a peaked cap rather over one eye; his trousers were of fustian, and cut – like a sailor's – with "bell bottoms". This fashion of the trousers was the most distinctive feature of his attire and make-up.'
Manchester Boys by C.E.B. Russell, 1905

1890: 'Police Court Missioner to Lads describes how the "professional scuttler" wears "narrow-go-wide" trousers.'
Hooligan by Geoffrey Pearson

Permapunk DJ and producer Kris Needs is the man behind Secret Knowledge and Irvine Welsh's band Hibee Nation. He has toured with the Prodigy and Primal Scream and runs Creation's dance wing, Emmissions. Here Kris reflects on the savage power of trouser width in popular music:

'When punk was starting everyone else was wearing enormous Dan Dares and if you didn't look normal you were hated. The punks really were shocking people with their fashion. I remember feeling really daring for sitting on the train wearing one single nappy pin. When I went to interview the Clash, I wore what I thought were outrageously tight trousers, but while I was talking to them I felt this tugging at my trouser leg and a voice said, "What are these, then?" There lying under the table was Joe Strummer. He was appalled by how baggy my legwear was. Some time later he took me to meet Sid Vicious, and the first thing he said was, "You can't go and see Sid like that." He took me to his granny's high-rise flat in Royal Oak to lend me some more suitable trousers. They were so tight they were like a pair of tights and I left walking like John Wayne. But we met Sid and I passed the test.'

Paul Ryder is Shaun's brother and was a key member of the Happy Mondays and in the original line-up of Black Grape. Here Paul spurns the Mondays' link with the inverted trouser taper:

'The Madchester flares thing was weird, because the Mondays weren't wearing them. We wore normal trousers, Chevignon. We had worn flares several years before the Mondays hit: we were wearing flares when the Stone Roses were still Goths. In the North, casuals used to go to the match in flares. We'd already been and done that.'

Des was manager of the legendary lost rock band of Acid House, Flowered Up. He describes a night ruined by flares:

'I'd done acid and people were sitting up against the wall wearing flares, looking really soapy, and I thought the place was full of tramps. I had to go and sit in the car. My mate that gave me the acid came to check on me and I was shouting at him, "You cunt, you've fucked my night up." But it could have been the flares.'

The flare has straddled the globe: Joe Bloggs now sells in the Middle East and Russia.

24 inches you say? Joe Bloggs' boss meets Princess Anne

DRUGS

'We could really dance on acid. You could pick up whole different rhythms and do really fast footwork. I remember dancing on acid at Genesis at Lea Bridge Road and I thought the floor was lighting up in squares like when Michael Jackson dances in "Billy Jean".'
Dale

MADE IN THE 'DAM BY A BLOKE FROM NASA
TOP TEN MYTHS ABOUT E (ONE OF THESE IS TRUE)

10. It comes to Britain via some oil-rig workers on shore leave, because they don't have passport checks. Do they?
9. There are huge drug factories in Amsterdam run by a former NASA researcher. It's so pure he tests it himself every day
8. Chemistry students in the Midlands have got this very big shed
7. It's a chemical version of nutmeg
6. It's made by a religious cult out of pure, uncut Love. They bless each tablet
5. A Harvard scientist comes over once a year with a briefcase full. He doesn't get stopped because he looks really old
4. The shed's where they make the E. The chemistry students
3. It's heroin and acid sort of blended, you know, like coffee
2. It was commissioned by the FA to wipe out soccer hooliganism
1. It's made by starving Russians who are forced to make it now the cabbage mines are empty

Answer: Nutmeg
Ecstasy has a similar chemical make-up to this natural spice. However, you would have to eat fifty billion nutmegs to get the effect of an E, by which time you would be incapacitated by a craving for rice pudding. And dead.

BAD ACID

Only For The Headstrong – Acid
Not to be confused with acid house. In a particularly stupid period in journalism's history, the tabloids created the impression that thousands of people were having a fantastic time thanks to LSD. This was very much not the case: by and large people were taking the much friendlier, cuddlier, fluffier ecstasy.

Think of ecstasy as a dog and acid as a cat. Dogs are by and large soppy creatures who want to have some exercise and maybe dry-hump your leg. Cats are moody fuckers who, while highly entertaining on Monday, on Tuesday will poo on your duvet out of spite.

Effective Ways Of Calming Down Acid
Nice hot bath (shallow: above the taps is too full), nice duvet on the sofa, nice cuddle, nice cup of tea. Removing hand from blender.

Ineffective Ways Of Calming Down Acid
No matter what anyone tells you, another trip does *not* cancel the first one out.

47

NIGHT PARALYSIS
Some regular users began to experience night paralysis, also nicknamed night-nurse syndrome. Seemingly caused by interrupted sleep patterns, it scared you senseless by giving you the feeling of being wide awake but unable to move – rather like in a dream when you want to run but can't. Other less fortunate souls could move, and did, randomly. You could also hallucinate sounds and sensations, for example clearly hearing footsteps walking across the room or feeling pressure as though someone had sat on the end of the bed. You usually wrenched yourself awake or went back to sleep.

WHAT ARE *YOU*? WEIRD PILLS 2
Kenny from Epsom, 27, and Karl from Enfield, 28, bought some very strange Es.

'I don't know what was in them, but basically what these pills did was put you out for three days. When you came to, you couldn't remember anything apart from what you'd hallucinated. All I remember is I thought people were sitting on the end of my bed, asking me what the fuck I was playing at. I tried to argue my way out of it but I could tell they didn't believe me.

'Karl was in a worse mess. He was wandering around Bristol talking to himself. He was arrested for breaking into an Austin Allegro. His defence was that he could see *me* sitting in the back seat shouting at him. That's ridiculous: I couldn't have been there – I was still talking to the people sitting on my bed.'

'I was sitting up in bed. I could see a young bloke, a raver, standing next to me. I was hallucinating but I could see him very clearly. I can still remember his curly hair.'
Kym Kennedy

Italian House – The Roman Conquest

His name was Gino. Latino. And he was the teacher of the house music. Sueno Latino, Black Box, Starlight – in 1989 the Italians showed us how it was done. No moody garage for our linguini-stuffing continental brethren: instead they churned out ascending scales, major chords, screaming choruses and baffling lyrics by the bucketful. 'Ride on time,' yelled the bird-looks-like-a-bloke out of Black Box. Right on, incomprehensible sister, concurred the British, their cheeks flushed with the summer weather and the discovery that they *could* get pissed and take E at the same time.

Don't Go

'After the last record, they wouldn't let me leave. I'd have to hide behind the lights in Heaven.'
Paul Oakenfold

'I played the last record at the Slough Centre and they offered me £200 just to play one more. I thought they were joking but I eventually stuck one on, then when I looked at my wages there was the £200 there.'
Trevor Fung

MUSIC

THE DAISY AGE: ANTHEMS FOR SUNRISE IN A FIELD

1989 introduced Britain to something it didn't see very often: sunrise. Until 1989, sunrise was something for milkmen, teething babies and druids. No one could have predicted that by summer hundreds of thousands of us would be not only awake at dawn, but dancing in a field.

Sunrise: the best time to study man's tenancy agreement with nature. After hours of hunting down parties and drugs, sunrise was the first chance you had to work out where you were, what shape the dancefloor was, whether you were dancing in rolling fields of gold or the back-end of a sileage tank, what that stuff on your shoes was and whether the person you'd spent two hours talking to really had the head of a horse.

EVENTS

NUDE, HACIENDA, MANCHESTER • BOY'S OWN, VARIOUS, SOUTH-WEST SUNRISE, VARIOUS ENERGY, VARIOUS • NEW MIAOW, LOCK-IN AT QUEENS, SLOUGH • BIOLOGY, VARIOUS • WORLD DANCE, ORBITAL RAVE • BACK II THE FUTURE, ORBITAL RAVE • WEEKEND WORLD, ORBITAL RAVE AMNESIA, KU, IBIZA • CLAPHAM COMMOM, SPONTANEOUS GATHERING, LONDON CLUB SUPERMAN, OCCASIONS, SHEFFIELD • RAW, YMCA, LONDON KONSPIRACY, MANCHESTER • SIN, ASTORIA, LONDON • EL METRO'S, WINE BAR AT HAMMERSMITH TUBE, LONDON • CHUFF CHUFF, ANUGRAHA, EGHAM • MUD CLUB, BUSBY'S, LONDON • SHABOOM, BLACKPOOL BLAST OFF, RAVES INC., BLACKPOOL • LIVE THE DREAM, VARIOUS, BLACKBURN • TRAX, CAMDEN PALAIS, LONDON • TALKING LOUD … SAYING SOMETHING, DINGWALLS, LONDON • SOLARIS, GRAY'S INN, LONDON LAND OF OZ, HEAVEN, LONDON • RAGE, HEAVEN, LONDON • CLUB DOG, SIR GEORGE ROBEY, LONDON • DOWNHAM TAVERN, TONY WILSON'S SOUTH-EAST LONDON ALTERNATIVE TO QUEENS • SERVICE STATIONS

SERVICE-STATION FRENZY

Looking back, it seems bizarre to think that, for a short golden era in the late twentieth century, the motorway service station, that soulless temple to reconstituted hash browns, lemon-scented washrooms and strangely unfamiliar sweets in tins, would be kindled into soppy great campfires of affection and dancing. Football away games had taught the service station to beware the descending swarm that would strip it of its Toblerones, Um Bongos and, in some cases, money. But nothing prepared the M4, the M6, the M23 and certainly not the brand-new M25 for their new role as dancefloor. Wry rock journalist Jack Barron, unable to find Biology, reviewed his night in a service station instead. Here are some memories from the glory days of the slip road.

'You'd go to Leicester service stations, and people'd have their car sound systems pumping away in the car park. It was a mass of people, who were so

friendly. You could be dancing next to someone who was probably your actual enemy from another city, another football club, a full-on nutter, but totally loved up, and it was an amazing experience.'
James Baillie, promoter

'The times I spent waiting at South Mimms petrol station … I remember the nerves, the excitement – this mad panic to keep up. One time I wrote my car off and just jumped in with someone else and left it there.'
Gemma Walker, raver

Up until a couple of years ago, you could still go to service stations and see little bundles of girls and boys with baggy jumpers and eyes like tube tunnels steering trays of orange juice around Burger King, desperately concentrating on keeping their walk straight while their faces wobbled all over the place.

BLAST OFF 1

'It was in a great big green field with a river running at its side and an ancient wood across the river. E-Zee Posse played "Everything Starts With An E" and the bass was bouncing off the trees. In those days some of us used to wear swimming trunks under our jeans because they had the little pocket for your you-know-what, and I ripped my pants off and waded into the river. I remember standing there getting these rushes off the fish tickling my legs. People looked at me and wondered what I'd found, waded in after me and we were all standing in the water together going, "Oh wow!" I met people that night I kept in touch with for years.'
Andy Carroll

THE BLACKBURN RAVES

'There was this woman who wandered around with a basket selling tangerines and peaches, like a modern day Nell Gwynne on E.'
Andy Carroll

'I'd say I went to 99 per cent of them. I went to the one where there was the big fight, ones where the whole motorway was blocked off. A lot of people from Manchester, Leeds and Liverpool used to go. You'd drive to a pub, wait for someone who knew where the party was and then all jump in your cars and follow them. One time the police knew where the rave was, I don't know how. The convoy got there, and the police got there soon after. It turned into this massive running battle. The police were charging, hitting people, and people were chucking things back at them. It got pretty horrible. There were loads of photographers there and it was in all the papers the next day. Another time I saw a guy get his eye gouged out.'
Andrew Barker, 808 State

PASSION AT VALBONNES

'With Valbonnes, you were really relying on the person who could stay together enough to drive – we had hundred-pound cab bills and shit like that. I don't think it would have been such a great thing if it had been down the Shepherd's Bush high street.'
Wayne Shires

KONSPIRACY IN MANCHESTER

'Konspiracy had five rooms. Upstairs was the harder side of things. People like Nipper and Justin Robinson played fiercer music upstairs that developed into a harder style of house. Downstairs it was very dark with more students and women. The music was a lot housier, like the Hacienda. A lot of London DJs played downstairs like Fabio and Grooverider. There were local ones as well like

NEW MIAOW
By 1989 it was pitiably hard to have a party without police attention. Even if raids didn't stop your do, they hardly improved the atmosphere. New Miaow was a radical concept: get there in the middle of the night, get locked in and not let out till morning.

1.. YOU MUST ARRIVE BETWEEN 3 AND 3.30 ONLY. THERE WILL BE NO ADMITTANCE AFTER THIS TIME WHETHER YOU HAVE A TICKET OR NOT.
2.. AT 3.30 THE BOTTOM GATES WILL BE LOCKED AND NOT RE OPENED UNTIL 8 IF YOU FEEL YOU CANNOT STAY FOR THIS PERIOD OF TIME WE SUGGEST YOU DONT BUY A TICKET!

'When we got there there was a security man saying, "Turn your lights off!" Every ticket had your name laminated in it. I remember taking magic mushrooms and rolling around on the floor, going to the toilet and seeing that it was daylight and running back into the club, not wanting it to be day yet.'
Wayne Shires, promoter

PLEASE KEEP ALL MATTERS CONCERNING N.M. TO YOURSELF ANYONE FOUND DISCUSSING N.M. INFO WITH NON MEMBERS WILL FIND THEMSELVES GOING TO BED EARLY ON CERTAIN DATES!!

'It started at midnight and went on till eight in the morning and you got locked in so you couldn't leave. Bob Jones played, Phil Perry – the music was fantastic. We used to try and hang around for Queens the next lunchtime. One time we stopped off at Heathrow Airport and we were walking around Arrivals going up to tourists going, "Welcome to England! Isn't it the most fantastic place you've ever been to? You'll *love* it here!"'
Beautiful Ben

'Below the venue was a bright-yellow field of rape. It was the morning after, the sun was shining and it looked too inviting not to run into. Polish Tony decided he could fly. He went straight in with his arms out like a bobsleigh. But the liquid manure van had been. Everyone else stopped dead and he kept on flying, like Superman on shit. We had to drive home with the roof open and our heads out the window.'
Martyn the poet

Pickering, Dave Haslam and Jason Boardman. In the caves at the back we were playing soul, funk and hip-hop. Justin Robertson and Greg Fenton's Spice Thing was eclectic as well.

'The two main rooms were as they were, with seventies decor. It was put together on the wing of a prayer, basically. The caves were done by a guy called Dimitri Banglestein and contoured out of some kind of moulded white material with stalactites hanging down. He painted the caves with faces of people like Aretha Franklin and Jimi Hendrix, famous people in music and poetry.

'On the opening night a guy called Johnny White did some wheels made in ice that turned around and melted throughout the evening. People came from everywhere. Tony Wilson queued to get in. Things started going wrong after about three months. Somebody got stabbed there and everyone had to be filed out of the building and video-taped. There was a lot of indiscriminate battering because some people have aggressive problems that just aren't dealt with on any other level and when they are pissed up and drugged up it's fun to them to beat people up.'
Chris Jam, Jam MCs

ROOSTERFISH
'Phil Dirtbox's club: mucky, full of ICF. In those days there wasn't the choice so you had to mix with all sorts. Maybe in retrospect that kept it a bit spicy!'
Terry Farley

WORLD DANCE
N-Joi did their first PA at World Dance. Unfortunately they also chose that night to do their first E.

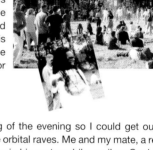

'Adamski had just played a wicked set as we walked on to the stage. I started to come up really fast on the E. I started this pathetic little keyboard line. It sounded so shit I said, "Turn up the bloody drums, Chris!" He looked at me reallly off his head and said, "What drums, man?" It was 8 a.m. and everyone at this huge rave was off their head waiting for us to be brilliant and we were barely audible and shit. After that I didn't dare perform for months.'
Nigel

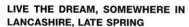

GENERAL ORBITAL NONSENSE
'I always tried to get the set at the beginning of the evening so I could get out on to the motorway and make it down to the M25 for the orbital raves. Me and my mate, a real Balearic god with long blond hair, used to go out raving in his partymobile, a silver Opel Manta with a really loud stereo. When we never made it to the rave or if it got shut down, we'd just throw open the doors of the partymobile, turn the sound up and have a party wherever we could. When we turned up people would say, "It's him with the kicking speakers!"'
DJ

LIVE THE DREAM, SOMEWHERE IN LANCASHIRE, LATE SPRING
Those notorious friendly rascals the Donnelly Brothers ran these. They went on to set up Gio Goi, the clothing company. The best one was in a huge deep valley with great rolling acres of fields on every side. It went all night, all day – it was so full of adrenaline. I remember clearly they ran out of DJs and played the Virgo 4 album all the way through, but it didn't matter – we just lay on the hillside with this beautiful warm bass tickling our stomachs, chunnering away with big smiles on our faces.'
Andy Carroll

BLAST OFF 2 – RICKMANSWORTH

'It was near a canal and, as light was breaking, the people who lived on the canal boats started waking up, looking at us and scratching their heads. A couple of joggers ran past staring at us. A few minutes later they came back with their mates. Finally the police, all staring up at us gobsmacked. And then the whole rave waved at the locals and cheered. It was the most moving show of unity. Halfway through the morning party, Harvey played Jimi Hendrix's version of "The Star Spangled Banner" and came over the PA and said "Her Majesty's forces are waiting for us at the bottom of the hill, so I think, if you've got anything on you that you shouldn't have, do it now before it's all a little bit too late." It sounded like your old man giving you sound advice. I looked around and everyone was nodding thoughtfully. Then everyone took their drugs out.'
Andy Carroll

LEGENDS, WARRINGTON

'Every Saturday morning I'd wake nauseous with excitement. On any other day Legends looked like a working-class social club, nearly concealed at the end of Priory Street's terraced houses. But Saturday night transformed it into a network of strange sounds, smells, colours and delights. The houses displayed banners saying PLEASE LEAVE QUIETLY REMEMBER THERE ARE RESIDENTS SLEEPING. The mythology of what occurred behind those four walls enticed them to their doorsteps at 2 a.m. They'd stare in disbelief as we left the club at our distorted pasty faces. Dozens of semi-naked bodies would skip past, immune to the severe November chill.

'The club opened at 9.30. Outside the girls exhibited their bodies in bright lycra moulded on to athletic figures in bikini tops and shorts. Caps, cricketers' hats, trainers were *de rigueur*. This sporty, sexy image was clumsily completed with oversize bubble jackets or Adidas parkas. In 1989 Legends played rich Italian house drenched in vocal. The interior of Legends resembled an oversized living room. Peeling wallpapaer, a damp carpet and a low ceiling ... a cosy warm environment, indispensable, of course, to a good E.'
Helen Walsh, Liverpool

CLAPHAM COMMON – A HAPPENING

Every Sunday in the summer of 1989, this bland stretch of South London municipal parkland became a free afternoon rave for up to 10,000 multicoloured loons.

'Anton the Pirate used to start it off sometimes. He came back from Sunrise, turned on some music. We'd finish working in Camden Market at five on

Sunday and it would still be going: thousands of ravers all sitting on the grass with music coming out of speakers, sitting by the Windmill pub.'
Haight Ashbury, Tooting

'We thought the Common would be the perfect place for the summer – we meant for the ten of us. I got back from Energy on Sunday lunchtime to see about two thousand people. By mid-afternoon, people were arriving from places like Southend and Bristol.

Ravers were turning up with their children – you didn't even know they were married. Members of the public brought picnics and sat down in the middle of us, saying, "Ooh, this is fun. What are you then?" A middle-aged lady in a real Laura Ashley dress was asking me if I could score her any blow.

'Clapham Common took the connections people had made with each other in clubs to another level. People weren't self-conscious yet and were still being silly with each other. Then some people printed flyers for Clapham Common and that was it: the police had to pull the plug on it.'
Anton Le Pirate

'There was a thing happening at Clapham Common. I remember Sunday afternoons when hundreds of people just used to descend on it, opposite the Windmill pub. That must've been what San Francisco park was like in the sixties. Clapham Common was where you could go when everyone was still buzzing but all the clubs were finished.

'Music would be booming out the back of cars – it was who had the biggest system. Proper sound systems did get strung up but the police broke them down. I remember one weekend when the police landed and everybody, the whole lot, got arrested. The police were after everybody who looked remotely like they might be into this acid house thing.

'Most of the people just went to watch the sun come up with their friends, or just to sit taking more Es and drinking beer. I remember Seal there. I remember him making daisy chains and selling them. Selling them! Mostly to girls, it must be said.'
DJ Dave Angel

THE TUNNEL CLUB, LONDON
'A group of about twenty young ravers all joined hands around a huge rotating lightball on the dancefloor, chanting. I said, "What are you doing?" They said, "We're opening up a gateway."'
Anton Le Pirate

'Evil-looking young men, like mature skinheads, were standing spread-eagled against the yard wall, being searched by police officers … sticks of chewing gum were on display, believed to be implanted with LSD …'
The London Evening Standard

'Out the back you used to get these amazing urban sunrises over these old gas tanks and wrecked cars. People used to be sitting there off it, staring at some old gas tanks, absolutely gobsmacked.'
Anton Le Pirate

'Drug dealers, a syndicate of ruthless black men, take command of these dances. In the yard at the rear of the pub, drug dealers and their customers converge for injecting, snorting and ecstasy-tab swallowing.'
Detective superintendents Thompson and Fullerlove (Yes, Fullerlove)

In January 1989, the Tunnel was raided by 390 officers. Six people were charged and eight bailed, seven pending analysis of substances (that'll be the chewing gum). Eleven were still being questioned the next day. But they got that LSD chewing gum, praise the Lord.

The Tunnel Club – London Evening Standard
'The landlady seemed shocked and incredulous at the sudden, totally unexpected invasion. With haunted, staring eyes that filled with tears as she spoke, she watched the damage to her dreams.'

Chapter Three
1990: MENTAL MENTAL RADIO RENTAL
– BETTER DEAD THAN AN ACID TED

ACID TEDS

Peter Hooton of Liverpool band The Farm explains:

'Ted is an old Liverpool word we used to use in *The End*. A ted was a dickhead. It originally described teddy boys because they were a laughing stock, and in the end it meant anybody.'

With acid house the term found its new home, as the Balearic contingent's name for the wide-eyed new clubbers flooding the dancefloors.

'I remember being in the toilet at Spectrum and two big blokes came in. One of them said, "What's this we're supposed to be shouting?" And the other said, "Acieed," and the first one said, "What does that mean?" and the other one said, "I dunno." And they both went out shouting it, fists in the air.'
Roger Beard

CLUBLAND DIVIDES

If you'd gone clubbing in 1990, you'd have noticed that all of a sudden people who'd been falling downstairs in yellow jogging bottoms were posing at the bar in black and white suits. Cool was back. What had happened? While the Balearic lot were voguing at the Limelight, Venus and Spice in John Richmond shirts and piling into the gents to do charlie, the nation at large was bombing around the countryside in a lilac hooded top with a speedy E in its stomach and a Vicks inhaler up its nose.

Q: Which group was having the best time?
A: They both were.

But 1990 began miserably for a lot of the original acid house crowd. Every last bod had access to an E and a ticket to a party somewhere. For people weaned on the small-scale, intimate house scene at Shoom and Future, the sheer scale of later parties made it impossible for them to let themselves go. Bluntly, it used to be about them and their friends and now they felt surrounded by a load of idiots. And there's nothing like ecstasy for turning out idiots.

January
The Public Entertainments Act is used to bring an injunction against a rave in Norfolk.
At a party in Rugby, Warwickshire, revellers stop dancing and attack the police.

February
Nelson Mandela is released from jail.
The Freedom To Party march goes through London to protest against the Pay Parties (Increased Penalties) Act sponsored by MP Graham Bright. Organisers claim fifteen thousand people; police two thousand. Shadow arts minister Mark Fisher fears the effect the Bill will have on barn dances. Graham Bright claims his Act 'doesn't affect things like the tennis club barbecue or the boy scouts' and says he is interested in 'protecting young people'.
Perrier mineral water is withdrawn worldwide after traces of benzene are found in several bottles. Shadow cabinet devastated.
Madchester is everywhere as the Inspiral Carpets sell six thousand 'Cool As Fuck' T-shirts.

March
At the court case in Dundee concerning an acid house party, the following exchange takes place:
Judge: 'What is acid house?'
Inspector Brown: 'I have seen it on *Top Of The Pops*. It is just a din, a noise which goes on and on. No rhythm, no words, but it seems to be in the current trend.'
Judge: 'What did you intend to charge them with?'
Inspector Brown: 'After I heard what kind of music was being played, I intended to charge them under the Misuse of Drugs Act.'
The Face predicts the return of mambo: 'What once looked likely to be consigned to the terpsichorean ghetto of *Come Dancing* is set to make a full-blooded return,' it says inaccurately. Five years later a Perez Prado tune is used in an advert for stout.
'What troubles me about this Bill is the smell of moral outrage attached to it. A politician is safer when he is slightly tipsy and accompanied by a prostitute than when he is under the influence of moral outrage' – William Deedes, former *Times* editor, on the Bright Bill.

April
The Poll Tax riots (see Events) do a lot of damage in London. Julian Cope attends, dressed as a six-foot alien called Mr Squbbsy.

May
Guru Josh tells the world, 'This summer will be very interesting because people are clued up to what's going on. The authorities think it's just a load of woofter kids out raving, but it's not. There's people with power and jobs and they won't tolerate being pushed around any more.' Quaver, evil-mister-fascist-prime-minister womanman!

June
231 people are taken for questioning by the West Yorkshire police after a Wakefield rave. 225 are released without charge.

July
The Bright Bill becomes law. You can now face a fine of up to £20,000 and/or six months in jail for organising parties on unlicensed premises and outside legal licensing hours. It is almost immediately used to arrest 836 people at a party in Leeds, one of the largest mass arrests of all time. £2000 worth of drugs are seized and the crowd retaliate with bottles and bricks. Most are released after a few hours and an official complaint is made against the police, who are sued for assault and unlawful arrest.

August
The DPP rules out criminal proceedings against Hillsborough police or officials.

September
Soviet troop withdrawal in Eastern Europe begins.
George Best goes on *Wogan*. 'Can I say "shit"?' he asks.
i-D run a music forum. 'As soon as it goes overground and as soon as the press arrives, they ruin it,' says Norman Cook, founder of PizzaMan, Beats International, Freak Power, Fat Boy Slim – the original underground king. (Underground Jonathan King, that is.)

October
Germany is reunified.

November
Margaret Thatcher resigns. National mood of exhilaration and sadistic triumph not greatly dampened by arrival of John Major.
Milli Vanilli are stripped of their Grammy for not singing on any of their records. 'We're so relieved. The past two years have been a nightmare,' says Rob Pilatus of the duo.

December
British teenagers Patricia Cahill and Karyn Smith, caught with 44 pounds of heroin, claim they didn't know they were carrying it or notice their luggage had just got three stone heavier. Just the girls you want to help you with the shopping.

'Later, it became very sceney and cliquey, because when you'd been into it for a while you could see the stages people went through when they started taking E. Firstly being totally into it, really losing their inhibitions. Then they started realising what they were involved in, who were the right names, what the right records to buy were. The ted thing came about because, when you're over the stage of being really into E yourself, you don't want some sweaty bloke with spit all over his face kissing you and telling you he loves you. At first you were really into your E too, but after a couple of months it was, "Yeah, all right, mate. Get off!"'
Chris, early Spectrum punter

Less sympathetic criticism came from the bastion of straight talking, *Boy's Own*. 'Stop moaning,' they wrote, 'that's what you can do.' But nobody did.

'The next time some plank in an E T-shirt grabs you in a sweaty embrace and shouts, "Can you feel it?" smile politely and say, "I certainly can … But you'll never understand, I'm afraid." Staying in moaning means these people have won.'
Boy's Own

Elitist, but *Boy's Own* expressed what a lot of people were feeling, bringing a choice old phrase from the Cold War era bang up to date: 'Better dead than an acid ted'.

The Balearic scene had a choice: adapt or die. It evolved dramatically. 'Anything goes' made way for smart dress and exclusive door policies. Kazoo, Spice, Monkey Drum and the Limelight had a new, sharper attitude. The great debate in 1990 was whether this was elitism or protecting your own. Opinion was divided, depending on whether they put you on the guest list or not. Either way, the Balearic crowd made the break from the rave crowd permanent.

1990 was a year in which a lot of people simply gave up and went home, particularly the original Shoomers. More of them were in their thirties and there were more E-babies around by 1990. Many people talked about the strange feeling of seeing a face in the street and realising that you used to have an intense bond with that person and the last time you saw them they were dancing with their eyes shut, grinning.

DID THE BIG RAVES RUIN IT?
'Bollocks. Absolute bollocks. I don't want to get into a slagging match but they thought they were special, they thought they were better than everybody else. The way I see it is, if they were doing something that good, their crowd would have stuck with them. In the end people wanted more; they wanted parties of ten thousand people. It's great to have these theme parties with three hundred beautiful exclusive trendy people, but the reality of it is the majority of people wanted to be in a warehouse with ten thousand other people.

'They thought they were all too good for everybody else. Their idea of having great gigs is all the really trendy beautiful people. They thought they were all too good for everybody else. There's more ugly fucking peple that want to go and 'ave it than there are beautiful people in this country. Our parties weren't directed to a particular kind of raver; they were just directed for everybody. Everybody who wants to come, cool. They were all on this egotistical ride that they didn't want anybody in apart from their special clique. If you weren't a designer, an artist, a singer, they didn't want to know. They just wanted to keep it to themselves.'
Wayne Anthony, promoter of Genesis, author of Class Of 88

TEDS – THE CASE FOR
'I went along to Norman Jay's club High On Hope and I was a bit the worse for wear. I was dancing like a lunatic and a total stranger told me to behave myself. My guess is he'd been a nutty dancer the year before and it embarrassed him now. For me, being an acid ted was the best thing about it. I expect it's like school: as you get older you learn a new system of behaviour and wouldn't dream of behaving like the new kids.'
Jack Barron

'All those blokes in waiters' shirts, people coming up to you saying "I've got a pair of trousers that cost £800" – it reminded me of the whole scene when we were really young and used to go out and really dress up. It started to get ridiculous, with all those stupid girls with perms and funny outfits. There wasn't enough dancing and really going for it.'
Ozman

'The essence of going out is dancing and going mad. If you can't do that you might as well stay in.'
Russell

Style magazines sneered at house the second it became popular. As early as September 1988, go-go and P-funk were two of the preposterous 'new' music fashions supposed to energise everybody 'now that acid house is dead'.

'Get on one, matey. You look as though you need it.'
Letter to the editor, i-D, November 1988

'Suddenly people were embarrassed to say they got on one. It was all standing in corners pretending to hide your cocaine when really they were going, "Here! Look at my fifty pounds' worth of drugs all in one wrap!"'
Anon

Dave Little (right)

'There were idiots with lights in their mouths, pulling all these faces. They'd be sweaty and they'd nick your drink. They'd come up to you and whip out a toy gun that sparked, and you'd go, "Oh, fuck off!"'
Anon

Dave Little was one of the early Spectrum/Future members who was not best pleased with the way it all went.

'From our point of view, the rave scene seemed something that was wrong, non-thinking and formulated. You're trying to keep something insular and here were all these people who didn't know what it was about. It used to have a balance between the partying and the ideology. There was definitely a hippie ideology when we started, a lot of peace and love and a very nice feeling for six months. The people who bought the smiley T-shirts didn't have the understanding of where it all came from. We had to watch it turn into this monstrosity that was all about money and big-time drug dealing. I used to stand on the balcony at Future with Terry Farley and Cymon Eckels shouting, "Better dead than an acid ted," at the people below, spitting pure venom at them.'

'One of the reasons that it was so great was that you stopped going out just to see which faces were there. We'd say, "Our scene's against all that." Then the Who's Who started to come through – and everyone thought they were part of the top end.'
Tall Chris

But, typically, *Boy's Own* could see the funny side:

'Downers: teds calling teds, teds'
Boy's Own

LIFESTYLE

ESSENTIAL CLUBBING ACCESSORY – SAVLON

Savlon ranks alongside mouth-ulcer tablets and little plastic money bags as a clubbing necessity. After two years of violent digestive incidents, the nation's brown starfish was a quivering, brutalised creature. Only with regular Savlon counselling sessions could it overcome its harsh treatment. Ruminating on the connection between Es and savage shitting, someone once remarked that 'once you pop you just can't stop'. An inevitable side effect of the country's favourite contraband is leaving an African face mask wherever you go. It's all a question of attitude: look forward to the anal cataclysm. Horror or poogasm? It's up to you.

'You always know you've had a good E when you go for that initial E-poo and suddenly come round, and realise you've been sat there twenty minutes. Then there's the stretch – oo-er! – and you're off.'
Andy Currie

SISTER EXPERIENCE TO THE E-POO – NO PISS SYNDROME
Speaks volumes. Which is more than you piss.

DETACHED FROM YOUR BODY
'I noticed that I stopped actually looking in the mirror – you might look in the toilet mirror in the motorway service station if you had a spot, but you weren't really concerned about the whole package. Plus, with your state of mind, the last thing you wanted to see was your own reflection. And diet went right out the window: we didn't eat food, we ate munchies and that was it.'
Anon

'I was DJing and doing the acid dance at the same time. I'm skipping away when some bloke comes up to me and says, "Do you think you could put another record on? Because that one finished ages ago."'
Johnny Walker

I USED TO BE A HOOLIGAN BUT NOW I'M ON ONE MATEY
'The Home Office reports that football violence has fallen in the previous year to its lowest level for five years, despite increased attendances.'
The Independent *August 1992*

The story of the hooligan-turned-ecstasy hippie sounds like a media invention, but the more you research it, the more testimonials turn up. Bluntly, the FA owes ecstasy a favour since it helped neuter football violence and pave the way to the reinstatement of British fans' rights abroad.

Football Violence: An Anonymous Testimonial
'I'm from the fringes. Me and my brothers used to go to Arsenal and I used to go to Millwall when I was a kid. When we went to a lot of the early acid house places especially the Poplar High Street dos and others around the South East, there were well-known faces from the football fraternity, Gooners, West Ham and Millwall, who were all well aware of each other. Whereas a few years previous it would have kicked off for definite, nothing was happening. We were really shocked, people were coming up to me saying, "Have you seen who's here?"'

'Why did the football lot go to acid house dos? I think it was the informality of the early dos. They weren't all blockheads, but apart from the odd cool club, if you went somewhere mob-handed or as a lot of blokes you wouldn't get in.

Also, I don't think anyone could do one of those early Calis and not have it affect them in the short term, or even the long term. It might click you into a new way of thinking. Some people were changed for good, it gave a lot of people a chance to relax. I bumped into quite a few Gooners who had chilled out. It still makes me laugh even now.'

Acid House Stopped Violence In The Clubs, But Did It Really, As Is Claimed, Stop Violence On The Terraces?

'Listen to this. When the 88-89 football season started, at the end of August 88, Millwall played at Aston Villa in the old Division One as was then, so they travelled up to Birmingham. Obviously Millwall have got quite a bad lot going up there. It's the usual thing, the whole big herd of them went up there for the first or second game of the season. There were the few minor stand-offs on the way to the match – you'd have the away fans arriving and there'll be the home fans shouting at them from the pubs on the way to the ground, with the police in between.

'So the game was over and they let the Millwall fans out of the grounds, the

police herding them down to the station. Some of the Villa fans were thugs and they wanted a bit of hooha. It was all a game to see if Millwall would live up to their reputation: these were people who, the season before, had been rampaging all over the place. But the Millwall fans didn't respond because they just wanted to home and get to a party or club that night. And a large number were still going from the Friday night. It's not widely known, but some of the police at football matches are really out of order and like to almost instigate it, winding people up. And at that match the Birmingham police were goading them into a rumpus, saying "You're supposed to be Millwall", pushing a few people around, trying to instigate a violent event. But a whole load of the Millwall fans were completely on one and no one wanted to know.

'Say you had a hardcore of about two hundred fans who were a bit naughty, up there for the usual beer and a fight, but a real big amount just wanted to get back and get back on one. I'm not saying it transformed Millwall into a family club, but it was quite a shock to the system. Quite a few people used to say that football was a priority, but these weekend missions became more of a priority. We used to go to a lot of away matches, and when house hit, without wanting too sound over-the-top, to us it was the kind of thing we'd always hoped for because you could go out in the evenings too and stay out all weekend. You can't quote my name on this one.'

Whether or not it stopped violence in the long term, house broke the habit for a generation of hooligans and, in the word of one former terrace warrior, 'it split up the pack'.

'Before house, I couldn't have gone to Leeds 'cos I'd have died. From my history in football, I'd have been killed. Now I was chief usher at the wedding of a bloke from Leeds. I used to follow Arsenal and fight this bloke from QPR. He's now a head of security for a club. Now me and him go to football together, and when they see us together the police shit themselves – they say to us, "What are you up to? What's this about?" I was talking about football to one guy from Up Yer Ronson at Leeds and I realised he was the very bloke that had started a scuffle years ago by throwing a coffee at me. We had a good laugh.'
Andy, former Gooner "on the register"

'I was talking to this man at Spectrum and he showed me a big scar down his face and said, "See that? I used to be a football hooligan but I've mellowed." I came straight out and said, "Why? Are you on drugs then?" He said, "I really quite fancy you but I don't know if I'm on a love trip or not. But I'll give you a free E though."'
Kym

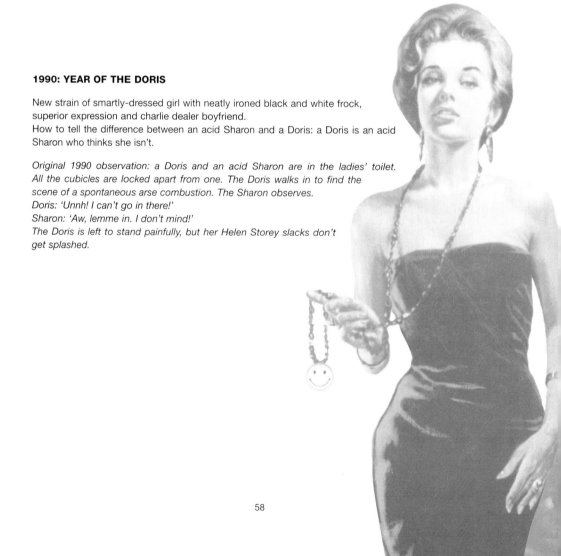

1990: YEAR OF THE DORIS

New strain of smartly-dressed girl with neatly ironed black and white frock, superior expression and charlie dealer boyfriend.
How to tell the difference between an acid Sharon and a Doris: a Doris is an acid Sharon who thinks she isn't.

Original 1990 observation: a Doris and an acid Sharon are in the ladies' toilet. All the cubicles are locked apart from one. The Doris walks in to find the scene of a spontaneous arse combustion. The Sharon observes.
Doris: 'Unnh! I can't go in there!'
Sharon: 'Aw, lemme in. I don't mind!'
The Doris is left to stand painfully, but her Helen Storey slacks don't get splashed.

FASHION

NEW AGE: THE SILLIEST LOOK EVER

OVERHEARD IN 1990
Two Shoomers, in New Age white tracksuits, are under the bonnet of their Mini

SHOOMER 1
The trouble with these white clothes is they get all messy

SHOOMER 2
(sighs)
It's just another new age problem...

There are two signs someone has sailed up their own arse without a paddle. The first: they start saying they hate the trappings of success. The second: they start dressing in white. The summer of 89 had seen a lot of off-white denim; people optimistically setting out to rave on a Friday night cream-coloured from head-to-toe. By Sunday, it looked like they'd waded through a lake of cow cud.

Come February 1990, however, a great silliness gripped the fashion scene. There was talk of a New Age, a new spirituality, a new super-sensitive colonically flushed elite. And how did this divinity express itself? The white shellsuit. And lo, they did take up 'healing' crystals and nonce about ambient rooms saying, 'Brian Eno, he doesn't date, you know.'

Even more unfortunately, this fashion caught on among the older clubbers, hence the bizarre sight of slightly tubby and over-the-hill club bods wobbling round in white cycle shorts and silver trainers the size of moonboots, wearing preposterous 'healing' crystals. By summer it became impossible to walk into a club without being deafened by the humming of hundreds of crystals promoting clear-headedness and reason among their idiot owners.

While all-white crystal-touting loonies skipped through city centres, everyone else in Britain billowed across the fields in baggy Chevs and flares the width of Ireland. In July, a windy spell blew the Stone Roses across the Pennines into the sea.

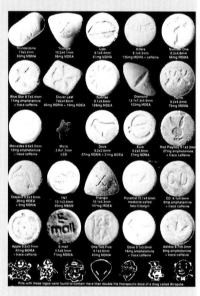

Warning: Some of these pills are filthy dirty nasty drugs, and dangerous – see Ecstacy Reconsidered *by Nicholas Saunders and the website below for futher details*
http://ecstasy.org

DRUGS

MEXICAN MUSHROOMS
Bigger, stronger and more colourful than conventional recreational fungi, these blue and yellow mushrooms were supposed to be from Mexico, but this could have been a ruse to get the price up.

'SPEEDY' ES: NOT LOVED UP MUCH
Blamed for the beginning of Tuesday Syndrome (see below). Everyone knew speed made you miserable, so they had to have speed in them, right?

'SMACKY' ES: I'LL GO AND DANCE IF YOU WILL
In 1990 this party-pooper's phrase made a reappearance for the first time since pre-acid, and gurning was the order of the day: some Es made you want to do nothing other than vegetate in a corner. In clubbers' understanding of drugs, old-fashioned E didn't do that, but heroin did, so clubs were full of people talking about new Es with heroin in them. These gurners' specials are now thought to be MDA as opposed to euphoric MDMA.

THE LATE NICHOLAS SAUNDERS, ECSTASY EXPERT, ON THE DIFFERENCE BETWEEN MDMA, MDEA AND MDA:
'MDEA and MDA are two common drugs similar to MDMA. All three are psychedelic amphetamines with fairly similar effects, although connoisseurs invariably prefer MDMA because of its empathic quality. MDA lasts twice as long (8-12 hours, while MDMA lasts 4-6 hours), is more speedy and has a psychedelic edge to it. MDEA (sometimes sold as Eve), lasts a rather shorter time (3-5 hours) and is nearer to MDMA in effect, but still lacks its communicative qualities.' This would account for a 'trippy' or 'speedy' E – probably MDA.
Ecstasy Reconsidered, top book with silver cover for blinding visuals

According to Nicholas Saunders, since the bust of a massive drug factory in Latvia, MDA has been rare. MDEA has been rare since it was made illegal in Holland in 1993. Saunders stated that as a result of this there has been more MDMA on the market... Time for another reconnaissance mission?

TUESDAY SYNDROME
Thanks to acid house, women got to experience that incredible communal buzz previously exclusive to men through football. And the female population gave something in return: thanks to acid house, men were able to share in a richly textured emotional experience previously exclusive to women – PMT. If a man really wants to discover his feminine side he has only to fill himself with speed and ecstasy for several months. Soon he too will feel all woman. Tuesday Syndrome perfectly simulates the murky depression, irritability and piquant despair of PMT. Done regularly, it guarantees that even the simplest household tasks will illustrate what a hopeless waste of space you are.

For most people, the physiological downside of ecstasy didn't materialise straight away. At first it was simple: fantastic euphoria on Saturday night, followed by a warm glow and very little interest in food until Tuesday when a mountain of pies would be in order. But by 1990, Tuesday was *not* a good day any more. The downer would kick in – feeling filthy-tempered, discouraged and, in particular, negative about yourself. Tuesday would find many partygoers marching down the street with a bag of fruit saying they had to sort their lives out.

MUSIC

The success of 'World In Motion' started a craze for drug references. EMF kicked it off with the alleged abbreviation of Ecstasy Mother Fuckers, but by winter things had gone too far with the release of Status Quo's Christmas single 'Raving Off Our Mental Drugnuts'.

SLOW DANCE MUSIC

Paul Oakenfold started *Movement 98* to foster slower dance music of 98 beats per minute, on the premise that everyone had had enough of fast dance music and wanted to chill out. This lasted until someone heard a fast dance record again and Paul Oakenfold is now heavily into trance, running Perfecto Fluoro to foster music with about four million bpm. Slow dance records that had that turn-of-the-decade feel included Frasier Chorus' 'Cloud 8', St. Etienne's 'Only Love Can Break Your Heart' and Doctor Mouthquake's 'Love On Love'. By now the Balearic tribe had a rhythm: James Brown's Funky Drummer slowed down by Soul II Soul, a constant unifying pulse wherever you went. George Michael, spotted at the Brain club dancing to his own record – badly – obviously picked something up. *The South Bank Show* showed the mildly terrifying sight of George Michael explaining to Melvyn Bragg how to mix in the Funky Drummer beat with a folky guitar for that perfect 1990 sound.

'I was ostracised for still playing house instead of all that "British" slow music.'
Phil Perry

'Happy Mondays – yuk! I probably shat my pants out of boredom in those days.'
Fiona Crawford

AMBIENT HOUSE – THERE'S NO SUCH THING

One lamentable trend that started in 1990 was so-called ambient house. Observing that clubbers were prepared to pay to sit on the floor listening to Brian Eno mixed in with the sound of whales whinging about the weather, ambient rooms opened up everywhere with their own made-up genre to go with it. José at the Café Del Mar in Ibiza had been playing relaxing music for years, but what he played was an inspired combination of anything from the Cocteau Twins to classical music. What he didn't play was cruddy dolphin noises and pan pipes from compilations with titles like *Flight of the Condor* and *Inca Moods*.

LET'S ROCK: PUT ON YOUR RIDICULOUS LEATHER TROUSERS, BABY. WE'RE GOING OUT TONIGHT

The Happy Mondays, the Stone Roses, Primal Scream, the Inspiral Carpets, two dancing gnomes called Candy Flip – in 1990, despite the fact that Britain now had several genuine electronic dance bands, a primeval urge to have guitars waved at them got the better of people. From the ashes of rock rose ... rock.

Never let it be forgotten that before acid house, no one danced to rock. For proof, see a Bruce Springsteen video. Any Bruce Springsteen video. Whatever Bruce is doing with his legs in that video is what people did to rock. After discovering they could dance in 1988, people were not going to suddenly stop, but by 1990 they were prepared to dance facing a band. However, house had made people's musical taste more sophisticated and, give or take the odd accidentally funky track, rock bands on their own couldn't cut it. Paul Oakenfold translated the Happy Mondays, Andy Weatherall became extremely close to Primal Scream, Terry Farley spin-doctored The Farm. By summer 1990 it was said that people would dance to Pink Floyd if someone put the Funky Drummer beat under it – and they did.

Rock bands were a relief to the music industry. Bands are in theory a long-term money spinner, and also rarely as heinously ugly as DJs, therefore able to appear on children's television. After the sheer naked terror of 1989 when it looked like no one would ever buy a record on a major label again, Britain's industry men could go back to a life of performance belching and digging encrusted cocaine out from under their manbreasts.

December 1990 – Clairol seek an injunction to stop Clint Boon using curling tongs.

LET'S ROCK: The Stone Roses
The Stone Roses made the best ecstasy rock album ever; apart from a moment where Ian Brown inexplicably launches into a foll-de-roll version of Simon and Garfunkel, The Stone Roses: *The Stone Roses* is a classic. *Waterfall* ranks alongside *Let The Music Use You* as a tears-to-your-eyes dance classic. Then they lost it. When the Stone Roses reappeared claiming to have been in the shower like Bobby Ewing, they were an embarrassing badly-acted version of themselves, obviously played by different actors.

David Geffen had clearly had a very bad day when he signed the Stone Roses, because he decided to give them five million pounds to go to the countryside and play with their instruments, thereby ending their careers. Journalists continue to blame the Stone Roses for losing it. This is nonsense: what else were a simple bunch of tiny orphan Goths going to do with five million pounds? To this day very old Welsh villagers talk of the piece of hash delivered to the Roses in their recording studio. Other village elders say that's ridiculous, something that size couldn't have been hash, it must have been an enormous turd left by a dragon in the night. Whatever it was it clearly got wedged against the studio door trapping The Stone Roses, because they didn't come out until sixty months later by which time the Tunes Fairy had got bored and gone to live with The Verve. Ian Brown is still alive.

LET'S ROCK: The Happy Mondays
In a sign of the times, the Mondays were the first band to employ a dancer, the skeletal Bez. Thousands kept time with this concave man as he grimly clutched death in one hand and a pair of maracas in the other. The louche Mondays duo Shaun and Bez were the Dr Johnson and Boswell of acid house, careering through the back alleys of the soul. By the end of their journey Bez had a right arm held together by surgical plates and pus and Shaun was trying to smoke his own feet. How did they break? Paul Oakenfold remixed them and let the rest of Britain in on the Monday's vibe. Good Christ, noted the musical establishment, look down there, between the smackhead scally's feet: it's the sinkhole of pop gold. A short while later they were international stars of the most rock'n'roll kind:

'We started in 1980. The best thing about the Mondays was it didn't matter whether Shaun could sing or not, whether we could play or not. It all came from going out – we were different. House at the Hacienda started out as ten people dancing under the balcony. Some Sharon or Tracy from Manchester would be staring at us with this nasty look.'
Paul Ryder

Jayne Houghton Had The Sticky Job Of Being Shaun's PR:
'At one point Shaun was chasing the dragon on stage behind the drum riser. The photographers could see, the front row could see – I was having to issue statements saying that the band weren't on drugs. Shaun didn't want us to cover for him but the record company did. Where drugs were concerned, Shaun had the constitution of an ox but everyone still expected him to die. The *Manchester Evening News* would ring me at seven in the morning and say, "Is it true that Shaun Ryder has died of an overdose in the Hacienda?" I'd panic and phone round and he'd be at home asleep.'

The Happy Mondays were so undeniably huge at one point that they played the Rock In Rio festival alongside George Michael and Lisa Stansfield. But the Mondays did it their way:

'The crowd were throwing things. We were throwing them back. We went to Ronnie Biggs' place. He was a great guy, very intellectual. Writes a lot of romantic poetry. His son was a child pop star, so there's photos of him up everywhere – nine years old in front of a stadium of people. Ronnie had an Irish guy living with him who was hiding out – he had something to do with the IRA. And he was a mercenary. And a diamond smuggler. Ronnie sent us to this bar where the girls were really stunning but they've still got a dick and balls. One of the photographers started necking one of them and I said, "Kevin, that's a lad." Prince sent us an invite to his

party – Piers Morgan was gutted, he didn't even know about it. When we got there the security on the door gave us this warning. He said, "These are the rules. You don't look at Prince. You don't talk to Prince. If Prince gets on the dancefloor, make way for him." Prince's party was rubbish.'
Paul Ryder

'Ronnie had a villa in Rio with sweeping views, but it really had the feeling of an East End house, with a teapot and everything. He did the barbecue himself. He took a shine to Shaun – he saw a lot of himself in Shaun. He said "If you're doing anything naughty, don't get caught," and told them where to get coke. We went to this tatty disco where it was a couple of quid for sex. The Mondays had wives but the crew were up for it. It was fairly foul – posh suits and sleazy tourists. I went to the loo and I was sitting on the loo when the door was kicked off its hinges by this huge prostitute who looked like Myra Hindley. I stood up and pulled my trousers up and started on her. Then I saw the knife and it went sur-real. Shaun pulled me off her – I think he saw me as his sister. I was too pissed to be taking on Brazilian prostitutes. Shaun really laid into me. "What were you doing? You should have been grovelling to her!" He's incredibly protective, very chivalrous.'
Jayne Houghton

Bez

'Bez is very cool. They were driving down a country road to Glastonbury in a double-decker bus and it crashed into a street lamp. Bez had his head down rolling a spliff when – it smashed through the top window at him. He just looked round and carried on.'
Jayne Houghton

Bez: The Lost Stephen Hawking Interview

It would have been the match of the century: as part of his 'job's a good 'un' series of handy tips on BBC2's *Sunday Show*, Bez was due to interview Professor Stephen Hawking. But this clash of the titans was not to be; despite Bez staying up all night to Hawking's show-off book *A Brief History of Time* (and it had 'done his head in, too') Hawking blew Bez out. Clearly he couldn't take the pressure.

'Recording the last album in the Caribbean was the end. Bez had gone home – Shaun seemed less of a loose cannon when Bez was around, it was a brother thing. Shaun had to finish writing the album on his own so they had to virtually lock him in a really remote part of the island with no money, just food and drink. Muzzer [Ryder's ex-manager] took everything out the house that he could have pawned and left him there. Then after three days Muzzer went to find him and as he got near he passed a dodgy-looking black kid walking along the beach – in Shaun's clothes. Just this kid in baggies. Muzzer gets into the house and there's Shaun, sitting there naked, smoking crack.'
Jayne Houghton

The Farm: left to right, Roy, Keith and Peter with Svengali Charlie Chester

LET'S ROCK: The Farm

Stereotypically lugubrious scousers The Farm went from obscurity to a Christmas number one with 'Altogether Now' in a few weeks. The Farm were unique in indie dance: they were able take the piss out of themselves, something they did constantly. When the Inspiral Carpets launched the 'Cool As Fuck' cow T-shirts, The Farm wasted no time putting out their own The Farm: 'Ugly As Fuck' version. The Farm once sacked a band member for turning up in an overcoat.

NEWSWEEK, JULY 23 1990
'Kids who weren't even born during the original summer of love in 1967 are slipping into paisley skirts and bell-bottom jeans, and heading for up-dated love-ins known as "raves". Scrubbed and mellow (and often stoned on the designer-drug ecstasy), their Monkees' haircuts bobbing and their bright, baggy clothes flapping, they dance until dawn ... The motto of this dance-mad generation: Fun Is Good.'

BLAG YOUR WAY IN FOOTBALL HOOLIGANISM
Millwall Brick – rolled up newspaper for whacking people
Tachini capsleeves – fashion blunder
Three-star jumpers – hugely popular then hugely dated
Schoolies – pre-pubescent totty
Beaut – dickhead
Knock-off – liberated merchandise
Twirlie – chewing gum
Women – no idea

PETER HOOTON AND *THE END*

A Liverpool hero, or at the very least in the words of his own manager Kevin Sampson, 'a flamboyant self-publicist', lead singer Peter Hooton was the anti-Cilla, anti-Carla Lane jolly scouse – a sardonic, oblique scally. Since the early eighties days of testicle-hugger jeans and wedges, Peter had been producing the magazine *The End*, the funniest tribute to the dole casual ever. Before Alan Bleasdale's Yosser, who wanted a job, there was Peter Hooton's Dossa, who, er, didn't.

'The Happy Mondays were not the original scallies – a scally is a scouser. At the time the scally thing was fresh and anarchistic; now all that "stealing scally" thing just makes me sick. That TV show, *Bread*, that's what did it. Most of *The End's* writers were self-confessed, convicted hooligans, or at least going through a period of challenging behaviour. There was violence all the time then. I remember I was selling issue four or five at Wembley when Liverpool played Tottenham when a fight broke out; people who'd just bought it were rucking with copies of *The End* in their back pockets. I was an observer not a hooligan, but I really nearly died once after getting my face beaten to a pulp by a few of the Tottenham lads from the Broadwater Farm estate. Mind you, that was after Liverpool fans had rampaged through Tottenham High Road punching everyone in sight.'
Peter Hooton

Perfectly capturing the atmosphere of being too smart for your life and stepping onto the terraces in gentleman's attire of tweed jacket from Dunne & Co., slip-ons and expensive beige sweaters. *The End* was the inspiration for *Boy's Own*. Uppers and Downers was a straight lift from Ins and Outs. In 1990 Peter was a drugs counsellor giving electric shocks to heroin addicts ('a short-lived trial scheme', Hooton insists) but spurred on by the irony of the Mondays getting all the credit for the scally image. Kevin Sampson says, 'No scally would be seen dead in the Joe Bloggs/Gio Goi/'baggy' clothing favoured by the Mondays. Their junk-rock tunes were sound, but they looked like the shopped at Eccles outdoor market. These were the things which obsessed The Farm.'

The Farm decided to cash in their cheque with *Boy's Own*. Kevin had just shot a Film On Four starring Suggs out of Madness, and soon Suggs joined the mission. Terry Farley put the old Mantronix/Snap! bassline on 'Stepping Stone' and it went straight into the midweek top 40. An insane period of doing the early-nineties Right Thing ensued. Kevin: 'the band wore Duffer and Mau-Mau and Michiko, with their own classic Puma Argentina and Adidas Gazelle – impossible to get in 1990, now in the front windows of Olympus and turned out by the bucketload – got their hair done at Cuts and hung out with Flowered Up at Danny Rampling's Pure. They were the trendiest thing in London.'

'We started the neo-casual look. We did stay true – Keith refused to wear a leather shirt on *Top Of The Pops*. We went to tremendous lengths to keep our fashion sense pure – in the early days, bands had to have a look, like Frankie Goes To Hollywood or Limahl, but we looked like "blokes who stand outside chip shops", as Terry Farley put it.'
Peter Hooton

The look was the Get Off My Land: 'We started out in Barbours, Harris tweed, two lambswool crewnecks over each other, brown cords and suedies. But we never wore deerstalkers – that was a real ted fashion. We wore mountaineering boots and bubble jackets. That was before tracksuits, bubble jacket were rare in those days. You had to go to expensive mountaineering shops or abroad – Smedley tops were impossible to get – we used to go to Dunne and Co. The look was related to the drug culture because scousers were all into smoking, Pink Floyd, Bob Dylan and Roy Harper. We were taking the piss.'

And so the London/Liverpool, *Boy's Own* crossover began. 'The strangest thing about it was to be transported into a completely different scene – not that dissimilar to a sort of heavy metal-meets-techno scene,' says Kevin Sampson. 'We weren't sure where we fitted in but we decided to just drink a lot and try to join in.'

The house scene took them from Merseyside to posh leafy North London. It gives you some idea about poverty in Liverpool to learn that, as a youth worker, Peter Hooton escorted an exchange trip between teenagers from Liverpool and Harlem.

'London was surreal. We were sat in a very upmarket old English pub and this elderly gentleman came in, looking very dapper in a herringbone suit. He sat down and said, "I used to hang out in Paris and there's not much I haven't seen in the way of fucking." Then he took his glass eye out, pointed in the hole and said, "You can fuck me in here if you like."'
Peter Hooton

Farm member Roy Boulter describes an early meeting between the Liverpool scene and the London scene:

'The night at Kazoo next to Paddington Station, we went on to a club called Ziggy's in Streatham. We piled out of the most unglamorous van to be met by loads of geezers with shoulder length hair, going, "Fackin' 'ell, it's the Farm boys!" It was Farley and some geezers, second generation Rocky and Diesels. We stayed at Charlie Chester's flat on an estate – I really liked Charlie and Karon. He had a huge bath. All I remember was it wasn't decorated, it just had top TV, top stereo and mountains of fliers.'

Then The Farm made the smartest move of their career and became one of the in-house bands on Charlie Chester's Ibiza 90 trip, filmed by Kevin and broadcast almost straightaway on Channel 4 as *A Short Film About Chilling.* Charlie Chester says, 'It was the most influential music programme that year. It had "Come Together" by Primal Scream, "U Got The Love" by The Source, "Groovy Train" by The Farm – it got the biggest audience for that slot and they still show it.' *A Short Film About Chilling* captured the house scene at its sun-soaked, post-E tingling, positive best at a time when you were lucky to hear half a Beloved single played on *The Chart Show*. 'Ibiza were my favourite memories,' says Peter, 'because it was still so positive, everyone was united, you didn't have the factions, the Tallyband and Hezbollah of acid house. The fact that we were from Liverpool and accepted by that crowd was fantastic.'

The Ibiza film went out on Channel 4 on Friday night and the next night the record moved up enough to get on *Top Of The Pops*. 'Ten year old vagabonds were chasing me down the street shouting Groovy Train!' said Peter. 'We listened to it on someone's car radio in Lark Lane. We walked round in our skinny white Levis being very cocky. We were the biggest Liverpool band since Echo and the Bunnymen.'

They went from Merseyside to an American tour. Roy Boulter, drummer, remembers the culture shock:
'We were late getting somewhere in Hollywood, when two kids in a car recognised us. They were like, "The Farm! You guys are so awesome!" and we were like, "Er – Please could you give us a lift?" We were driving along when a dirty old pick-up truck pulled up next to us and I looked in and there was David Lynch. And the kids are still saying, "Wow, the Farm!" And we're going, "Wow! David Lynch." We were just English chancers in baggy kecks.'

Becoming heroes of the dance scene was also quite a stunt, especially when you consider they got to number one without being able to dance. Phil Perry remarked that 'I think it was the dancing that put the lid on their career.' Peter says his dancing has got better.

THE FARM: WHERE ARE THEY NOW?
Kevin has just signed a handsome book deal for his two novels, the first of which is *Awaydays,* out now. Peter and Keith have a new band, Hunkpapa named after the Sioux tribe, which Peter describes as 'The Sex Pistols meets the Beach Boys' and Roy Boulter writes *Hollyoaks* and *Brookside*, no less. Carl makes documentaries and Steve reckons he has achieved perfection with the anthem 'Altogether Now'.

***THE END'S* GUIDE TO LIVERPOOL**
Toxteth: quiet residential suburb renowned for its street parties
Tonka tits: playthings
UB40: scouser's wage card
Understanding: a scallies mum after he comes in bevvied and bloodied
Uncle: your mam's fella

ARE YOU A REAL SCAL?
Did you play for the school team?
Yes: 5 points
No: 0 points
Yes, but refused to play because you couldn't swear: 15 points
Yes, but got banned because you were caught robbing: 25 points
Have you had a job since you left school?
Yes: 5 points
No: 10 points
Yes, but on the sly: 20 points
Do you like playing videos again in slow motion during televised crowd disturbances?
Yes: 10 points
No: 0 points
Don't own a video: 0 points
Have you had a girlfriend for more than a week?
Yes: minus 20 points
No: 10 points
Only when you're skint: 20 points

1. Name the hardest dog in your neighbourhood
2. Does your dog go for Busies/Warrant Officers?
3. Can your dog get into all the clubs in town without paying?

SCOUSERS V COCKNEYS: DAGENHAM DAVE

Dave's as cool as can be
In his top by Tachini
Round the shop floor he will hike
in his dazzling flash red Nike
But he had to lead the way
Down to Harrods with his pay
Buys Cerutti, like a fool
Ain't for them in Liverpool
Now he'll be the king of Fords
'Till they follow in their hordes
Setting trends throughout the land
Dave will blow his hundred "parnd"
Yes, we know this much is true
Spandau were scalls in 72
Truer still my trendy chap
You can't beat a Cockney
For buying crap.

FLOWERED UP

Flowered Up appeared in a fireball of publicity in 1990 and disappeared what seemed like seconds later. Flowered Up should have been the acid house dream made rock, but somehow it never worked out like that.

FLOWERED UP'S BUSINESS CARD:

YEEE-HA!
CONGRATULATIONS
YOU HAVE BEEN SPANKED AND CARDED OFF COURTESY OF FLOWERED UP

'It should have been Spanked, Wanked and Carded,' adds Liam, thoughtfully.

Eight years after the heady days of Flowered Up mania, pocket singer Liam is still as angel-faced as ever and Des their manager still has his hands full playing Dad.

30 SECONDS IN THE LIFE OF FLOWERED UP

A GENUINE CONVERSATION, 7.1.98

LIAM
(AS SON)
Bill up, Des.

DES
(AS DAD)
No, fuck off. You nicked the last one.

LIAM
I did not fucking nick it off you.

DES
You fucking did you cunt.

HUGE PILE OF CARDS AND TAPES FALLS OFF THE DESK

DES
Look what you've fucking done! You fucking cunt!

LIAM
Fuck off! That wasn't me!

LIAM BENDS TO PICK UP STUFF, INSTEAD HAS HUGE COUGHING FIT

DES
It fucking *was* you, you cunt.

LIAM
Where's the weed?

LIAM GOES FOR BOX WITH PUFF IN IT. DES SNATCHES IT

DES
No! You've had enough! Fuck off!

BEER BOTTLE SPILLS ON THE FLOOR. PAUL TRIES TO KEEP BEER OFF CARPET, MAKES IT WORSE

DES
No! Not on the floor! Keep it on the carpet!

LIAM'S COUGHING FIT GETS FRIGHTENING, DES RUNS OUT, RUNS BACK IN AGAIN WITH CLOTH

DES
That *was* you, you fucker.

DES MOPS UP, PAUL SPILLS MORE BEER. LIAM RUNS OUT

(O.S.) SOUND OF LIAM VOMITING

LIAM RUNS BACK IN AGAIN

LIAM
This keeps happening.

LIAM REACHES FOR DRAW

DES
Fuck - off - you - cunt!

DES ROLLS A SPLIFF, GIVES IT TO LIAM

DES
Now *don't* fucking do it again!

REALLY WEIRD BLOKE WHO LOOKS LIKE THE CHILD CATCHER OFF
CHITTY CHITTY BANG BANG COMES IN

DES
All right, mate!

'TONY' GOONER WALKS IN WITH A BEAUTIFUL BLONDE GIRL IN A PUFFA

DES
If anyone can give you a line, this man can.

GOONER
A couple of Es and anything's yours, babe.

'TONY' GOONER RACKS OUT COCAINE

GOONER
Do you want another line?

EVERYONE HAS A LINE. CHILD CATCHER GETS UP TO LEAVE

WEIRD BLOKE
I'm off to France. I know these blokes do it for the duty free.

DES
See you mate. Get us some CS gas!

A FRIEND WHO'S COME TO STAY HAS TO BE SENT UPSTAIRS DURING DINNER

DES
Keep him in the bedroom, he's nutting out in front of my Mum.

Welcome to the world of the former Flowered Up.

Jeff Barrett

Boss of Heavenly Records, Jeff Barrett seems to have all the wrong
qualifications to work in the music industry: he is a completely affable man and
he never stopped going out. In 1989, as one of the few music industry people
who had an idea what was going on, Jeff was regarded as the Balearic Svengali.
'People were always approaching me because they had musical ambitions and
to tell you the truth I wasn't so into it – but then I met Des and Liam. I saw Liam
sat on an island in the middle of these puddles, just sat there off his tits rolling
up, and it struck me as a defining image. I thought if he were already famous that
image would be reproduced thousands of times, with kids wanting to look like
that. When I met Des, he wanted to do a festival on his estate – a couple of
bands, Farley and Weatherall playing. The council was never going to let him do
it, it's surrounded by flats – but his energy blew me away.' Jeff took on the
rascals from the Regents Park council estate.

LIFE WITH FLOWERED UP – REPRISE

A FIGHT HAS ESCALATED OVER WHETHER OR NOT DES LOOKS LIKE MARK THATCHER

DES
You can take my clothes off if you're starting.

LIAM
I had a bit of an embarrassing moment last night. You see, I thought I'd farted. It was all down the back of my leg by the time I got home. I was extremely distressed.

DES
They were my trousers too.

LIAM
I had a shower but I thought, if this is going to happen again I ain't wearing my own trousers. So I put another pair of his on. Do you still do E? I had the best one I've had for ages last night. In fact I had three and a half.

Flowered Up made their astonishing London debut with scenes straight out of Beatlemania. No one remembers whether they were any good or not; if they do remember anything, it was a tiny little singer shouting into two microphones and their dancer Barry Mooncult, an alarming-looking bald man wearing a four-foot purple cardboard flower round his neck. But that didn't matter – in a city still quivering with excitement from the nuclear bomb of acid house, everyone was looking for something. Manchester had the Mondays and the Stone Roses, London had… Brother Beyond. Suddenly, from nowhere, came a rumour about a band that were going to be the mouthpiece of the dance scene. Still smarting from having missed those first weeks at Future and Shoom, London's three-quarters of a million clubbers weren't going to miss out this time. Within 24 hours of their first gig being announced there was hysteria.

'A&R men were on the phone all day, desperate – I wouldn't even tell them where it was. I kept saying to them, "It's not about that…"'
Jeff Barrett

Flowered Up At The Africa Centre
'It was the best night I ever had. The whole day had been scrambling for tickets, outside the Africa Centre everyone in London was trying to get in. It was anarchy – inside, literally everyone was off their tits, right in the middle of Covent Garden, and they got away with it.'
Stuart Powles

'You couldn't get past the crush to get to the toilets so I puked in a pint glass and gave it to Cymon Eckel.'
Emma Cooperthwaite

Within weeks, and without even releasing a record, Flowered Up were on the front cover of the *NME*.

LIAM
'Flowered Up began with us seeing the Stone Roses at Dingwalls. I thought, well, I'm as handsome as Ian Brown so we might as well start a band. We've got the same heads as the Happy Mondays, the same fucking upbringing. We were the same kind of boys, robbing people and thieving. We used to hire a space cruiser and drive up to Manchester to sell E.'

DES
'We first got spotted in 89, when *Bummed* by Happy Mondays came out. People liked us – they'd see Liam and go, "Who's yer mate?"'

JEFF
'I asked them, have you got a name yet? And they got a bit shy and said, "Yeah, it's, er, Flowered Up."'

LIAM

'Flowered Up weren't phoneys. We walked it like we talked it. The day we signed Des took an eighth of coke to the meeting and wrote FU in coke on the table in the record company's office.'

Were Flowered Up Really Villains?

DES

'People had the wrong idea about Flowered Up. I've never been a football thug. I could never be dealing with the thought of getting my stomach slit open by a twelve year old.'

Flowered Up Held One Of The Most Notorious Parties Ever, 'Debauchery', Dubbed The Black Album Party

LIAM

'Barry was a glazier, doing up someone's mansion while they were away. He had the keys and we ended up running round for ten days with no clothes on in a four million pounds house with crystal chandeliers. We were smacked up, cracked up, E'd up. We found a wardrobe with top hats and tails in so were sat by this massive heated swimming pool naked in top hats going, "Shall we have a line of cocaine, old chap?" Finally after a week we decided to make some money, so we had a huge party in the house.'

JEFF BARRATT

'Hanif Kureshi was there and I'm sure it's the party he's describing in his book, *The Black Album*.'

LIAM

'Gerry Conlon was there in a big three-quarter length leather coat, really buzzing because he'd just got out. The mansion got trashed, the police got called …'

BY NOW, TO HIS PARANOIA, LIAM WAS BEING ASKED FOR AUTOGRAPHS. ('I THOUGHT IF I SIGNED THEM, THEY'D TURN ROUND AND GO, "SEE THAT CUNT?"'). FLOWERED UP WENT ON A NATIONAL TOUR, FEATURING SCREAMING CROWDS, PUNCH-UPS AND GROUPIES THAT SCARED EVEN THEM

DES

'You've got to understand they were really Jekyll girls, soppy Doris. That's why we wrote the song "Doris Is A Little Bit Partial". They were throwing themselves at us.'

LIAM

'Every time they'd let you go further than you'd think they would.'

DES

'One night we met these three student nurses. We went so far we couldn't believe it. In the van the next day we never said a word to each other the whole journey. We slapped and spanked them all night. It's what we were into – we used to shout *Yee Haa!* – that was our chant. We were into spreading pots of treacle over them, oranges, all sorts.'

THE NAME FLOWERED UP SEEMS SLIGHTLY SOPPY FOR TOUGH FELLOWS FROM NORTH LONDON, BUT IT WAS THE SPIRIT OF THE TIMES. IT CAME FROM THE BUDDLEA, OR BUTTERFLY BUSH – THE BIG PURPLE CANDLE-SHAPED FLOWERS YOU SEE GROWING OUT THE SIDE OF CHIMNEYS FOUR STORIES UP, A WEED SO TOUGH IT CAN GROW IN A FART.

WITH ONLY EIGHT SONGS WRITTEN, FLOWERED UP SIGNED A SEVEN ALBUM DEAL WITH LONDON FOR A QUARTER OF A MILLION.

Barry Mooncult, Des, Liam and their chauffeur have never taken drugs. Ever

LIAM

'I threw a chair at her, she laughed. I threw a sofa at her, she was still laughing. Finally I threw a wardrobe at her and she still wouldn't stop laughing.'

DES

'We tied them up. Finally we had one of them in the bath and we CS gassed them. And they were still laughing. We went to find her fifteen minutes later, we went into Jacko's room and he's got one of them on the bed shaving her. Fifteen minutes later and she's half shaved.'

FLOWERED UP WENT ON TO MAKE THE ONLY ACCURATE FILM ABOUT THE ACID HOUSE SCENE, THE VIDEO FOR THEIR SINGLE 'WEEKENDER': *QUADROPHENIA*'S ENERGY, HOPES (AND SAMPLES), UPDATED.

'WEEKENDER' AND LED ZEPPELIN ANTICS ASIDE, FLOWERED UP NEVER GOT AS HUGE AS IT LOOKED LIKE THEY WOULD. THERE WAS ONE MINOR PROBLEM.

DES

'The band could have carried on. I hate the way if you're on heroin you instantly become a second class citizen. You can't get a flat, a job. The truth is you can carry on as normal on smack, you can live your whole life on it. People would be a lot healthier! I haven't had a cold or flu in seven years! How do you think you get people living to 150 in Malaysia and places like that? Opium! They say it makes you become a thief and a liar and it *does* because you have to hide it all the time. Everybody knows you're doing it, they can smell it on you when you come out the toilet. It's the lying and the hiding it that makes you look worse. Why aren't you allowed to just say you're on smack and carry on?'

While waiting for the Patents Office to overcome their tiresomely arcane attitudes to his cure for the common cold (side-effects: may cause drowsiness and death), Des is still managing Liam. You can catch the legend that was Flowered Up in potted form – Liam ('I'm off the smack and back') is fronting a new band called Vegetable Man with Phil from Sabres.

FLOWERED UP: REPRISE

We go back to Des' mum's house to study some possible illustrations for this book by Paul Cannell, the artist behind the *Screamadelica* sleeve, who this summer will celebrate ten years of acid house by putting on The E Exhibition. Des' mum Clare opens the door, sees Liam, shouts 'Oh no,' and storms upstairs. Des lurches up to his room and comes back down with a portfolio. Liam has also been up to Des' room and has rather fortuitously found an old bottle of red wine. Des drinks half a glass and falls over, landing in a painful position on the floor. Without moving, he opens the portfolio and shows me some pictures. 'These pictures are work of genius,' he says, his legs bent under him. 'Look, it's Christ being carried to the cross.' The pictures are excellent. Des' mum walks in, points at Des, laughs her head off and leaves. Des, from his position coiled round the back of an armchair, shouts 'Mum! There's cat shit on the floor!' Des rolls over and comes eye-to-eye with a cat shit. 'I'm going out,' says his mother. 'See?' says Liam. 'See what I have to put up with?' Des' eyes close and Liam quickly searches him for cigarettes.

PRIMAL SCREAM

'I got Bobby Gillespie into E and introduced him to Andy Weatherall. It's my fault!'
Jayne Houghton

Bobby Gillespie is possibly the most delightful man in rock. The leather Superwaif had been around long before *Screamadelica* and even *Loaded*: former Goths will remember The Jesus and Mary Chain, simply the loudest white noise band of the eighties and Glasgow's inaudible answer to The Stooges. Bobby formed Primal Scream and set out on a mission to outdo the entire line-up of the Rolling Stones in one slim Scotsman.

'It was like a *Carry On* film on that tour bus. It reminded my of being on the road with The Clash when we used to make up animals, Paul Simenon would say, "A fish with a penis." He'd be silent for ten minutes and then suddenly go, "A budgie with human arms." The words memories and Primal Scream don't go together, but a typical day on tour would begin with waking up on some floor. One time we couldn't even find Duffy at all. He'd gone to sleep in the drum riser. The bus was a cross between a floating prison and Pontins. Me and Throb would be investigating what was left of the previous night's rider, Bobby would be talking about Iggy Pop and the MC5, Innes would be going on about World War Two bi-planes and Duffy talking about this plan he had to patent corduroy underpants. The sessions started getting longer and longer. Frog went four or five days without sleep. I went a week once. It was fun but I started seeing things crawling out of ashtrays.'
Kris Needs, Primal Scream's remixer and tour DJ, recounts life on the road

EVENTS

LAND OF OZ, HEAVEN, LONDON • MADCHESTER, G-MEX, MANCHESTER LOVE DECADE, YORKSHIRE • GLASTONBURY FESTIVAL, SOMERSET • THE STONE ROSES AT SPIKE ISLAND • CIRCUS WARP, WEST COUNTRY BOUNCE, MARCUS GARVEY CENTRE, NOTTINGHAM • COMPULSION, THE PALAIS, SHEFFIELD • RAINDANCE, BARKING • KONSPIRACY, MANCHESTER SOHO THEATRE CLUB, SOHO, LONDON • SYNERGY, NATIONWIDE • RAGE, LONDON • VARIOUS NIGHTS AT THE BRAIN • SPICE • JOY IN LEEDS • BOYS OWN, THE ZAP, BRIGHTON • KGB, WAREHOUSES • PURE AT THE MILK BAR • THE POLL TAX RIOTS, TRAFALGAR SQUARE, LONDON

IBIZA 90

Ibiza was a lifestyle all of its own. First and foremost, the need to save money to spend on drugs meant Ibizan trips had a special flavour. Ibiza is a place where you can live six to a room, taking turns to sleep. A place where you discover that banana Nesquik can be nourishing, round-the-clock nutrient. Where brandy like embalming fluid become a classy aperitif in a glass of chocolate milk. Where the Seat Panda, whilst looking from the outside almost like a real car, is in fact a tin ferret that hates the British and will kill you if you relax your guard for a second. And a place where the price of vodka and orange will drive a heterosexual young man to giving a queen the eye.

Charlie Chester, half-man, half-good-time, is a former hairdresser and market trader from the south west of England ' selling horrible denim ra-ra skirts'. Following a long and messy encounter with acid house, he gave up ra-ra skirts to turn club promoter. In 1989, with his wife Karon, he organised package holidays dedicated to the Balearic dance scene. In 1990 he tried to do it again. It was a landmark trip for the British indie music scene. It was also an administrational nightmare from beginning to end.

'Of our little firm, five of us couldn't get on the plane. We were being calmed down when they came back to us and told us we were going to be driven to Bristol because it was the only flight they could get us on. We got there to find Charlie had put us as far away from everyone else as possible because we were the Chelsea set with gold teeth and Chelsea tats. No sovs though! We decided to play up for the rest of the holiday. We took acid and finally caught up with the others at Summums and there was Harvey B. He blew us away. He mixed "Kung Fu Fighting" with Michael Jackson – what a swerve. I was doing huge Kung Fu kicks on the dancefloor. It was that time when the music was shit, our DJs were playing that slow indie crap and it wasn't working. Everyone was just standing around combing their hair. Our DJs should have been left in the toolbox that holiday because the Spanish DJs had it, playing banging Italian house. Everyone used to go on about this great indie music but I'll tell you something: when we got out there it was the banging Italian house they were all dancing to. After that holiday people started playing proper Italian piano stuff again.'
Steve

Charlie Chester, Heather Thatcher, Sean, Ian and friends

Ibiza 90 Was Lucy, Mandy And Elaine's First Time Abroad:

'Four people were killed in road accidents when we were over there; we had an accident because the bloke that was driving went down the wrong side of the road. We didn't know he was tripping. He told us after that HE thought he was on the M4. We had a rota after that – we all took acid but the person doing the driving could only take E. It made sense at the time.

'That night it was a Flying party at Ku. Ku was full of glamour people: lots of trannies and dancers who didn't seem to have tits or dicks. Most bizarre. A Red Indian guy would take his clothes off and go into a prayer to the sunrise. I thought it looked a bit fake but it was in the spirit of the thing. We were drinking Coco Loco – coconut cocktail with E in it. We were dancing

to Raven Maize – "Together Forever" – when a huge storm started just as the sun came up. The whole club was dancing in the storm, the rain dance. Fucking fantastic. We got a lift with The Farm and their mates automatically robbed the local shop when we stopped for wine. Two blokes tripping with bottles of brandy sticking out their anorak pockets.'

Es Paradis, Ibiza: The fountains on the dance floor

In 1990 Margaret Thatcher announced the assisted death of rates and the forceps delivery of her unpopular child, the Poll Tax. This grossly unjust tax was widely seen as forcing you to pay several hundred pounds for your right to vote. Whether or not registering to vote automatically led to a Poll Tax summons isn't known, but certainly in 1990 it was the general belief. And the Tories were in no rush to correct this opinion, since young people are more likely to vote Labour. Thousands of young people simply evaporated from electoral registers, meaning they couldn't join libraries, the local swimming pool, not even register with a local GP – all the things that are the difference between civilisation and living in a hedge. The last time a government had tried this on, in the fourteen century, a huge mob marched to London, rioted and cut off the Archbishop of Canterbury's head. In 1990, even revoltingly ugly Tory Rhodes Boyson – the one with the mutton chop whiskers who looks like a Victorian abortionist – described it as a 'political cyanide pill'. Sure enough...

Riot!

'Suddenly this huge mob loomed up from one side of Trafalgar Square, and from my previous football violence experience, I knew there was going to be a riot. The police wouldn't let them march up a street and the whole thing exploded. I remember looking to the right and just seeing this army of people running towards me. I heard someone shouting "Revolution!" and it was Ben and Anne, our two soap dodger mates standing right up on top of a lamp post.'

Anon

The Scots wouldn't take this crap, and a whopping three quarters of a million simply adopted the can't-pay-won't-pay stance and got court orders sending the bailiffs in.

'At the villa one girl didn't waste time dragging Harvey into the bedroom. She took her clothes off and got right into bed. Harvey said he was going to get a drink and came running out of there. Next thing we knew Harvey and the boys had put our clothes on – these strapping great lads off their face in miniskirts and orange bikinis. The people in the village were probably having their lunch. Harvey remembered the girl he'd pulled and ran back into the bedroom – wearing my French knickers. She fucked off pretty fast after that. I don't remember anything after that but I woke up the next evening under a sheet with a fly crawling in my mouth. Oh God. Back in England, The Farm became massive stars all of a sudden. We just stared at them on the telly – six months ago we were all sitting on the floor covered in watermelon pips.'

THE HOUSE ON THE HILL

'I'd met DJ Harvey in Ku and he'd made a big impression on me. He was wearing a construction helmet, and I thought, this fellow is a leader of men. At the end of the night he said, "Why don't you come to the mountain?" It seemed biblical – here was Jesus and the mountain. So we told our driver he had to take us there. Our driver was unaffectionately nicknamed dumbhead, and he walked around in a T-shirt that said "I'm so happy I could shit." He refused but we forced him to drive us, the van and all the band's equipment up this sheer track to the villa. When we got there there were all these girls dressed exactly the same – black jodhpurs and motorcycle boots, all with long hair. It seemed like a religious cult, so the image was complete. We stayed for hours. They were fantastic times – I'm cynical, but it got my guard down – it made people realise there was more to life than jealousy and hate.

'Later we heard this screech of tyres and he was off down the mountain with our van. He left us this brilliantly written letter saying, "How dare you! Never in my time as a driver etc., etc." We had to fly someone out from Liverpool to come and pick us up.'

Peter Hooton

73

IBIZA SHOPPING

In most countries nightclubs were viewed as seedy. In Ibiza they were temples of bohemian sophistication. There was also a considerably more cosmopolitan attitude to the place of drugs in society.

'I used to buy cocaine on a credit card over the bar at *[FAMOUS CLUB]* in Ibiza. The bar staff would bill the card, pocket the money and give you the coke. I did go to jail once when I got caught coming out the bar with two grammes of coke, but it was coke for the owner of one of the clubs so I got out of jail pretty fast.'
Anon

Arden (left) and Darren Emerson of Underwo

Acid house worker bee Arden had every acid house job going: podium dancer, DJ driver, bugle player and manager of the Sandals and later Bandulu.

'I was working as a casino pit boss – scummy business – I probably threw myself into the euphoria of the ecstasy experience because I was fed up with my job. E came into the country and defined a period. The whole acid house experience is inextricably linked to ecstasy, and if you pretend it's not then you're not really part of it. It's to do with drugs and technological development. The sampler, the computer, the E and the reaction to eighties wealthy clubbing was what fuelled it. It expanded because people could travel in to London. Before the eighties, young people had less money, they didn't go from one person's culture to another person's culture. People in Leeds looked different to people in London, talked different, dressed differently and did different things. In the eighties, people from outside of London came into London; they came from Rickmansworth, Uxbridge, all those places, which hadn't happened before.

'Acid house inspired me to give up my regular job and my personal pension and private health, and pull up anchor. I needed to get out and change my life pattern. People always said that acid house was about anonymity, but I disagree. If you went out to an acid house do in 1989, you were doing your own performance. By 1989 I was 33. I'd been a clubber, but it had always been different. It had been cocaine, or girls, or West End, or money or going to Milan for the fashion shows. It hadn't been democratic. People talk about the first Glastonbury or whatever, but the proportion of the population that was aspiring to that alternative lifestyle, to the attitude and consuming of narcotics was much, much smaller.'

RIMINI, 1990

'People went from having been in places like The Soho Theatre, your classic grubby London club, to the Mafia-owned clubs out there. Riccioni is like Blackpool for Italians – massive, marbled clubs with glass windows and swimming pools looking over the hills. If you're Mafia, a good way to launder lots of money is to build a nice club. A nice club is a status thing for a Don. I just got involved by going out and getting off my head.'

THE SANDALS

'They'd do anarchic things like making music with washing machines on, anything wacky and diverse and surreal. They were in that post-surrealist tradition, I suppose. There was a club, Violets. Derrick used to do his performance painting in the middle of the gig. He had the canvas up, missed the canvas and covered the entire front row with paint. They spent a year paying back the cost of everyone's clothing.'
Arden

PURE

'The most fun I ever had was those wet Wednesday nights in London. We'd spill out of there on our second or third pill, determined to carry on and end up causing havoc in Bar Italia in Soho. There'd always be someone with some sort of stolen credit card, or their own card they'd reported stolen, or caning dodgy chequebooks. We'd end up standing drinking in Frith Street drinking with cases of champagne in the boot of a car.'
Richard, TIP Records

ECLIPSE AT THE DIORAMA, LONDON

Wayne Shires and his partner Rod put on a classier, better dressed kind of event, and the Diorama, an unusual, ornate round building hidden away in Regents Park, served the purpose.
'Me and Rod got sick of going to warehouse parties with warm beer that you'd never heard of. We insisted that at the Diorama the toilet would always have paper and the bar would have Absolut vodka and Sapporo beer. The fact that it was all out of date and we got it cheap was beside the point! Fat Tony was looking at the Sapporo cans, going, "What do these stars mean?" and I was saying, "Shut up! Shut up!!"'

SPIKE ISLAND AND GLASTONBURY

Everyone's hopes were with both these events in 1990. People hoped the house vibe might have taken them over, even though they were essentially white, middle-class rock concerts. Spike Island sounded like a historical happening like Eel Pie Island or the Stones in Hyde Park. But the Island itself seemed nothing more than an industrial estate in a pond. Religious protesters picketed the route to Spike Island with placards warning about the dangers of rock excess, when they should have read, 'Warning: Last gig before band lose it'. *Record Mirror* reported that the Stone Roses planned to follow it up with a big festival in Hyde Park. With hindsight, a box full of dying butterflies might have been appropriate.

GLASTONBURY 90: A BIT OF A MAD ONE

Top three quotes overheard at Glastonbury 90
1
Baby Madchester Raver on the payphone (panicking):
'There's fifty-year-old hippies here, Mum, it's not like a rave at all'

2
Crustie in the travellers' field:
'Will somebody please buy my bastard drugs?'

3.
Graffiti on a traveller's lorry:
'20,000 dirty hippies on the rampage without giros'

THE TONKA TENT

The Cambridge-based Tonka Sound System were the stars of this epic Glastonbury. Their Bacchanalian dance tent featured a naked man riding a horse and another man dancing naked apart from his wellingtons. DJs Harvey and Rev went on the disco warpath with classics like Atmosfear: 'Dancing In Outer Space' and Hamilton Bohannon's 'Let's Start The Dance'. Or it could have been something else completely – memories of this event are not reliable.

'I mostly remember the Tonka Tent and Archaos, the anarchist circus troupe, had a man who sealed himself into a car full of goldfish and drove it off the stage. I met a journalist that night who was well off it. She wrote this long, intricate review of the evening and I asked her how she'd remembered it all, and she said, "I didn't, I made the whole lot up. It seemed more in keeping with the spirit of the thing."'
DJ Andy Carroll

THE BLACKBURN RAVES – ANARCHY UP HILLSIDES

Rougher, readier and initially free, the Blackburn raves kept the original anarchic acid house vibe going long after other people had gone indoors to pose and have paroxysms about getting on the guest list.

John Kelly, the irrepressible Liverpool DJ, reflects on a golden era of spirituality and falling down holes.

'One I went to was in a factory, and every three feet or so there was a two-foot gully in the floor. It was the most dangerous place you'd ever seen but there were people all over it, dancing. The organisers used to have a sacrificial sound system playing a tape, and when everyone was safe inside the rave they'd lock the door, bring in the proper sound system and turn it on. Then when they split, they'd take the big one, leave the tape playing on the small sound system and let it be confiscated.

'We'd just bought a cup of tea from a hot dog van outside. As I walked away, I turned round and my wife had fallen down an open manhole. Another one we went to had giant automatic shutters, and when they came down she got its chains wrapped around her legs. Dangerous places.'

'The worst scrape I ever had was in Nelson in 1990. There was a massive police presence from all over Lancashire but still the party went ahead. It held about ten thousand people and was the biggest one I had been to. There was always a massive mixture of music, just really nice house tunes. Acid house had died out by then. At about 7 a.m. I was stood on top of a wall dancing my heart out. I could see the tops of everyone's heads and all the light sticks, then the police just ran in from one corner of the building, hundreds of them, all in riot gear, spraying stuff. All of a sudden the music stopped. The last record was The Beatles' "Strawberry Fields". Everyone was running out of one end while the police ran in the other.

 'I was really scared because I had Es, dope and acid in my bumbag. I was already off my head and started emptying my bag while I ran. Outside it was daylight. I'd lost all my friends, therefore I'd lost my lift. Everyone was just frantic, trying to get to their cars. The police were letting dogs chase after people, who were running up the banking on to the motorway and letting them bite their legs to pull them down. They were being really rough, like at a football match. I was stuck in the middle of Nelson with no money. I finally found a friend about 200 yards away and legged it. I never went again. It was scary as fuck.'
Mandy, raver

THE LAST NIGHT OF SHOOM
The love leader closed its doors for the final time. Boy George did a highly emotive version of 'After The Love' as 'After The Shoom Has Gone'. The good vibes were spoiled rather by Jenni Rampling climbing on the bar and shouting with venom – 'To all of you who've criticised us over the years – you're all JEALOUS BASTARDS!' 'Shoom Shoom Shoom,' commented one punter drily, and another moved away from them so as not to fuck their buzz up.

HOW THE ORIGINAL IBIZA FAMILY WAS BROKEN UP
'My mate, one of my lovely scally mates from Ibiza, set me up with 12,000 Es, sprayed me in the face with ammonia and took them. I was blind for weeks. Only a friend could have done that to me because only a friend could have got that close. That was it, that was the end of the whole thing – I closed up the flat, got taken to a private hospital with my own armed security outside my door. I sent two men to have the guy killed and at the last minute I paged them and told them not to do it, I couldn't have a friend killed. I thought, this is it, it's got too serious now – and sure enough, two days after I'd left my flat the drug squad kicked the doors off. What he did ended everything. He was a top dude, a player, we all loved him as much as we hated him, but he did that to me. It changed the inner circle, it fucked the family, after that it was gone. I moved to Hampshire and bought a house and a horse and went horse riding for two years.'
Anon

TROUBLE WITH THE LAW: EASTERN BLOC
'We were prosecuted by James Anderton for selling the tickets – there was no legal precedent at the time. People used to come to us, 'cos I suppose we were the only outlet in Manchester at that time, in the north west even, but events without an entertainment's licence are illegal. At the time the police were getting hysterical, trying to shut them down, but they were trying to say that we were organising them. Typical. James Anderton [God's Cop, the chief of Manchester police, who believed he was on a mission from God to clean up the city] prosecuted us, barristers got involved, it was very expensive and in the end they offered us a deal where they said you stop selling the tickets for events without a licence, and we'll stop the prosecution.'
John Berry, Eastern Bloc

SPICE – JUSTIN ROBERTSON

The Balearic 'smart clothes and attitude' spread to the north. It hit Manchester at Justin Robertson's terrific small club Spice, prior to Most Excellent.

'Spice? I hate to admit it but Spice was an elitist thing. But we didn't deliberately exclude anyone. We felt like a lot of idiots were getting into acid house and it got really boring. We were all into hearing newer, different things so we started our own night playing Balearic music.

'Spice was the greatest club that never was. It was never that busy but it was good fun. A hard-core group of people would come down, people from the Mondays, Sasha and a few celebs. It was a drinking club mainly. We had a clear agenda with a fanzine and we all dressed differently. We used to call it the Spice uniform: white Levis, old school football tops and shelltoe trainers or desert boots – a kind of "neo-mod" thing. We even had silver pendants made. It was a weird cult in a way.'

CHANTS

'We used to have all these chants that developed at Spice and ended up at Most Excellent like, "Up up and away". A friend of mine used to shout, "Lummee, it's the Jerrys!" when he was really going for it at Spice. It was from those war books that you used to get as a kid with cartoons of the Tommies fighting the Japanese.

'We used to do the Spicey Shuffle. It was like a sixties northern soul dance mixed with a trance dance. You shuffled your feet and hips and stabbed the air with your fists. It was a bit like driving a tank, like pulling two levers the opposite way. It was a calmed down version of trance dancing.'
Justin Robertson

ACID HOUSE NAMES

High Street Pete
Tall Chris
Ginger Steve
Mark Mellow
Crisis Chris
Plug
Lofty
Muggsy
Frog
Acid Eric
Bisleri Bastard (assumes yogic positions on the dancefloor, pulls mental face and holds it there for forty minutes)
The Mad Midwife
Smelly Benny
Belcher
Fat Steve
Big Pete Feet
Bootleg Bill and Chips
Jeggsy
Half Head

JANUARY

Saddam Hussein says he is ready for the mother of all battles. Britain is put on a war footing and Operation Desert Storm begins.

Queer Nation is up and running. Promoter Patrick Lillee says 'I always thought there was an irony in a gay club like Heaven hosting a rave night with hundreds of straight men hugging each other and saying, "I love you, matey."'

Iraq begins Scud missile attacks on Israel.

Brian Harvey out of East 17 samples one of these ecstasy tablets he's heard about and finds it quite a pleasurable experience.

The return of style as *The Face* interviews a chair.

FEBRUARY

The trial of Winnie Mandela for kidnapping and murder begins; she is found guilty but released on bail pending an appeal.

The IRA fire three mortar bombs at Downing Street from a van parked in Whitehall. Two bombs explode at Victoria station. One man is killed.

The Gulf War begins. The '100 Hour War' turns out to be violent, bloody and not over in 100 hours at all. The war is hailed as a triumph of high-tech arms: our soldiers were shot at with all the best weaponry – and, by jingo, it was Made In Britain. The allies drop the equivalent of seven Hiroshimas in explosives on the Iraqi people yet somehow manage to miss Saddam Hussein. More British soldiers are killed by Americans than by Iraqis probably, but heck, there were bugs on the windshield. The government hails our soldiers as Brave Desert Rats but when they start feeling alarmingly unwell afterwards calls them silly hypochondriacs.

Geri Spice is 42.

MARCH

The Birmingham Six are released. Seventeen years in a British jail for a crime they didn't commit, but like the Murphy's, they're not bitter (David Quantick, writer).

Firefighters begin to put out burning oil wells in Kuwait.

The Hillsborough inquest jury return a 9-2 verdict of accidental death.

Unpopular handballer and cocaine user Diego Maradona suspended.

The nine children taken into care in Orkney are returned to their parents.

MAY

US troops complete their withdrawal from Southern Iraq.

William Kennedy Smith, nephew of Teddy 'pantsdropper' Kennedy, is charged with rape.

After a six-year-old girl is savaged by a pit bull terrier, the Government announce plans to introduce legislation controlling the dogs.

JUNE

Prince William is operated on after accidentally being hit with a golf club at school.

JULY

Gazza goes to Lazio for £5.5 million.

AUGUST

Hostage John McCarthy is released. Iraq admits to the UN that it had produced small amounts of plutonium, much as a small boy might admit to soiling the bed.

SEPTEMBER

There is a new club trend – friendly headbutting.

Hostage Jackie Mann released, to the joy of the world and his enormo-spectacled wife Sunnie.

OCTOBER

Vivienne Westwood is named British Fashion Designer of the year for second year in a row.

Walks around with no pants to celebrate.

NOVEMBER

Freddie Mercury dies of AIDS.

Newspaper tub Robert Maxwell falls off a boat and goes to Hell for ever.

The last British hostage in Lebanon, Terry Waite, is released.

Police break up 1000 people raves in Woodstock, Oxfordshire, and Gloucester.

DECEMBER

The Soviet Union ends when Russia, Ukraine and Belarus meet to form the Commonwealth of Independent States.

Chapter Four

1991: 3000 KILOWATT TURBO MEGA LASER SOUND VISUALS BOUNCY CASTLE NIGHTMARE BIGGEST MENTAL EVIL PROMOTIONS PRESENTS

Adamski and girlfriend Natalie

RAVES BIGGER THAN TOWNS

'Halfway through, Adamski stopped the whole thing and said, "I want everybody to put their hands in the air because this is bigger than Sunrise, this is bigger than anything else – *there's 25,000 people here.*" And the crowd went insane.'
Jane Waring

'I had no idea how big it was going to be. The promoter took me in the back way, a door opened up and we got to the top of the scaffolding, to the DJ box. We got to the top, and there were 15,000 people, video screens, the lot. It hit me - *"Bang!* Oh my God."'
Sasha

'The KLF were playing and it was about 5 a.m., a really nice summer's morning. I looked out over the people, and walking through the middle of them all comes this housewife in a velour tracksuit, carrying the Sunday papers. She came up to me and said, "You look like a nice person," and I said, "I have my moments," She said, "in that case could you please get them to turn the music off? I live three miles away and I can hear it in my living room."'
Boy George

'At one point the crowds were tripling every weekend...'
Anton Le Pirate

RAVE IS ALL THE FAVE, THE *SUN*:
'Raving is the new dance craze sweeping Britain... but you can forget the shock and horror of acid house. Raving is about good clean fun. Drugs, booze and dancefloor brawling have been given the elbow by the teenage armies who pile into clubs each week simply to dance the night away."

RAVE GUIDE, *TODAY* NEWSPAPER:
'Credit cards are considered hugely frumpy, especially if they are gold or platinum. Ravers like to dress, eat and drink cheap and cheerfully and pay for everything in cash.'

When it comes to rave, historians will look back and scratch their heads. At any other time in the records, if 25,000 young people got together in a field they were either waiting to see if Keith Richards would die or sent there to hack each other to bits in battle. Either that or there was word of a really good stoning.

Whether you thought raves were the new emotional revolution or just ten thousand boggle-faced loons dressed as Andy Pandy, the very act of being in a group that size *on the same wavelength* had a weird power.

'You couldn't beat 5000 people dancing in synchrony – the energy it put off was phenomenal. It connected to something.'
Jack Barron, journalist and raver

People power aside, rave was a once in a lifetime chance to get together with a massive group of others the same age before everyone disappeared off into normal jobs, having children and Saturday night in front of the telly for ever. Nowadays some of us celebrate Valentine's Day by putting The Samaritans on Friends and Family, but in those days in any one weekend you could have ten thousand partners to choose from, and the national catch phrase was 'come and meet my friend'. In the average life, school is the one chance you get to socialise with a big group of your peers and make some friends and partners, and school unfortunately coincides with being young and stupid. Men might have football, and a fairly small percentage go on to college, but short of the odd house party, prison or the Merchant Navy, school is the only opportunity you get. House, rave and its million bastard offspring gave people a second chance.

Q: Where have all the nice women/men gone?
A: Home.

'I went straight from school to college, did a year there and then it was straight into a nine-to-five. It was a bit like, "Oh – is this it? Where is everyone?"'
Bill

'Me and Ginger Steve met more people than we'd ever met in our lives. I went on holiday to Europe and ended up getting stranded out there, and while I'm away Steve's meeting 500-odd people. I was only gone three weeks but when I got back people I'd never met were coming up to me saying, "Chris! Man, so sorry you got stranded – good to have you back!" I was thinking, who the fuck are you?'
Tall Chris

It's a tough job, but someone's got to do it

VICKS
Dancing in cycle masks filled with Vaporub and Deep Heat, heady preparations that previously only served the Holy Trinity of tennis elbow, rheumatism and gay sex.

CONVOYS – FOOT TO THE FLOOR FUN
With the police likely to shut down the rave when you got there, you had to make the most of the rest of the evening. Luckily, by 1991 people were having such a good time that even driving up and down the motorway for six hours was a party.

'You always followed a yellow Capri. It always knew where it was going. All you could see when you looked back were headlights for miles. Everybody had to go through the red traffic lights just to keep up with the person in front. If you were the one that stopped, because you were scared you were going to get nicked, that was it, you were lost. I remember once, my friend stopped and we lost the convoy so we decided to come home over the moors. When we looked back there were hundreds of cars following us.'
Mandy

'We used to call our M25 missions *church*. One weekend we ended at a petrol station with no party but hundreds of people waiting to see if one would come off. In the end one guy just pulled off in his car and that was it – run! We all followed him on to the motorway. Miles later he pulled up outside his house. He got out the car and said, "What are you doing?" There were dozens of cars lined up in his road. We said, "Where's the party?" and he looked at all the faces, desperate for a party. We ended raving in his house for two days. All of us. There wasn't nothing stolen, nothing ruined – any animosity was lost. Everyone whipped round to get some money together, when people were hungry, food was brought in, drinks...'
Timmi Magic

'I'd be sitting in a bar with a mobile phone that looked like a ghetto blaster, trying to find out the address. It was like Russian roulette. You'd pay £25 for a ticket, and then it was like "Is it going to happen?". That was the whole excitement of it. It was a revolution, a dance revolution. You felt like you were underground Russian revolutionaries.'
James Baillie

WHAT IF RAVES HAD NEVER BEEN STOPPED?

By 1991, there were raves bigger than towns. A government clampdown put a stop to the crazy days of rave, but for a short while you could spend 24 hours in these independent communities, with their own cafés, shops, toilets, doctors ... self-ruling mini-cities that appeared on Saturday afternoon and were gone by Sunday, leaving no trace apart from a mountain of Evian bottles and a man no one knows in a poncho asleep in a hedge. But what if they hadn't packed up and gone? What if the government had allowed raves to continue as long as they liked?

THE NEVER-ENDING RAVE

Daily Mirror, *2041:*
Live The Dream Fiftieth Birthday Celebrations: Major given Keys to the Rave

LIFE IN THE RAVE
Year 1: nothing to eat except ice cream and ecstasy. Raver eat dud Es for the roughage
Year 2: Raindance Harvester opens, offers Rave Platter
Year 10: never-ending car boot sale sets up at the back of the rave, where ravers can buy back the things they've had stolen
Year 15: public transport established. Until then, Sandra, 68, remembers: 'To travel about, you'd spread a rumour that Carl Cox had come on at the other end of the rave and lift your feet off the ground.'
Year 20: still has no elected mayor: instead, every four years the ravers elect a new energy drink to govern. This year a can of Red Bull opened the controversial Radio Rental art gallery. The art collection is continually updated, since it consists of patterns traced in the air by ravers that only other ravers can see
Year 50: rave suburbs appear, full of older ravers who sit among twenty foot high piles of coats and moan about the way things are going

Manchester Evening News, *June 2042*
Ravers have gone feral and eaten the DJ

HUGE FLYERS

Rave flyers were a strange contradiction: lavishly produced in glossy full colour, but with terrible illustrations that looked like the doodles of the weird kid into Heavy Metal: large-breasted girls getting their heads chewed off by snotty-mouthed snakes. They had whole paragraphs of carefully-worded text that just made them sound worse.

Why *were* rave flyers so embarrassing? Probably because they were very upfront about what was on offer – mind expansion, peace and love, sexual fantasies, hobgoblins, interplanetary travel, Celtic warrior stuff – all the psychedelic stuff. Among the 'cooler' clubs, Spectrum was fairly unique in wearing its psychedelic heart on its sleeve – as people got more self-conscious about love and peace, club flyers started to get more and more uptight, getting further away from the spiritual side. Soon many were nothing more than stark typefaces and blocks of colour. By 1997, the Ministry of Sound just had a picture of a Technics.
Rave flyers expressed levels of emotional honesty the trendies had lost. Either that or they were just shit.

RAVE THE BOARD GAME

The now contraband table entertainment *Rave* is a classic of its genre. Ranking alongside the early pornographic *Monopoly* sets as a collectible (opium den: $400) it contains fake *Rave* money with a smiley instead of the Queen's head which looks disconcertingly normal. The fivers say Five Moody Pounds and players have to make their way to the rave across the board past landmarks like Mental Meadows, El-Esdee Green and the Nocombe Downs. Best of all, it comes with a big bag of plastic Es. Kerr-plunk!

FALLING DOWN

'We went to raves all over Norfolk, Thetford and Cambridge. One night I was running around a barn in Thetford selling E, I remember I was singing, "E, E! Give it to me! Eat it up! Yum yum!" then I fell down a hole.'
Gemma Walker, raver

TALES FROM THE RAVE 1

'Energy at Heston Services was like a medieval bartering town. Traders were just turning up on spec with their vans selling anything. Two guys turned up and sold Bedouin tents and rugs. Ice-cream, scarves, umbrellas – people were selling anything.'
Anton Le Pirate

Reproduced with kind permission of John Brown Publishing/House of Viz

THE ACID SHARON: A BIRDWATCHER'S GUIDE

Appearance

Pastel Lycra tops, stonewash jeans and blonde hair in a Mandy Smith/Sigue Sigue Sputnik pineapple style: the colder their natural habitat, the darker the tan

Dances

Alarming repertoire of vigorous moves. Run if it looks like their eyes are about to close: the full teeth-bared, eyes-rolled-back-in-the-head gurn is imminent

Age

No limits. Somewhere in a warehouse, the sun will come up, the steam will clear to reveal a middle-aged woman jacking furiously with her eyebrows knotted and her stomach muscles rippling in the dawn's early light

LIFESTYLE

I'LL DO YOU THREE FOR A SCORE: GLORY DAYS OF THE BLACK ECONOMY

Money in carrier bags, money in shoeboxes, money more often than not rolled up down the side of a sock... In the glory days of the black economy, oceans of money changed hands without seeing a till, let alone an Inland Revenue account. The best thing about house was its anarchic attitude. It existed totally independently from mainstream culture for one simple reason: for your own private theatre of madness, you had to have privacy. In the beginning tickets were printed up by friends, handed out personally, paid for in cash; the drinks people needed were bought from cash-and-carries, and sold by little brothers from a bar made out of a cardboard box. The side effect of this need to stay underground was a huge black economy.

House didn't start as an avaricious quest for wealth. There were some intensely idealistic people at the centre of the house movement, passionately devoted to its spirituality and freedom. Some parties like Hedonism and the Blackburn Raves were put on over and over again for free, just to keep the thing going, it was that fucking good. All the best party 'organisations' were a couple of people running the whole thing from their front room. Or, for all their swishing their bobbed hair about, their Mum's front room. The thing was, if your party was popular enough, vast sums of money kept appearing...

SILLY MONEY

'I used to stuff it down my trousers to see what it felt like.'
John

'One Monday morning I paid in ten thousand pounds cash at the bank, a huge carrier bag full. It was a very weird thing – by the time she'd finished counting it, the till girl was red in the face and giggling.'
Anon

'Me and Ali literally used to squeeze the money, we never counted it. We'd squeeze it into the shape of two bricks, and say, "Right – that's yours, that's mine."'
Dave Beer, Jockey Slut

YOU SPEND	YOU ARE
£1	An attractive young girl (cloakroom will always cost as run by other attractive young girl or tranny)
£30-50	Out with the girls
£40-60	Not doing it any more oh all right then
£80-100	A mug
£100+	A beast
You seem to be £20 up	A DJ's girlfriend: 'Anyfink you want girl, you can 'ave.'

To misquote Irvine Welsh, think of the best weekend you ever had, think how much money you spent, multiply by a thousand and you're still nowhere near the amount we ploughed into the business of going out and staying out. Now take that sum of money, multiply it by all the ravers in the country, all the raves they went to and the years they went raving – and imagine it as cash. These days you might spend anywhere from ten to two hundred pounds in a night but nearly all of it passes through a till. In those days house was a self-contained economy and this was a further snub to the authorities. No wonder the government was spitting.

'I'd make so much money I'd have to leave the party and come back again, because my pockets were so stuffed with notes I literally couldn't walk properly.'
Stuart from Devon

Suddenly there was a whole new currency.

'That night Frank Bruno fought Tyson, the night of my party, I went shopping for an outfit on the Kings Road. I went into *[FAMOUS DESIGNER SHOP]* and I got talking to the sales assistant and I said "I want this, I want that, I've got this party in Battersea." He said, "What, the one in the film studios?" I said, "Yeah, it's me that's putting it on" He asked me if he could have some tickets. I said, "Boy, we can trade clothes for tickets." That day I shopped all over London and I exchanged paper that I had printed up for clothes. I found that highly amusing. There was such a buzz on this party it was like luck to people that I was in their shop. It was like – "Here! *Have* the garm!"'
Jarvis Sandy

Jarvis would like to add that the 'supercool five-hundred-pound suit' he bartered for was stolen the same night, so if anyone at Linford Studios found a supercool suit to fit a six-foot-four man, he'd like it back.

HI-TECH SCAM

Then there were the phone lines. All weekend the premium rate lines were buzzing, racking up the profits of BT, as everyone scrambled to get the answer to that deceptively simple question – *where is it?* The difference with this phone line system was that BT didn't keep all the profit. You, the party organiser, would set up the phone line with BT, everyone who phoned in was billed at premium rate, and BT would split the profit with you. And like all the most professional premium lines, you took as long as possible to give your callers any information. You may even have told them to phone again later.

'The lads picked up on it and started putting posses in London. You could sort out an arrangement with the phone lines to have people calling in for the address of the party, do a few flyers and get the money off the phone call – without even doing a party. Even if you only had a thousand people call the number, you've made a few hundred quid in a night without lifting a finger.'
Liam, Flowered Up

LOW-TECH SCAM

Then there's the more straightforward scam: never mind phone lines, just sell a few bits of paper and fuck off.

And then there were the bottom feeders. Ecstasy was everywhere and the shifty characters moved in and started rubbing their hands with glee.

TALES FROM THE RAVE

'The rave was nearly over and we went up to this one stall and said, "Have you got any chewing gum?" And the guy goes, "NO! No! I've sold out of chewing gum. I've got one stick left" But my friend goes, "I'll give you three quid for a stick!" and the guy's going, "No fucking way! I can get a fiver for this stick!" and she's saying "No, no, I'll give you four!" He was totally serious. There were people standing round bidding for this single stick of chewing gum.'

'My friend came up to us, really E'd up and said, "I've found twenty quid on the floor – I'm going to buy everyone water!" He went off and bought twenty big bottles. Later we saw that the guy selling it had a van with a big tub of water in the back and he was picking up filthy bottles off the floor and filling them and selling them for a quid.'
Jane, former raver

SPUNKING IT UP THE WALL

'When it comes to the money we made, I know one thing – I spent a million pounds. Me personally. It took me seven years but I did it. And I am proud. What did I spend it on? Catering. Every city we went they'd say, "What do the guys want for special catering?" and the best supplies would be waiting for us from one city to the next. The *best* supplies.'
Paul Ryder, Happy Mondays

Wayne Anthony with his well-gotten gains

WAYNE ANTHONY, PROMOTER, GENESIS

'So here's me in the main restaurant at the Savoy hotel – a little black boy from Hackney – ignorant, arrogant, with loads of money. I'm staying there for the weekend with Tony Colston-Hayter and my partner. By this time we're pissed, we're E'd up, we're charlie'd up and we've got four of the most sexiest girls upstairs. They were really well-known women – we had pop star status at the time. We ordered champagne and the waiter was really snotty about it, expecting us not to know anything. So we said, "Well, what have you got?" He rattled off a few and we said, "What's the most expensive?" And he said, "That would be the 82" or some year; they were like, a thousand quid. So we said, "OK, we'll have two."

'Then we decided we were going to snort charlie off the table at the Savoy. We didn't try to hide it; we were like kids. We just chopped it out and did a load. We could have got away with it if we'd just had one line, but we were on a roll. The waiter's come over and he's like, "Are you doing drugs?" We're like, *"What?* Go and get the manager, right now." He backed down. So we did a load more and he caught us bang to rights. He said, "We're calling the police." But we had these lines already chopped out on the table – so we said, "All right," and we sniffed it. With the dinner our bill was about sixteen grand. We're lurching round reception fucked, *fucked,* going, "'Ow much is it?" and taking cash out a bag.'

bumble bees = Es

'You'd go to the pub, there'd be a lock-in, the jukebox would be up loud and there'd be eighty people dancing on the tables in sunglasses.'
John Kelly, DJ

'I was talking to a man I hardly knew in his office. We were talking about how we didn't know how anyone could take Es, being full of crap. He said, "I mean, look at this," and he reaches under his desk and brings out a bag of 500 Es. "This lot are going back tomorrow." he says, completely matter-of-fact.'
Anon

'One dealer I knew said he used to go to his local pub and there were so many people taking E he could sell the lot there before he even went to the club.'
Dom

'I was in the changing room at the gym and I was listening to this posh woman planning a picnic on her mobile phone. It sounded like your average toffs' day out and then she said, "Don't bring the kids, there'll be bumbles."'
Anon

'When I got the Shoom tattoo, the big Hell's Angel that was doing it said, "What's this about then?" and next week him and his mates were doing Es.'
Anon

BLURTINGS

'You've lost my carrier bag.'
'What carrier bag?'
'I had a carrier bag, now it's gone.'
'What was in it?'
'Garden peas.'
'PEAS??'
'It's all right, I've remembered where it is – it's in the lost property of the glue factory across the road.'

FASHION

I CAN'T BELIEVE I USED TO GO OUT IN DUNGAREES
'We all had psychedelic shirts and dungarees and friendship bangles right up our arms. Then one day I said, "Janet, this is a load of fucking bollocks" and we cut them all off.'
Ann

Rave went one way, Balearic went the other. In World of Balearic it was absolutely necessary not to look like a Ted, so there was a lot of black and white clothing. In rave, it was absolutely necessary not to look like a plainclothes, so there wasn't.

The world looked on in horror as Britain found its inner child and expressed it with vigour:
'The new look, a seventies revival in all its horror, can best be described in its own vernacular in which "BAF" stands for "baggy as fuck" and sums up the stylistic aspirations of a generation'.
Details *magazine, USA*

MONSTROUS STYLE BLUNDER OF THE EARLY NINETIES
And an expensive one at that: Pucci leggings. A cross between Elizabeth Taylor in her drinking years and an ashtray full of Quality Street wrappers, these skin-tight technicolour nightmares only ever looked good on Lady Miss Keir, and she was a hologram. DJ Dimitri was Pete Waterman in a girdle.

THE SARTORIAL GROUND WAR CONTINUES WITH CLEVER T-SHIRTS...
Wild Green Fairly Hip Kid
Johnson's Babe Power/Powder
Matey Bubble Bath – Are You On One?

THAT'LL BE A NO SUCH SOUL SKIRT THEN
EARLY 1900s: 'the Scuttler's *(hooligan's)* girlfriend also had her own style of dress – "clogs and shawl and a skirt with vertical stripes"'
Geoffrey Pearson, Hooligan

DRUGS

FOUND IT, WASHED IT, WOOFED IT – THE RETURN OF COCAINE

'"Found it, washed it, and woofed it" – parlance commonly used to describe the partaking of Bolivian medication.'
Boy's Own

Question 3. Acid house: what stopped it?

a)	**b)**	**c)**

Toilet lids, cisterns, shelves, dashboards, CD boxes, desks, notebooks, kitchen counters, car bonnets, urinals, penknives, video library cards, pub tables, the back of your hand – stand still too long and some would rack out on your forehead. It felt like *Brewster's Millions II – The Teethgrinder*: everyone given a ton of Columbian fine blend and told they had thirty days to get rid of it or lose their inheritance.

'Three grammes in one hit. I chased a whole table four foot long. I can't remember how it felt but I think my heart nearly packed up.'
Brandon Block

It was getting ridiculous. Every time you opened a door in 1991 you walked in on someone bent over and sniffing. You couldn't sit in the park for an hour without meeting someone who was 'just off for a little one'. Lean forward to say hello to someone in the pub and they'd put a wrap in your hand. In every toilet cubicle the feet were facing the wrong way. And there were four of them. Either the nation had been gripped by a crazed, lock-jawed lust for taking each other up the wrong 'un, or there was a cocaine epidemic.

Saying of the summer, from one cubicle to another: What are you using for a shelf?

Everyone started to behave like they were in a movie: the girls were sexier, in shorter skirts and tight tops; the men were looking flasher, in Gucci loafers, smart strides; and unlike 1989's loved-up speechlessness, conversation was running sharp and fast. Stand at the bar too long and someone with a saliva deficiency would grab you and explain at great length exactly what in their tetchy opinion was going wrong with the scene.

'It was about being part of a movement – something that was really good. I remember hearing some people talking at Rage saying they'd waited ten years for this to happen, but in the next breath they were saying it was all over and ruined. People got very precious about it. It was exactly like a band – "We saw them first," it was ego shite. There was a lot of snobbery starting at Shoom – a lot of people wouldn't give you the time of day if they thought you were off your head, even though they were and didn't show it. There was an inverted snobbery at Shoom against ecstasy – people started doing coke instead.'
Anon

SLANG
mashed
nutted
I am off my head/tits/nut
mullahed
trolleyed
mashed
bollocksed
monged
fucked
spangled
sledging
chonged
battered

'Slang? I made half of it up, love. Cheesy, pear-shaped, bangin', nish, havin' it, the bollocks, disco buscuits. The lot man. It was all made up in Manchester.'
MC Tunes

COCAINE 1

'I was in a drinking club listening to a record producer tell me in fine detail why his divorce wasn't his fault. I was doing my best to listen but every time he got agitated a tiny lump of cocaine fell out off his nose.'
Anon

COCAINE 2

The well-known comedian who couldn't pay for his meal because he'd lost his gold AMEX card down the ladies loo.

'The humour became really barbed, constant digs at each other. They were winding people up for their entertainment. On a personal level people were being very snide. I can remember being passed dud twenty pound notes by friends of mine happy to rip me off.'
Dealer, anon

For all the gibbering hysteria ecstasy generated, it had one undeniable advantage over other social drugs: it's non-addictive. If they put enough effort in, people with addictive personalities can build up a fair 'addiction', but as they are the first to admit, they'd have got addicted to facing west if that's all there was on offer. Most people hit the ecstasy ceiling and stopped. The cocaine ceiling was easy to pass through and on the next floor was a room full of cocaine.

'"I get no kick from cocaine", sang Frank Sinatra. You want to lay off it for a bit, mate.'
David Quantick, writer

The first benefit of cocaine is it reveals your own greatness. It goes on to sharpen your senses, helping you realise how inferior, badly-dressed, dull, poor and irritating everyone else is. But does it stop there, leaving you alone with the burden of this knowledge? No! It furnishes you with immense powers of arsiness to let the world know the way it is. What a drug! Take enough cocaine and you get spectacularly good at contempt. Feel that peace'n'love fuck right off.

YOU LOOKING AT ME?

'One of the first time I saw cocaine violence creep into it was at a fancy dress party at the ICA, down by Buckingham Palace. Coming out of there I could hear the sound of tables and chairs being smashed. I looked back and what I saw was surreal: on one side of me was the Palace, and on the other were people dressed as droogs out of *A Clockwork Orange* with painted faces and white outfits. They're caricatures of violent behaviour, and there they were, really charlied up and smacking the bouncers.'
Anon

With half the nostrils above you running, the early nineties were no time to be short. Noses served firstly as cocaine immigration ports and secondly for looking down.

'It got to the point where I saw a fight every night I went out. I got involved in a lot of disputes over drug dealing territory in Love Ranch all the time. There was definitely a point where real gangsters were stepping in but mostly it was ordinary people playing up to the gangster image. There was a flyer for Kinky Disco that had Sid Vicious walking down some stairs in a tuxedo with a gun. The imagery got harder. People liked to think they were hard.'
John, drug dealer

NO, YOUR NAME IS NOT TONY MONTANA

For months it was fun. Then it got silly. As the year passed, the look in the cities became blatantly aggressive. Michiko Koshino turned out bourgeois Rambo outfits for the clubland mercenary. Women were stomping round in humourless versions of the Tank Girl outfit. Men were swaggering into nightclubs in leather commando waistcoats complete with ammo holders for the guns they didn't have, the silly suburban sods. And the fashion item *everybody* was after were the cold, hard mirror sunglasses Robert Duvall wore to administer the morning napalm in *Apocalpse Now*.

Cocaine costs a fortune and everyone knows it. Handing it out makes you look flash. Sad, but unfailingly flash. Now that house had spawned a new music industry, the traditional industry conversation tool was back in business. Cocaine is a pharmaceutical greeting, a thank you, an apology.

A&R: Didn't I call you? Sorry, mate, it's been really on top... Here...
SUBTITLE: *I still can't be arsed to talk to you but let me apologise pharmaceutically.*

'Cocaine changed the whole scene. All of us were taking it. It's an aggressive, mean drug. Because it's so expensive it's "You can have some, and you, but not your mate because I don't know them." And if you get given some it's "Oh, I should be so honoured that you've included me in your gang." All of a sudden you're dividing the room up. The Limelight was cocaine central. There were some heavy people appearing, one dealer in particular was a nasty little prick. I saw a lot of people lose it. I remember thinking, hang on a minute – we've started freebasing! I think when I designed the Land of Oz flyer it was an inadvertent gut reaction to the cocaine scene. It was a mean, nasty face with piecing white eyes. Where had the peaceful Spectrum logo gone?'
Dave Little, designer

'I went out with a charlie dealer and got on this real ego buzz. It was a power thing – you think that your shit doesn't stink. At one stage I got so thin my mum started bringing me food around. Mind you, I was also doing twenty to twenty-five Es a weekend.'
Gemma Walker, raver

Dave Little's flyer for the club that didn't happen:
Phantazia, it turned out, was a popular
young folks' drug.
Became Land of Oz, which wasn't

I'M NOT THE ONE THAT'S PARANOID

With the irony of a self-fulfilling prophecy, everyone got moody about everyone being moody. Two parallel conversations ran through clubland: the first was a eulogy to how great the scene used to be before all this grumpiness set in. The second was a long grumpy moan about the state of things.

'All the clubs got moody, everybody started standing round looking at each other. Northern clubs are more up for it because they can't afford cocaine. Down south everybody's doing cocaine, even 21 year olds who don't work. Maybe they're selling it, I don't know.'
Karon Dunn

As debate rages over which millennium monument would best depict life in the twentieth century, there is a strong argument for a hundred-foot bronze model of a rolled-up tenner in Soho Square.

MUSIC

HARDCORE YOU KNOW THE SCORE
The Magic Roundabout, Trumpton, Rhubarb And Custard – rave took every TV theme from your Ribena years and remixed it for your second, unpredicted, Ribena revival. 'Charly' by The Prodigy brought the public information film with the lisping idiot child and his unhelpful cat into the charts. It was very easy to take the piss out of rave and many did. *i-D* sniffed about 'the distinctly non-ambient mindset of the Barry Grant good-time raver'. There was only one answer to that:

SHUT UP AND DANCE
Because most record labels wouldn't touch rave with a shitty stick, this produer/ label duo sold their own records out of the back of their car. Shut Up And Dance had the coolest record titles of the rave scene: 'Dance Before The Police Come' and '£10 To Get In'. What was the remix called? '£20 To Get In'. Now that's satire. They were also responsible for the greatest record ever made, 'Raving I'm Raving'. Singer Peter Bouncer, that's *Peter Bouncer*, gets through a rave version of 'Walking In Memphis' without physically splitting from laughter. 'Put on my raving shoes and boarded the plane...'

WAR!
The authorities go into wartime censorship. Massive Attack are renamed Massive as the British record buying public are obviously so stupid they thought Attack means Train Your Vast Gunbarrel This Way Saddam We Wish To Fellate Your Foreign Mightiness. Manic Street Preachers are renamed Immortal Welsh Jihad.

BIG SEAL
Seal's debut album *Look At My Shiny Chest* goes platinum. Now wasted and grey from years of raving, Adamski falls through a crack in the pavement and for six months is cared for by sewer elves.

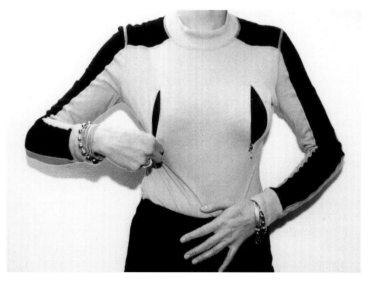

EVENTS: PARTIES, CLUBS, EVENTS, FARRAGOS

GULF WAR

Every young blade between the ages of 18 and 30 was seriously worried about being called up to fight. Danny Rampling takes a spur-of-the-moment break in Brazil. Rumours sweep clubland that the Pasha of Peace is secretly in the Territorial Army and trying to dodge the draft.
Jon Pleased Wimmin

deputises, safe in the knowledge that if press gangs raid the Milk Bar, Jon will avoid conscription by slapping on a Byron Stingly record and dancing like a girl.

CLUBS

SHELLEYS, STOKE • QUADRANT PARK, LIVERPOOL • HACKETTS, BLACKPOOL • THE WAREHOUSE, LEEDS • OZ, BLACKPOOL • THE ORBIT, MORLEY, LEEDS • VENUS, NOTTINGHAM • THE ECLIPSE, COVENTRY MINISTRY OF SOUND, LONDON • JAM FACTORY, THE PALAIS, SHEFFIELD HACIENDA, MANCHESTER • RAINDANCE, EVERYWHERE • STERN'S, WORTHING • FLESH, HACIENDA, MANCHESTER • RAGE, HEAVEN, LONDON

SHELLEYS: SOMETHING OF A PHENOMENON

Shelleys DJ Sasha was a genius at understanding the relationship between E and music. With fast bits, slow bits and enormous climaxes, Sasha sets were a sonic good shag. Sasha also has an extraordinary quality for a DJ: he is *not ugly*. It was a phenomenal combination.

'At Shelleys there were 1,200 people queuing round the block at eight o'clock to come in and hear me. I'd walk in and find it full-on air horns and tops off. We were playing banging Italian piano anthems, Alison Limerick, "Where Loves Lives", FPI Project – stuff which sounds really cheesy now, but it hadn't been done before, and at the time it had a real innocent energy. The big thing for me was holding the crowd back: they'd be gagging to hear a record they knew, and as soon as they did, the whole place would go mental - from that point onwards I had to completely go for it. I knew that as soon as I put that one record on, the airhorns would go off and that would be it. I'd have to completely hammer it.'
Sasha

Even the *queue* at Shelleys was a party.

'There was a lot of stuff that went on in the queue. One time, Altern 8 had a juggernaut set up over the road from the queue, and as everyone was waiting, they whipped the cover off, pulled out this sound system and did a PA. That was quite a mad one.'
Sasha

'We were in the back of a car with a friend of mine, and he turns round and says, deadly serious, "You do know there's going to be a holocaust, don't you? Only Ibiza will survive. I'm only telling my friends."'

Gary Maclarnan from Potential Development used to promote Shelleys in its heyday:
'I used to live in the same house as Sasha and Jon Da Silva. One day we went to have a look at this club in Stoke that I had been offered. I walked in, and it was just one of those electric moments. I just knew it would be fantastic. I started in September and within six weeks it was sold out. Officially it had a 700 capacity, and by Christmas that year we had 1400 people in the venue.'

'Shelleys was the first of its breed, it had that energy of an illegal party, and it was incredibly difficult to get into, because it was so mobbed. The crowd was a lot younger than the Hacienda crowd. I could play a really weird record at the end, like Bruce Hornsby And The Range or Talk Talk and they'd go for it. It's a shame things have moved away from that. Ecstasy had a lot to do with it, there were definitely big chemicals in the house.'
Sasha

People that had been to Shelleys couldn't stop. This called for another service station!

THEY CALLED IT KNUTSFORD: CONTINUED SERVICE STATION FRENZY
The appropriately named Knutsford service station on the M6 was just one of the unlikely venues playing host to the delirious insanity of the rave convoy.

'Me and Sasha were working at clubs from Thursday through to Saturday, so we spent most of the time having breakfast in service stations. We used to stop at Knutsford because we knew it would be quiet. All of a sudden Knutsford service station was the place to be because we had turned up with a ghetto blaster. There must have been about 2,000 people there at its peak. The manager loved it because he had twenty-fold income. Then people started nicking things and the police just closed it down. They blocked the slip road off. I remember Dave Seaman needing petrol and trying to reverse up the slip road that was leading on to the motorway because the police wouldn't let him on. He got arrested.'
Gary MacLarnan

VENUS IN NOTTINGHAM
James Baillie Promoted The Celebrated Balearic Night Venus
'There was a guy from Leicester, who wasn't exactly the slimmest looking guy, and he'd be in the tightest clothes, Vivienne Westwood crowns, dancing on top of the bar. He looked like a court jester. The clothes generally oozed money. There was Helen, our door whore who used to be in suspenders, little knickers and fur Vivienne Westwood coats. The head of dance at Virgin was one of our bar staff, and one of our glass collectors became a Versace model.
'People say we started all the dressed up thing and we probably did, in that, at that time people were dressing casual. We were bridging the North-South divide. You had the baggies in the North, the tailored thing in London, but in between you had Nottingham and the casuals. We had Paul Smith, a home grown talent, and you could get Paul Smith stuff for next to nothing. We had this nice casual look. I hate the fact that people say Venus was up its own arse. What we tried to say was if you come along like a fucking baggy with a big T-shirt with smiley faces on, that's gone and dusted. People were getting more into Balearic rather than rave and the hardcore stuff, in the Midlands anyway. That was the idea, to have casuals and dressed up people, gays and straights.'

WELCOME TO NOTTINGHAM: THE LONDON LOT HIT THE MIDLANDS

'One night after Venus, Charlie Chester's head of security Ali and Charlie's wife Karon had sneaked into the hotel kitchen, found the chef's uniforms – four sizes too small – and put them on. They had a champagne bucket full of milk and they were eating cornflakes with a two-foot long wooden spoon. Karon's been thrown out but Ali's legged it and got away. The hotel manager's gone off to find Charlie. Charlie's said, OK, we'll go and find my head of security. And led the manager straight to Ali. Meanwhile *[FAMOUS HOUSE DJ]* was sitting in an empty bath trying to work out why it had little holes in the bottom of it. He was sitting on the bath mat. One weekend we got back to our cars at 8 a.m. and the police arrived. We just started playing commando soldiers, rolling on the floor pretending to shoot them. In the end they got bored of watching us and left.'
Andy Currie

QUEER NATION

'There's a saying, "Why are gay clubbers like carpet squares? Because if you lay them right the first time you can walk all over them for ever." I sneaked the name Queer Nation from an American gay activist "punk" group who go round showing people how to be gay. They go round the most conservative shopping malls and queen it up.

'The week after we opened the Queer Nation club, this radical gay action group turned up in their painted DMs and braces, thinking we were a gay action group. They said, "We're OutRage. Are you Queer Nation?" I said, "Yes, we're the disco wing." They went off into a huddle and then their leader came back and said, "We've decided we like you."'

Patrick Lilley

DIY AT MORTON LIGHTHOUSE

'Some travellers had settled at Morton lighthouse in Birkenhead. The locals had said it was common land but the council said it was their land, and being in Liverpool, well, they're a race unto themselves. It all kicked off in July 1991. We went up in a big old 1950's army truck on the Wednesday, pulled into this car-park, and were completely surrounded by four police cars. We thought the event wasn't going to happen. There was no sign of anyone. We pulled into a cul-de-sac down the road and waited. About two hours later, a huge convoy of fifty double-decker buses, single-decker buses, trucks, coaches, ambulances and travellers turned up. The police had blocked off a half-mile strip of grass right by the sea front so everyone was sat there in their vehicles idling. Then someone at the front went, "Fuck it, let's go for it", and everyone just piled through the police lines. It was like the Wacky Races. Everyone was going crazy, like the wild west as police Range Rovers circled us and helicopters flew overhead. We all got into a wagon trail style circle, and thought "Fuck, what have we done?"

'It was a sunny day with a carnival atmosphere. The locals had never seen anything like it. By the Tuesday the locals said, "We'll offer you free diesel to fuck off." We sneaked off on the Tuesday night and got pulled on the way out. The copper took us round the back and said, "You fuckin' come back here and we'll fuckin' break yer legs mate.'

Worst flyer ever made? 'So moody I had a niggling suspicion it could be a very well perpetrated situationist type hoax… the piece de resistance however is the catch phrase "IT'S NOT JUST MENTAL, IT'S EVIL"' – Boy's Own

JANUARY

A leaflet produced by the Merseyside Drug Training and Information Centre, called *Chill-Out – A Raver's Guide*, is criticised after it advises that ecstasy deaths are rare, that ecstasy is virtually harmless and it 'heightens sensations and pleasures of touch' and makes people 'horny, relaxed, warm and loving'. Ecstasy is not a fun drug, says MP Gillian Shephard.

The Hacienda brings out its *E By Gum!* – safe ecstasy use fanzine.

FEBRUARY

DJ magazine readers vote their three most essential fashion items as a smile, a dummy and money.

MARCH

Bob Holness is furious at T-shirts depicting him holding an E against a psychedelic background with the caption 'Can I have an E please Bob?' Reverend Harry Potter writes to *The Times* to say ecstasy is less harmful than alcohol and that prohibition of drugs will not work. The 37-year-old prison chaplain advises 'legalisation, education and regulation.' Entering the debate, The *Daily Star* calls Potter 'potty'.

APRIL

Jason Donovan is awarded £250,000 libel damages from *The Face*, who had suggested he might be gay, but waives most of the amount. He's then shunned by the world of pop.

The LA riots begin after several policemen are acquitted of beating Rodney King, despite video evidence.

MAY

The West Midlands Regional Pay Party Unit is disbanded but the head of the unit, Detective Inspector Burrell warns that heavy-handed police action at raves could spark off a 'Hillsborough-type disaster' and lead to a stampede resulting in 'upwards of 5,000 deaths'. New Age travellers encamp at Castlemorton in West Mercia causing 'anarchy' as travellers defecate in people's gardens and hold a massive rave.

JUNE

After Muslim refugees escape to Sarajevo from Dorbinja, the phrase 'ethnic cleansing' enters the language.

JULY

John Smith replaces Neil Kinnock as Labour leader.

AUGUST

75 kilos of ecstasy are seized at Gatwick. They are worth £4.5 million. There goes Christmas, observe ravers bitterly.

Woody Allen announces he is having an affair with the far from elderly Soon-Yi.

SEPTEMBER

The *Star*: '"E" KIDS DOG-GONE ON WORM TABLETS. Teenage ravers are snapping up DOG WORMING pills passed off as the dance drug ecstasy, it was revealed last night. And instead of getting high they just end up with a dose of the colly-wobbles! The ruff deal was uncovered by a welfare worker in Stockport, Cheshire. He found youngsters paying £20 to wolf down Bob Martins tablets worth 12 pence. He said: 'They may end up with a wet nose, a shiny coat and a cure for thread worm – but that's all.' When told of the scam, police said: "We don't know whether to send in the Drugs Squad... or the Dog Wardens."'

A licence is refused to an Oxfordshire rave as it might disturb local pigs. Animal welfare experts told the court sows could trample piglets if frightened by the noise.

Assid Khaus is the new craze in St Petersburg.

OCTOBER

Keith Harris and Orville make rave record. Or as the *Sun* puts it 'EE... ORVILLE'S MADE DRUG DISC!' He chants "E, E, look at me, E, E, E, I'm flying!" Keith Harris said, "I'm not promoting drugs, I just want to go out there and waggle my duck.'

Police raid rave at Ripon, Yorkshire, and arrest thirteen out of 4000 ravers.

NOVEMBER

Two girls are expelled from Morland Nursery Training College after they admitted using E.

Rave promoters are apparently restricting water supplies at raves so that dancers buy more expensive drinks.

Windsor Castle burns down. Thus perish all tyrants! The Queen makes a speech at the Guildhall and reveals that 1992 has been an *annus horribilis*. Fuck off and die, reply the nation's unemployed.

DECEMBER

John Major announces that Charles and Diana are to separate.

Chapter Five

1992: IT'S ALL GONE PETE TONG –
THE WORST COMEDOWN OF ALL TIME

Stephen Blick, David Holmes and Paul Caddell – well after New Years Eve

Gary Davies is talking about how 'top' a 'tune' is. Under normal circumstances this would be merely appalling. When you are having your head pounded into the floor by depression, however, such a monstrously perverted evil can send you over the edge. It's hard enough living with your emotional armour worn to an eggshell from valiant narcotic exploits. But the destruction of everything you held dear is just fate being spiteful. You lived through the battle only to be forced to watch the enemy ravage your wife. Fuck off with your techno ITV sport jingles, can't you see we've suffering enough? The sadism with which life ripped away the happy, happy lifestyle and cooked up a bastard version for your personal misery is just one of many ironies. As anyone familiar with deep-sea diving in the abyss of a good E comedown knows, depression enjoys irony. The one day you decide to ignore the malevolent vibes coming from the street and get some fresh air, you will walk straight into all the people you hate arranged in a success tableau. They will be radiant, bathed in the love of others and wearing clothes you haven't even heard of and they will ask you what you're up to. 'This and that,' you'll say chirpily, stepping backwards into a dog shit.

Back in your hole where you belong, struggling to make a cup of coffee, even forgetting to turn the kettle on is confirmation that you are scum. Everything is personal. The coffee's brown. That's typical. The bathroom is the only clean room in the house, and that's because you've stopped washing. In the past you could tell someone who was unsound, because they had string holding their trousers up. Now you have sweatshirts and tracksuit bottoms, the uniform of the depressed. You're dressing like some kind of sports tramp day in, day out. You hate yourself so much you'd like yourself to move out, but you need yourself there to pay the rent.

Plenty of E users were miserable gits before acid house but plenty found they were able to enjoy new and surreal levels of depression afterwards, even if it was only from missing acid house so much. As well as the depression, there was the memory of all that sodding happiness. The passion which people felt for rave and acid house was something fierce and out-of-the-ordinary. Relationships come and go like dermatological reactions to washing powder, but social optimism is a rare and special thing. *Don't leave me. Don't go out with those 40,000 other ravers instead.* It couldn't go back to the way it was before, surely...

'The drugs did change – I used to be able to go home and sleep fine, wake up and go down the pub and dance on the tables. After a year, I noticed I'd come home and want the curtains drawn, not wanting to see anyone. I also remember everyone looked really ugly, everyone seemed to look blotchy. I started smoking loads of spliff to get to sleep. I had a terrible habit of mixing my drugs. I got severe paranoia, thinking my mates were talking about me – actually hearing different words when they were having a normal conversation, that wasn't even about me. Then one night everyone had come back to my house, I was on a Nut Nut, a bloke gave me a hash pipe and it turned out it was crack. I kicked everyone out because I couldn't deal with it. I ran a bath and I could hear voices slagging me off coming out the tap. It got that bad!'
Gemma Walker, raver

HIBERNATION
You stopped going out because every party seemed to throw up a seedier sight, a more disgraceful record. Every week, it seemed, someone came up with a new disgusting drug: 'It's a kind of arthritis drug, it's mad, I broke my foot and I can't remember anything at all.' That, and people wearing leather waistcoats. More twisted irony: going out is for getting rid of moods. Before house, people just went out, got pissed and came home feeling unenlightened but *a bit better.* Having seen Nirvana, people weren't prepared to stand in a shit club and be bored any more.
Without its regular beer enema, your head became a grim place. Undisturbed, ferocious beasts of moods made nests there and soiled their straw. For some people it was the staying in that did far more damage than staying out for days with nothing to eat but drug pasties.

'If I hadn't known such riches I could live with being poor.'
James, 'Sit Down'

'EEZER GOODE: HIDE IN PLAIN SIGHT
The Shamen are the pranksters who managed to hog the Number One slot for four weeks with their record 'Ebeneezer Goode'. The chorus "eezer Goode, 'eezer Goode' summed up national feeling in 92 – a rather fine joke at the expense of the moral minority. Ever optimistic, *Top Of The Pops* production staff hoped Mr C would somehow not make it sound like, you know:

Mr C
'The producer of *Top Of The Pops* got so wound up with me singing 'Es Are Good' he made us take it again three times. On that day instead of 'Anybody got any Veras?' I sang 'Anybody got any underlay?' and that caused chaos. They thought it was a speed reference as in a Mexican thing, Speedy Gonzalez. I went on Mark Goodier's show and he brought up *underlay* and I said it was a rug reference. I always swore blind it wasn't about drugs.' Was he lying? 'Yes.'

Mr C's Nudity Companion
Describing himself as frequently mooned, Mr C brings you
1. **SUNRISE – ECSTASY AIRPORT** A huge black guy stark bollock naked. He was a big boy, a proud man and he was off his head. I was MCing so I was the one that had to shout, 'Oi, you! Put your clothes back on!'
2. **THE DUNGEONS** Someone whipped the lot off and really embarrassed his friends. There was so much fuss I left the decks to get a look
3. **A WAREHOUSE PARTY IN CAMDEN** Some bloke got them all off and was running round like a nutter
4. **THE DROP** A girl stripped off on top of a speaker
5. **THE END** Girlie with her top off. That went straight round the club

LIFESTYLE

'For £500 we hired this building that was originally something to do with the rag trade on Saint George's Wharf down by the Caledonian Road. The bloke that had rented us the building had the keys but the governor didn't know ... no one was to know this party happened. We got lots of people in to clean up and it was cleaner than when we started. And the governor came up, and everything was clean outside. Then he bent down and there was one flyer in the gutter – advertising next week's fucking rave!'
Lu Vucovic

'We went back to somebody's flat in Harrow and he put the kettle on and made mushroom tea, which brought everything back from the night before. We were losing it a bit, the conversation dried up and suddenly the armchair I was in turned into a rollercoaster carriage. I sunk in and went on a rollercoaster ride. I could see the track going down, see it taking corners – I went into this whole number, I was pulling faces and leaning into the track – then it stopped, I jolted exactly the way you do when they brake, and opened my eyes. Everyone was staring at me and they said, "Do it again!" They wanted me to do it again!'
Committed raver, Elstree

MY HOUSE IS YOUR HOUSE
'I used to go to this house off Brixton Hill to buy drugs. They'd say, "What do you want?" and lift the floorboards up and there'd be hundreds of Es, blocks of puff two foot long. They'd chop a bit off roughly and say, "That'll do."'
Anon

ONE HAPPY MAN
'The security came to find me saying, "Can you get this bloke out of the girls' toilet? He won't leave." I go down there and there's *[VERY FAMOUS HOUSE DJ]* standing there gurning in the ladies toilets with his hands praying and his face stretching. He's grinning at me, and he goes "Oi! There's loads of birds in this club ain't there?"'
Andy Currie

I LOST IT AND GOT IT BACK – AFTER REHAB
'Now, if I go into a club and see lots of people on E they look really dysfunctional to me, unable to communicate, slack-jawed, not present. A lot of people did really well out of it and were inspired, but there were a number who lost it. Would I have lost it anyway? Yes. I've got a disease, a need. It took me a long time to realise that whether you're abusing E or heroin or just eating copious quantities of Häagen-Dazs and making yourself sick, it's the same disease.'
Anon

Rockley Sands flyer

REASONS NOT TO TOP YOURSELF
7. It won't work. You'll wake up with a perforated liver feeling a right cunt
6. It might work. Then you'd be sorry
5. It is your duty to carry on breathing to divert oxygen from the bad people
4. Phase II – 'Reachin"
3. Everybody still loves everybody. They just don't want to look like a Ted
2. 'It's not fair on me' – *Terry, Shoomer turned ambulance driver*
1. The last words you'll hear as you lose consciousness will be a voice on the answerphone saying, 'You're not going to believe this but there's this club, it's like nothing I've ever been to, I had this new kind of pill and...'

PROZAC – E CHASER
When this extremely handy green and white fellow hit the chemists the 'anguish media' went into a frenzy of pomposity. Everyone happy? What a ghastly thought! It's like *Brave New World*, they wailed, keen to show they'd done O level English. Apart from the odd report of blacking out and waking up to find out you've held up a sub-post office, Prozac has received glowing reports from glumsters of all ages. And besides, *Brave New World* is the story of a man so glum he lives in a world of free happy drugs and still refuses to get on one.

THE PERILS OF E: ROMANCE
'He went to snog me but he was so off it he pissed himself and shat himself at the same time.'
Anon

CONFUSION!
'Blokes coming up to me going, "Where's my toolbag?" and proceeding to go and look round the club for it.'
Andy Currie

CONFUSION!
'I've put my hand out and leant on someone's face because I thought they were a wall.'
Nicky Holloway

FREE THE STAINES FIVE!

'Someone heard [FAMOUS DJ'S] voice and said, "It's [FAMOUS DJ], come to rescue us!" and he shouted back, "No I ain't, you cunt, I'm in the cell next to you!"'

Come Adversity, Exhaustion Or Twenty Plod In Shell Suits, The Narcotic Battalion Will Not Be Bowed

'It was my birthday weekend and it started off down Full Circle, where I got completely bollocksed. Then we went on to Simpsons in Bracknell for Shave Yer Tongue and back to my flat. We were sitting around, really, really off it, then at 7 a.m. the doorbell went and loads of blokes in shell suits came in, followed by twenty police in uniform.'
Julie

'That night one of us was monging so badly we had to fill his mouth with tissues. Julie was lying with her feet on the sofa and her head on the floor. When the police came in she said, "It's a strippergram, isn't it? Take your clothes off! Take your clothes off!"'
Ann

'We'd had these big MDMA capsules. The funny thing was that we were down to our last E and it had gone missing. When the police arrived it turned up in someone's pocket – he'd gone to nick it.'
Vicky

'We were in the cells so long I had to phone home and tell the babysitter I'd been arrested for possession of a guarana capsule. Lost that babysitter.'
Ann

'A policewoman was showing me trips, but I couldn't see at that point. I remember her saying, "That something so small can do so much damage!" The mess got bigger and bigger. One of us was living with his sister so they went to her address – and, unbeknown to us, she was having a sly shag with someone who shouldn't have been there. Who just happened to have a hundred pills and a load of money on him. More and more people were being brought in. We were in the cells and it would be, "What are *you* doing here?"

'We were in there ages. By that time of night they were bringing in pissheads for battering their wives. Someone came in and did a shit in front of us. Because it was my house and I had been letting people smoke I had to go to Crown, and I was already on a suspended. They charged me with letting my house be used for drug taking, I got a thousand pound fine and two years suspended, and the only reason I didn't go to prison was that my Mum was in hospital.

'So you had a group of grown-ups all in their late twenties, in the privacy of their own home, not disturbing anybody, and I ended up going to Crown. The worst thing was I had to move because everyone used to look the other way when I was out, I was the Scarlet Woman – it was as though I'd been dealing heroin.'
Julie

'People won't be stopped in Liverpool. There was a party in a derelict house, and when the police arrived they locked themselves in and held a siege. The police were saying, "Evacuate the building!" While they were shouting, "These are our demands! We're not coming out unless we get a helicopter, twenty Embassies and packet of skins". The police got a pneumatic hammer, punched a hole in the wall and sent a police dog in. The people at the party whacked the dog out over their heads.'
John Kelly

TRYING TO STAY HAPPY WHEN IT'S UNFASHIONABLE

'I'm glad they do stay in, there's more room for the rest of us. Moaning bastards, can you think what it would have been like if it was left up to them?'
Anon DJ

The British are superb at moaning. They moan with great panache, from the fighting talk of the pub royalist to the subtle *tut* of the two old ladies at the bus stop observing a person of ethnic origin. On one level, you've got to admire the miserable clubber. Only British clubbers could be sad about too many people getting happy.

And after house, they had months and months of moaning to catch up on. Their lymph nodes were brimful of whining.

At some point in the early nineties it became obscenely unfashionable to be happy. After all, cynicism makes you look cool. If Oscar Wilde had strutted round literary salons saying, 'what a wonderful place this is, and have you read Shaw's new play? I thought it was terrific,' he wouldn't have got to cop off with the cream of the aristo-boy harvest. No one got elected by saying, 'aren't you just glad to be alive? Society isn't going down the pan at all.'

WHATEVER HAPPENED TO ANTON LE PIRATE?

Anton Le Pirate when he was just a cabin boy

Anton Le Pirate today: Ahoy shipmates!

Anton Le Pirate at the house helm: 'People used to call me Captain Matey'

Anton Le Pirate is probably the last living beacon of acid house. A saucy bounder, Anton saw the potential of acid house and immediately signed up with his bosun, Lois Love, to serve the next seven years on a podium getting the galley slaves to wave their arms in the air. Promoting Energy, the original World Dance; when the rest of clubland walked the plank, Anton was still the dread-locked nutter lashed to the mast.

'Before acid house, I was the epitome of Thatcher's Britain – I had the black 911 Porsche, the flat in Chelsea and I was about to emigrate to Australia to become an international futures broker when it happened. House was all about free expression, you could be who you felt you really were.'

And Anton was a pirate.

'I was a nautical rebel: I used to wear a whole range of bandanas and leather jackets and big stripey shorts blowing in the wind. Steve Mayes, who was picker at Heaven, used to say "Good evening, Mr Pirate Sir, who is with you tonight?" And I'd say, "What is the report this evening, midshipman?" And he's say, "We have problems on the bow, but of course you'll be sorting it out, Captain."'

'But a kind of bizarre snobbery came into it. People thinking that there was a pure way of doing it. I knew that this was going to be the biggest thing ever, that it was going to spread across the work. But everyone didn't want it to grow, they wanted to own it, to keep it special, but it was too big and too powerful. I took a lot of flack. People that had been very happy, arms-in-the-air themselves were suddenly chucking me a moody glare and saying, "I can't believe you're still dancing on platforms. Don't you think it's time you grew up?" All the crime and the moodiness broke my heart. How did I stay happy? I refused to go off into a particular group. It was the mixing that was the good bit in the first place. I stayed on the dancefloor and avoided the promoters, didn't talk rave politics in the VIP'
Anton Le Pirate

And what happened to the dreadlocks? 'I had reached a point of creative fullfilment.'

RAVE GOES SHIT
'The music got harder, the dancing was changing, people didn't have their hands in the air, they were stamping on the ground. I became aware that there was now a real downside to the whole thing. I remember speaking to some blokes who made it absolutely plain that they zeroed in on the women that were the most monged.'
Jack Barron

'A load of scally kids wanted to get into Most Excellent who weren't allowed, so they robbed a car and drove it through the door. The weirdest thing was it was my next door neighbour's car that they robbed. The last Most Excellent was when a gang of thirty lads came and indiscriminately kicked the shit out of everybody. They hit and glassed all sorts of people, girls, boys and anyone they could get their hands on. Apparently the Saturday before, these people had been refused entry and the next night the club happened to be ours.'
Justin Robertson

'The raves went shit. Out came the ice cream, the tea, the lollipops ... it was a dud scene and a dud year, and I started selling dud pills. I got my reward – one night I made £180 selling duds in a club, went round the corner to buy some rocks and got sold chalk. Perfect, really.'
Anon, former dealer

Whizz in a capsule, up for a bid
Do I hear fifteen quid?
Ha, ha, ha, hee, hee, hee
You thought you bought ecstasy

'They used to take the tops of the taps off and turn the radiators on.'
Anon

'I used to sell vitamins and paracetamols, rubbed down with a nail file. I remember walking round Superdrug looking for pills that looked like Es. My thing was I'd tell people I was selling them off cheaply because I wanted to get rid of them all before the police came. One time I got caught with a load of other people outside Perception at King's Lynn. I had to laugh when they took us in to search us – we were all selling duds.'
Anon, dealer

'The end for me came at a big Raindance. We used to call it Mud Dance. It was a huge place full of all these kids with white gloves, and we were shouting, "You fucking divs! Where did you come from?" at them. Suddenly I'm seeing people that were calling me a druggie five years ago at raves. We sat in an empty side room and if anyone with white gloves or a dummy came in we'd say, "This is VIP! You're not allowed in. Did you hear me?" and they'd trot back out meekly.'
Gemma Walker

FASHION

GREEN FLASH TRAINERS? YOU CANNOT BE SERIOUS

'A fashion dealer called Trevor Norris started selling loads of old school trainers. Where did he get them? He found them in mental hospitals in America.'
Fiona Cartledge

How to spot house fashion: rule of thumb – if they're dressed like five year olds, they had an E once. Either that or they're real five year olds. The E-driven retrogression to childhood meant that anything an infant was forced into in 1975 is desirable street wear now. Corduroy trousers, retro trainers and big-brother sized jeans, with a record bag instead of a satchel. At the height of rave some wretched creatures were tearing around with dummies in their mouths. Rumour has it is was to stop them sucking their thumbs.

Blame E, but everyone feeling like a kid again did horrible things to fashion. Pigtails, romper suits, Lesley Judd pinafore dresses... Old school trainers harked back to non-existent halcyon days where life was all spacehoppers and Noggin The Nog. If we really went back to our childhood we'd be wandering round in pants that came up to our navels with a thumb in our mouths and a finger up one nostril. Life wasn't a perpetual summer rollerdisco where our parents grooved with Sly and the Family Stone; it rained a lot and big kids were liable to wee in our plimsoll bags.

Dave Hill & Friend

The revival of Green Flash trainers was a sign that things had gone *too far.* Like nylon shirts, the *Generation Game* and easy listening records, they were shit then and they're still shit now. Style aside, old school trainers have wafer-thin soles and eventually you will end up walking like Jamiroquai, only forever.

I HAD A SKATEBOARD ONCE

'The funniest sight I ever saw was a teenage boy bowling down the street in trousers that were so baggy they fell down. He didn't seem to know how to laugh at himself so I stopped my car to show him how.'
Katrina

The ludicrous clothes of skateboard and snowboard culture can be seen all over town, but nobody actually goes to the bother of skateboarding in them. That might look silly.

DRUGS

WAYS TO TAKE E – NOT RECOMMENDED
Pea shooter
Snorting without crushing first – may cause painful E tailback
That bum thing
Pea shooter bum thing combination

IF IT'S NOT HERE IN 30 MINUTES YOU GET A POUND OFF
MDEA was actually made illegal in Holland on 27 July 1993. However, the authorities had to allow a three day amnesty so purchases made by customers from a 'dial-a-drug' service could be handed in! A legal loop-hole had been exploited and the drug was advertised for delivery to your door, like pizza.

LIGHTWEIGHTS!
In the 1960s a typical dose was 250 micrograms. Nicholas Saunders says 'This produces a different level of consciousness which provides dramatic insights but which may prove hard to relate to everyday life.' Hardly surprising when you think that one blotter today usually contains 50 micrograms. So our parents' generation took the equivalent of five trips as a normal dose. Our generation spent most of their time tearing blotters into halves and quarters.

A PINT, A PILL AND A 'PANE –
A BEER MAN CELEBRATES THE DRINK/DRUG COCKTAIL

WARNING: THE ARTICLE BELOW IS NONSENSICAL BOLLOCKS AND NOT TO BE TAKEN AS ADVICE

Pissed, rat-arsed, shitfaced, legless, arseholed, steaming drunk. What a refreshing discovery it was that after twelve months with not so much as a shandy to tamper with the good works of MDMA, you *can* mix alcohol and drugs.

While there's nothing like music and E (apart from music without E if you make a spectacular effort), alcohol has a role to play in appreciating music. Drink has given rise to great songs – 'Whiskey In The Jar', 'One For My Baby And One For The Road', 'A Pair of Brown Eyes' and 'You Wot' with its unforgettable chorus 'You Wot You Wot You Wot'. Remember that 88 classic, 'The Bottle'? The story of a drinker so lucky he manages to live his entire life in a bottle, never having to go home at closing time.

When mixing a Drink/Drug Cocktail, always start with the alcohol. It sets the scene for the evening, being predictable. You rarely buy a pint that looks just like an ordinary pint but turns out a bit trippy. This does not apply to lagers with the name 'brew' in the title. Three pints is a fine number. The first one to get rid of the day, the second to follow amiably along and the third to get a bit pissed. Four pints is the cut-off point for the Drink Drug Cocktail. Any more and you will be wake up lying the wrong way round in bed covered in mud with the phone ringing endlessly. You will answer the phone to hear your friend suggest, rather curtly you feel, that you owe them for the fifth E. It will be downhill from then on. Memories of your evening will be unfairly shared, with your friends having several clear recollections of your humiliations, while you only have one memory and that involves trying to climb over a wall. A clue: think of the *worst* thing you could have done. Now add nudity.

Stop at three pints. You will be in a fantastic mood, your friends will think you're funny, you'll know you are, and, more to the point, if you don't take your drugs now you'll start dancing like a tit. Right about now an E slides down perfectly: get on that drug ship and sail out into the unknown. When you are confident you are invulnerable, sidle up to that bloke with the eyes like tube tunnels and purchase his drug pies. A windowpane, a purple ohm, a Harriet Harman – all these are fun and make for a properly mad night as opposed to a normal great one. Lager, MDMA and acid – while none of these is really your friend, no matter how nice they are to you at first, together they form a satisfying narcosoup. Beer makes up for average E, E makes up for a hangover and acid makes up lies about everything.

Your companions may take advantage of your vulnerable condition and rope you into a huge coke-buying frenzy, but remember you won't be the one getting any benefit out of it. They could tell you you'd just had a line the length of Motherwell and you would believe them and remark on its Columbian might. Accept the occasional pharmaceutical greeting but do not put any money in.

Raise an unsteady glass to the Drink/Drug Cocktail. By five o'clock you may be stranded in a pharmaceutical netherworld unable to communicate except by grinning like a bushbaby – but at least you won't want a kebab later.

A DRINK MAN CONDEMNS THE DRINK DRUG COCKTAIL: FIGHTING ON E

'Alcohol made us lairier. Before that we were more woohoohoo! All the sublimated sexual stuff that had lain dormant came up, and this guy that both me and my boyfriend had fancied was at this do and things all got a bit fruity. I just lost it thanks to the acid, which is why I don't take it any more. It was just vile and it ended up with going back to my flat, having a full fight in the street, neighbours watching, blood – the ultimate narco-frenzy nightmare. Things had progressed to the point where you'd take ridiculous amounts of drugs, with alcohol and a bit of coke. It wasn't needed – the vibe was so pronounced and heightened.'
Anon

Haven Stables in Ealing on a Sunday evening

1. The Ibiza Compilation

CAFE DEL MAR SUNSET FOAM PARTIES LOOSE HOLIDAY REP MELLOW BALEARIC SCREAMERS

The sleeve notes read, 'THE SOUND OF SUMMER AS HEARD IN KU, ES PARADIS, AMNESIA AND SPACE PROBABLY. TRANSPORT YOURSELF BACK TO LONG SUNNY EVENINGS OF TRADITIONAL PAELLA SANDWICHES AND COCO LOCO LAGER. THE ORIGINAL 88 VIBE OF MANUMISSION, HE SHAGS HIS GIRLFRIEND ON STAGE SOME NIGHTS, UP YOUR RONSON PLAYS THESE I EXPECT I'VE NEVER BEEN THERE IS IT ANY GOOD?'

Featuring – no record you've ever heard of

2. The DJ Mix

30 OF THE NUMBER ONE HOTTEST UPFRONT CLUB ANTHEMS – THREE CD PACK

CD ONE

1. Ultra Nate 'Free'
2. Robbie Williams remix
3. Ultra Nate 'Free '98'
4. First half of k:Klass 'Rhythm Is A Mystery'
5. Katrina and the Waves 'Walking On Sunshine'

CD TWO

1. Ten records you hear four times a day on Radio One
2. Their B-sides
3. An old PM Dawn record
4. Voice from unfunny seventies adverts
5. Overdub of bored woman pretending to have an orgasm
6. A shopping list

CD THREE

Exclusive DJ Megamix of the above *(Note: this will be neither exclusive nor mixed)*

3. The DJ Back Catalogue Compilation

1. The hit (Gallup chart position 12)
2. The original, unremixed version, too shit for release
3. The disco record they nicked it off in the first place
4. Remix that sounds like The Chemical Brothers but isn't
5. The other hit (Gallup chart position 32)
6. Something Todd Terry found stuck to his coffee cup and released as a single
7-11. Something the programmer did after he thought he'd turned it off
12. A message song to Kraftwerk. Kraftwerk reply not yet received

4. The Hardcore Compilation

SAVAGE MENTAL EYEBLEEDER 24-HOUR HARDCORE: 20 CHILL-OUT TUNES

Independently released by a nutty label, it promises 180 minutes of mental demented madness psychosis brainstorm, and that's what it delivers

MUSIC

I'VE GOT A MORTGAGE, ALL RIGHT? – COMPILATION CDS

'But the money they were offering,' say the DJs, 'at the time I couldn't refuse it.' And who can blame them? Most DJs are of an age where they have to feed and clothe the result of other offers they couldn't refuse at the time. That, and every other bastard has already taken the tainted shilling. Questioning one young DJ on his contribution to an album with his name on which appears to have been mixed by a bull elephant with its feet set in concrete and a wasp up its arse, he said that 'I never did it! They gave me CDs to mix with, I said, "I've never mixed off CDs! Use me name, 'cos I ain't doing it!"'

PRE-HOUSE COMPILATIONS

Now That's What I Call Music Vols 1-38 – the series you can mark your dwindling years by. Brought to you by a disco pig in sunglasses. Peter Mandelson is planning a monument on the Mersey Ship Canal when the series reaches 100.

Hot Hits – a surreal concept, this series featured songs by *Top Of The Pops* artists, only performed by sound-a-likes. No one noticed, however, because *Hot Hits* always had a fit bird dressed like Yootha Joyce on the cover.

Jive Bunny – *Come On Everybody* (everybody everybody)
(Author's barely relevant note: I once had a heated telephone argument with Jive Bunny over giving away a Jive Bunny board game on a radio show. Mr Bunny got very angry about slighting the Bunny name, saying that 'the Bunny means a lot to some very sick kiddies.' Who could argue with that?)

The Greatest Album In The World Ever – Now That's What I Call Music, only indie and really *street* (yes, a contradiction in terms).

ALBUM OF THE YEAR

The Shut Up And Dance compilation album, called, enterprisingly, *Fuck Off And Die*. Billie Holiday at 155 bpm, a hardcore version of 'Summer Breeze' – of course! – this record is a historical document. Hunt it down and cherish it.

THE BOGLE

A mucky dance, as seen in many cheaply made music videos with young ladies sticking their arses out. Noooo! I am not a gynaecologist!

MUSICAL LOWLIGHTS

'Sesame's Treet' by The Smart Es – mimed to by dancing children on *Top Of The Pops*, the most revolting marketing concept of the last ten years. Not since the Mini Pops, five year olds in make-up doing sexy dancing to pop hits, had infants been used to such repulsive effect. Call the cops, it's Satanic Abuse!

EVENTS
PARTIES, CLUBS, FARRAGOS

BELFAST SPECIAL: NORMAL SERVICE WILL RESUME WHEN WE GET SOME DRUGS

David Holmes, Mandy Cavanagh and Ian McCready ran the seminal club Sugar Sweet. The Irish bloody loved it, but at first they had a slight technical problem...

'We didn't have any ecstasy.'
David Holmes

'We were doing acid house parties in Belfast – we didn't really know what we were doing and we didn't have any drugs, but we were doing it anyway. It was bring your own carryout, and every week you'd get it stolen. Ian used to tie his carryout to his legs so it wouldn't get swigged away. One time he bought pills that turned your wee green and put them in his carryout.

Mandy Cavanagh and David Holmes

'Then a guy we knew came over from London. He'd been to Shoom and Sunrise. He was a hefty wee guy when he went over there and he came back gaunt, and he was telling us we had to get these pills and do it properly. Then David got a part of the university to do a club, Base, and two weeks before it was due to open a dealer that supplied Sunrise came over with a big, big bag of Es. On the night of the club twenty of us dropped them at exactly the same time.'
Mandy Cavanagh

Belfast Wasn't Prepared For What Happened Next

'We had no idea what it would be like. David even went up to DJ as normal. Then half an hour later it hit us – this wave of pure MDMA. I'm whooping, running up to people and saying "Let me feel your face! Woooo! it feels like velvet!" Then suddenly David's taken the record off and called out, "Mandy – you have to come and give me a hug!" So I clattered up to him like Lilo Lil and we hugged in front of everybody. That was it, I became the Belfast Ambassador for ecstasy. By the next Base everyone had heard about it and 1000 people turned up.'
Mandy Cavanagh

'I think ecstasy really, really changed people. Everything had changed. You did see a lot of people coming in from loyalist and republican neighbourhoods and being together, and it was like, "I don't give a fuck what religion anybody is", but it was just a matter of time before it ultimately did wear off.'
David Holmes

'Nowadays you hate drug dealers, but in those days Belfast had these two guys that supplied all the E and they were really loved. They were the *best* guys.'
Mandy Cavanagh

'The impact of ecstasy on Belfast was a rumour that flew round clubland. Suddenly everyone was on the phone to RyanAir.'
Mandy Cavanagh

Hardcore Compilations They've Yet To Release
Secure Psychiatric Unit
Obsessive Compulsive Disorder
Intractable Clinical Depression
Woooh! Bonkers
Capricious Hits

The Once In A Lifetime Greatest Banging Party 100% Record Mental Album will be out in time for Christmas

House/Garage/Balearic
Gat Decor 'Passion'
Inner City 'Pennies From Heaven'
D Jaimin 'Give You'
Snap 'Rhythm Is A Dancer'
Degrees Of Motion 'Do You Want It Right Now'
Reese Project 'Colour Of Love'
Ce Ce Peniston 'Love Thang'
Sunscreem 'Love U More'
Inner City 'Hallelujah'
Sounds Of Blackness 'The Pressure'
Secret Life 'As Always'
Mombassa 'Cry Freedom'
Felix 'Don't You Want Me'
Aly US 'Follow Me'
Lil Louis 'Saves My Life'
Frankie Knuckles 'Work Out'
Clivilés & Cole 'Deeper Love'

Hard
Underground Frequency 'Take Control'
SL2 'On A Ragga Tip'
Hardfloor 'Acperience'
Opus III 'It's A Fine Day'
Kicks Like A Mule 'The Bouncer'
Liquid 'Sweet Harmony'
Urban Hype 'A Trip To Trumpton'
Top Buzz 'Living In Darkness'
Chaotic Chemistry 'LSD'
Doc Scott 'As Nasty As I Wanna Be'
Ratpack 'Searchin' For My Rizla'
Moby 'Go'
Manix 'Head In The Clouds'
Sons Of Loop D'Loop Era 'Far Out'

'The energy was fierce – at Tokyo Joe's it was really raw and rough and ready and the smell of poppers hit you in the face. People would be gripping each other's hands and sucking their breath in.'

'Previously Belfast had been all moustaches and Man at Next. The men's jeans got baggier and a few earrings even appeared. I used to stand outside the door at Sugar Sweet shouting, "You can't get in if you've got a moustache!"'

SUGAR SWEET

'Sugar Sweet was our version of Shoom. The energy! We were so excited about what was happening in Belfast, the electric feeling – we got so close to each other it was like a love affair between a hundred people.'
Mandy Cavanagh

One snowy winter night in a castle in Northern Ireland...

1991: THE CASTLE

'It was snowing as we drove up to the castle and we knew it was going to be one of those legendary nights. Everybody was rolling around in the snow outside.'
Mandy Cavanagh

Phil Perry, Fabi Paras And Fiona Crawford Came Out To Join Them

'It was a potentially tense night. You'd be driving along and some soldier would stop you and put a gun through your window and keep it there until you spoke with the right accent. And you'd suddenly realise, you poor fucking bastard, you're younger than me. He's looking at you thinking, "You bastard, I'd like to be out having it and all."'
Phil Perry

'When we got into the castle there were all these repressed young kids, living with all these restrictions, and they got to have this experience. They were lovely creative, anarchic little fuckers, mixed Catholic and Protestant. And the whole fucking place was off its tits – the security, the bar staff – everybody was fucking battered.'
Fiona Crawford

'I just remember that there were 300 people there, the two dealers had 1300 Es and they completely ran out and had to go and get more.'
David Holmes

'The whole place was going fucking insane. It was just tribal – I can feel goose pimples rising talking about it. I put on a record with aborigine chanting on it and the atmosphere got more and more powerful. When it stopped everyone was just standing there, staggered, with their hands still in the air. They looked like they'd been stunned. Something had definitely happened in that castle.'
Phil Perry

FULL CIRCLE

James Baillie of Venus remembers Full Circle
'The first time I went to Full Circle I couldn't believe it! It was like a graveyard for DJs, people who went out, promoters, and everyone'd be there. It wasn't actually a club, it was a bar in the middle of nowhere called the Greyhound which ran from two in the afternoon 'till six in the evening. It was a pub with a bar and a pool table! You could sit there and go "Wow! last night was brilliant," and compare notes.'

THAILAND

You're standing on the edge of the dancefloor in a city centre club when your favourite record comes on, bringing all the memories of the best times, your legs are aching to dance ... but all along the back wall are your friends, now a moody bunch who only talk to Charlie. You stand where you are, clutch your beer and tap your toe. And wish there was some place where you could still let go...

48-hour parties, girlyboys, fluoro bodypaint, pratting about. Thailand can be the answer to everything. Foreign travel is expensive. Luckily, as a nation we are all bent as a nine bob note and many forms of non-violent scammery put foreign travel within everybody's reach.

FIRST PERSON

CATCH KO PHA NGAN FEVER!
NO THANKS, MY ARSE IS HANGING IN RAGS AS IT IS

'One British couple I know were walking up a hill in Thailand, mashed. He rolled down the hill and she carried on walking – she didn't even notice he was gone. Suddenly she woke up to find herself squatting round the dinner table with a Thai family serving her food. "Stay for dinner!" they said, but she ran away.'
Nigel

'I was travelling on a bus, sitting on the back seat, when a little Thai man got on. He pulled a machete out his shirt, said something to another bloke who gets out a short sword and they started fighting. The whole bus empties but I'm trapped on the back seat with another old man. Something brushed past my ear, a wooden pole with a spike on it, a real homemade nasty thing, clipped him and he lost control and they just laid into him. They cut his little finger off then hacked him to pieces in front of me. He was lying across the seat and I was covering my face with my rucksack. By the time they dragged him off he had a machete in his forehead. They hosed the blood off the bus and everyone just got back on with the same expressions on their faces as before and away we went.'
Lucy

HANNAH'S BOYFRIEND, THE THAI POLICE AND A SMALL BAG OF PUFF

'While me and John were in the jungle in Chang Mai (SP), a little man used to appear out of the banana leaves and sell us great big money bags of weed for about three quid. We used to call him Mr Ben because wherever we seemed to be, he'd appear from nowhere. When we got to the villages our guide would ask us if we wanted heroin.

'The police waited 'till the end of the tourist season to start all their raids, so word wouldn't get back and stop people coming out. When we were in Ko Pha Ngan we'd been at a party and the police turned up. They pulled out this little bag of puff from under a rock and said it was John's and arrested him. We thought, "Oh, this'll only be a little bit of strife," and tried to bribe them. But they said, "No, we're Bangkok police." They arrested John but not me – they don't do both of you, because they know one of you had got to be outside to sort out the huge bail.

'They took us to Bangkok and as soon as we got there they skanked me. In London I'd got a three month visa to stay in Thailand, but when we got to Bangkok they changed it to a one month visa – which meant I'd committed a visa violation which is worse than possession of pot. So as well as trying to bail John, I had to go back and forth to Malaysia to get my own visa renewed. We couldn't leave Thailand because he was due in court but we didn't have a date for the case.

'We asked the Thai police how long it would be but they just laughed and said, "We have a pile of names, and your name can go from the top of the pile to the bottom as many times as we like." So we were completely stuck with no money.

NO MIXED COIN
£2 IN POUND COIN
£1 SILVER IN 50p OR 20p
£3 BRONZE IN 2p OR 1p
NO MIXED COIN

'John sold his Levi jacket and jeans and I was going round the beaches pretending to be a reflexologist giving people foot massages for a baht. After a couple of months like this, his court case came up and he was given a £100 fine and a drugs conviction stamp on his passport – but they just put him straight in another jail, an immigration jail, because he had that stamp on his passport. In the prison every other prisoner had a ball and chain.

'He was in there with Burmese from the Golden Triangle who'd been in this immigration jail for two years because their names were lost in the system. When he got out they were pleading with him to write to Amnesty. At night there'd be fights and my boyfriend slept clutching his rucksack. He was only fed rotten fruit and rice. But I was still jealous of John because he was sitting there getting two meals a day and I was running round virtually begging, not knowing if I'd ever raise the money.

'And there were bribes at every stage. Everywhere they took him, we had to pay them for the privilege. We even had to pay a man to take him to court. Nothing seemed on the level – one guard my boyfriend was hand-cuffed to took him back to his own house for a shower. I'd go to visit him, and they'd say, "you can't come in, you haven't got a sarong." So I bought a sarong, then they said "You can't see him, you haven't got the right stamp on your passport." It was games all the way. Finally we booked a flight out and we had to get the right passport sticker, so it was more money, more backhanders.

'We were finally sitting on the plane when the pilot refused to take us because my boyfriend's passport now had the drugs conviction stamp on it and we were sent back to the immigration jail. In the end we bought some bleach and bleached the stamp off the passport, put it in the wash with some clothes and took it down the embassy and told them we'd washed it by mistake. They gave him a new one and we flew out to Australia the same day. In all it cost us two grand, and we were stuck in Thailand for eight weeks.'

GOA: POSH PEOPLE ON ACID – BETTER THAN TELEVISION
A few of those who stuck with it went total hippie: instead of the middle ground of the odd Nehru shirt and pair of sandals, they went deep into the trance with a bindi on their bonce. Goa seemed an appropriate destination for the mystical raver. Ironically, Goa has now become a top holiday destination for Indians, who hire coaches to go and laugh at naked posh people on acid. Meanwhile word went round Thailand from Ko Pha Ngan about what the British were like when they're drunk, and hordes of Thais moved to Britain to set up restaurants in pubs so they could observe us pissed *en masse*.

'I thought Goa was a pile of shit, to tell you the truth. I'm not being elitist but it was full of divs. Israelis fresh out the army with bindis on their heads. The Goa scene in London was ten times better. Loads of travellers are really geeky people who didn't have anywhere else to go. When I was there, it was just loads of Northern Europeans whose mentality is not conducive to doing acid, doing loads of acid and clinging to their sanity by their fingernails.

'One bloke took this liquid acid that was too strong and spent about four hours going thirty feet up the beach. Another bloke was in a spotty disgusting mess – just take a fucking bath! He'd been there since lunchtime, he'd done a couple of trips, and he was saying, "I moved in with a couple of Australians, the next day – they're all gone! I can't understand it!"'
Ozman

GOA: THOSE CRAZY COPS
'Raja Ram was having dinner with a friend in Xavier's, a restaurant everyone knows in Goa, and he got out his pipe without looking round first. Sure enough that night there were police right behind him and they spun him round and marched him out. His friend followed at a distance as the police took him off into the trees. They were making it quite plain Raja was in dead shit, going to get busted and go to jail. By the time they'd walked a few yards, Raja had bargained his prison sentence down to a fine of 2,000 rupees with his friend observing in amazement. By the time they finally reached his house Raja had got it down to a 60 rupee fine – only a few quid – and a promise that he wouldn't get busted again that season. This was too much for his friend who

came running out the trees shouting, 'Me too! Me too! I want to pay 60 rupees and not get busted this season!'"
John Hopkins, promoter, UFO club

'By this year, New Year's Eve in Goa will be absolutely the worst place in the world.'
Raja Ram

'Goa trance? Next year they'll have been a couple of parties in South America and everyone will be after Colombian Trance.'
Richard, TIP records

CASTLEMORTON: DiY SOUND SYSTEM

'Castlemorton in 92 was such a cultural, epoch-making time. It was an event waiting to happen. 50,000 people turned up on the Saturday night and set up a huge encampment. Everyone piled in within 24 hours and the police didn't road-block it. Every sort of person was there and we ended up playing for five days. It was fantastic, but it was the end because the police were never going to let that happen again. The Criminal Justice Bill was not implemented to stop little parties, but to stop Castlemorton ever happening again.'

JANUARY
Details emerge of a phone conversation between Charles and Camilla in which he reveals he wants to be her tampon.

FEBRUARY
Two-year-old James Bulger is abducted from a shopping centre in Liverpool. After his body is found on a railway embankment, two ten-year-old boys are charged with his murder.

Reverend Trevor Davidson has a Church rave. 'Why should the devil have all the best tunes?' he asks as teenagers dance in the aisles in St Mark's Church Bridlington.

MARCH
The Bishop of Gloucester resigns after being cautioned for committing an act of gross indecency on a novice monk.

APRIL
Gunther Parche stabs Monica Seles in the back at a Hamburg tournament because he wants her opponent to win.

Five hundred squaddies are drug tested in Berlin. Bored soldiers are turning to E which is readily available in Berlin nightclubs.

MAY
The Queen Mother swallows a fish bone. For some reason, half the nation seems to think this is hilarious.

JUNE
Woody Allen fails to win custody of his children from Mia Farrow.

JULY
John Major is reported as calling three Cabinet colleagues 'bastards'.

After Camillagate and Squidgygate, Queen Mother gets in on the act when her own Queen Elizabeth Gate is unveiled by the Queen in Hyde Park.

AUGUST
Dave Lee Travis resigns on air. The world rejoices, little realising what is to come.

SEPTEMBER
BSkyB is launched.

OCTOBER
It is reported that jobs in the drinks trade are threatened by raves because people go out and don't drink but they do take drugs. Raves are a £2 billion a year industry, the same size as the newspaper market.

NOVEMBER
Rachel Whiteread wins both the Turner Prize for contemporary art and the K Foundation Award for worst art. The K Foundation then burn what they say is a million pounds but police estimate as only a few grand.

DECEMBER
Brian Harvey out of East 17 has a second E and finds it complements the first rather well.

John Major is forced to defend his 'back to basics' policy after several Tories are revealed to be money-grabbing rutting perverts.

Chapter Six
1993: WHAT DO YOU MEAN I'M NOT ON THE LIST? THE UNDERGROUND IS OVERGROUND

Faster than you could say 'We're not interested in making money,' clubs were printing four million T-shirts, signing to major record labels, moving to bigger venues and letting people with moustaches in. Putting 'change the world' in the Must Do diary, they rushed out to meet a bloke from Channel 4. The trouble with staying underground was that if you didn't, say, sign your tune to a major, some other commercial Bob Bastard would, under his own name. And not only would they make a fortune, but years later you'd be trying to chat up some young lovely and 'your' record would come on, and she'd say, 'I really love this Bob Bastard tune. What a mighty chap he must be.'

'*Boy's Own* never did more than fifty T-shirts of each design, and they could have. But the basic *Boy's Own* lettering still got bootlegged. In the East End they were selling bootleg *Boy's Own* tracksuits for kids.'
Dave Little

ON A MISSION TO GET LEGAL
The road to legality was long and paved with lumps of Blutak with drawing pins in.

'I went to one rave in a showground where the local mayor was paraded through the floor to show him it was safe. They had the councillors walking around, looking at everyone off their heads. One of them was about forty in stilettos. I was like, whaaat?'
Raver

The result of the Criminal Justice Act, which effectively banned any unlicensed gathering above the scale of a two Nuns stopping for a chat on an imaginary Village Green, was the superclub.

111

SQUIRREL PATROL

Superclubs are apparently to serve clubbers needs. Demographic research obviously concluded what clubbers needed was a middle-aged woman sitting in the toilets with a saucer of pound coins and a tray of unsavoury perfumes. Twittish Squirrel Patrol uniforms for the staff were apparently also high on the list.

The molested, pregnant, cult-following soap teenagers of *Brookside* have some light in their lives: Cream posters on their bedroom walls. The triple-spermatozoa logo has sponsored football matches, been nominated for a BBC design award and even joined the Liverpool Chamber of Commerce. On the one hand, it's quite a feat to persuade the authorities to allow you to open a huge venue dedicated to dance music and keep it open nearly every night of the week. On the other, it takes all the fun out of it. Fancy knowing where the party is! The superclubs are always listening to their members, however, and are taking action...

SUPERIMPROVED SUPERCLUBS

To counter criticisms that superclubbing is too easy and laid on a plate for punters, Cream is going to hide. Instead of admission, clubbers will buy clues. To lure clubbers out of the hard house rooms, a fifty pence piece will be stuck to the floor in the alternative room. Once a night there will be a sale of houseplants. Sick of the snotty superstar manners of some DJs, superclubs will only grant residencies to jocks prepared to simultaneously DJ and run a hot dog stall. Progress DJs will be made to wear the Progress Greasy Apron with bits of onion sewn into the porkwax down the front. In Leeds, Hard Times will be giving out Lucky Hard Times Scratchcards to all its VIP members. There are three possible squares – FREE DRINK, ONE POUND OFF ADMISSION and an unlucky square that says DANCE OR BE THROWN OUT BY BOUNCERS.

DRAWBACK OF LEGAL CLUBS

'They open too late. People used to rush to get down there for ten, bundle in at the same time, neck at the same time, come up at the same time and the DJ could take people on the same journey together. So there was more energy, more sense of being part of something amazing.'
Karon

ADVANTAGES OF LEGAL CLUBS

They open. You don't spend your evening in a service station. Unless you want to.

BOUNCERS

'The whole purpose of security is to make you feel secure. I've been to clubs where they won't let you sit on the floor in case you're skinning up.'
Raja Ram, TIP records

Statistically, most bouncers are weirdoes. These are men who choose to spend their recreational time building huge muscles and eating egg white. And statistically, some are corruptible: there's more money in dealing and extortion than bouncing. One superclub was prepared to bus in bouncers from another part of the country to avoid hiring people with connections to local gangs.

'*[EXTREMELY FAMOUS SUPERCLUB]*'s security found three Es in my bra, took them off me and made a big show of telling the police officer on duty. It made me really angry because earlier in the day I'd been with someone who had sold a hundred E to the same security. So they were all knocking them out anyway.'
Clubber

LIFESTYLE

BAD BEHAVIOUR
Take It All, Parrot

'On holiday this parrot in the bar used to drive me mad. We gave it a few blow-backs and people were saying, "Fuck me, that parrot's quiet." Then on the last day as the coach pulled up I've picked up the parrot and thrown it in the pool. It was in its cage, it couldn't go nowhere, could it? I'm not proud of that.'
Jono

I HAD THIS WEIRD DREAM 1

'One time this bloke was really monged out in this club, so we pulled his trousers down, put his knob in one hand, a bottle of poppers under his nose, and woke him up.'
Ann

I HAD THIS WEIRD DREAM 2

'If anyone fell asleep at my flat, the Party Penis would come out: I'd put bits of bread under the end of it and drop it in people's mouths while they were asleep. Then they'd have this half-memory and come round my flat a few days later and say, "Did you – did we – did anything happen?" No of course it didn't, I'm gay, do you think I'm *that* desperate?'
Lance

CORRUPTING PEOPLE: THE STORY OF TIMOTHY

'This guy in our hotel in Ibiza was a post office worker, as straight as you can get. We called him Timothy after Ronnie Corbett in *Sorry – Timothy!* "Sorry mother". I ain't being funny, he was about 5'5", a lovely, lovely guy. We took him under our wing and he looked up to us. He started coming out with us. And he properly, totally lost it. He was on the dancefloor, lying on the floor with no clothes on, walking around on broken glass saying "I am Jesus, I don't feel pain" with blood pumping out his feet.

'Romantic couples used to walk along the beach outside out hotel so we sent Timothy after them. We watched him from our window running up to them in the nude and going RAARH! Then he went missing for about four days, and we were in the Ku club watching one of the bands when all of a sudden Timothy has run onstage, grabbed the mike and started singing.

'By the end of the holiday he was wandering round clubs in the only clothes he had left – a pair or pants, proper old man's underpants. He ended up in jail after beating up the bouncers and one of Charlie Chester's team had to get him out.'
Dave

WARNING: THIS IS FILTH

'I've seen people walking around with erections in clubs, people wanking in clubs … Mind you I've caught Dave wanking outside a newsagent.'
Ann

'I used to get so off my head it was too much effort to talk to girls, and I didn't used to get off on sex anyway, I was a voyeur. So I used to go and sit in the motor and call birds over to the window and have a wank. It was all planned – a proper perv, I was.'
Dave

FLAMING BEARD IN BELFAST

'We'd been going all night and Derek out the Sandals decided he wanted to walk through town in a racey No Such Soul halter-neck dress with Adidas stripes and crisscross back. So we all came out to cheer him on. After a while we just forgot he was wearing it. Until he got so fucked he set fire to his beard. All I remember is this man in a dress with his beard on fire saying, "Don't worry; be cool."'
Mandy Cavanagh

'I got a lift off this couple who were so fucked, they were arguing about which of them was too fucked to drive. We're on the M4 flyover, he's overtook a coach at 110 miles an hour, hit the coach and spun round – this is no word of a lie – we're overtaking the coach backwards. The car spins across the front of the coach, I'm clutching my mate as a cushion because I think this is the one, I'm going to die, and we flew down the flyover and stopped a foot short of the grass verge. It had the front wing peeled off, the strut was way out, it had no headlights...'
Jono

1993: A YEAR OF EXCESS – HELICOPTER AT CHUFF CHUFF

'It was that era where promoters had started turning up in limos and giving it the large salad. So I thought, right! I'm going to go one better – I'm going to turn up in a helicopter. I got some models, because I wanted them carrying the record boxes, and I told everyone what I was going to do. And I didn't even think about getting home so I had to go round asking for a lift, didn't I?'
Nicky Holloway, promoter with sense of humour

Now things are just getting silly:
Nicky Holloway's Sartorial Helicopter Stunt

NAILING ONE'S COLOURS TO THE MAST
TALES OF BEASTLINESS

'Our eyes looked like bloodshot pickled onions. Our eyes were chaos...'
Anon

'I had a bottle of poppers. It was seeing how many sniffs you could do without passing out. Your arm becomes rigid after you've taken a certain amount and it becomes so much effort – "That's ten..." Wooargh... "That's eleven..." You'd get to fifteen and suddenly you'd lose a minute and find your hand was wet with poppers and you're like, "Fuck!" You managed to get the lid on, and passed it to someone else...'
Russell

'I was in the toilets puking my guts up, and I could hear the girl in the next cubicle puking as well. She heard me throwing up and said, "it's a brilliant feeling isn't it?" and we both carried on.'
Amy Simmons

Mick Robinson and long suffering flatmate Del

114

'There was a girl at Solaris who used to drink amyl nitrate.'
Gaynor

'One of us got so messy he passed out with half an E stuck to his lip. We took it off him and swallowed it.'
Lance and Richard

'Excess? The time when I actually stopped caning it big time was after I had been up nearly three or four days. I was sat in bed and thought I was at a railway station. I was going, "Do you want to get a hamburger, I'm just waiting for someone on this train, they should be here in a minute and then we'll just go and get something to eat." About five years ago I remember I was in bed going to my girlfriend, "For God's sake put some clothes on we're sat in a bar." That was the moment when I decided it had gone too far.'
Justin Robertson

'I was outside Haven Stables and this man showed me huge burns on his hand and said he'd got it trying to make crack in a microwave. Blimey, I thought, things are a bit hardcore all of a sudden.'
Anon

LESSON FROM THE NARCOMEISTER

I got this phone call – it was Keith Richards calling me from the Savoy. I went to see him and he said, "I've got a problem. I'm flying to Jamaica in 48 hours and I've got to get rid of this lot," and produced a carrier bag of drugs and Jack Daniels. What followed was 48 hours of heroic consumption: he made it seem like the Duke of Edinburgh's Award scheme. After 48 hours he said, "Fuck the plane!" and collapsed. I left.'
Kris Needs

A DRUG DUEL IN HULL

'I was in a club and this promoter comes up to me and said, "Oi! Can you have it?" I looked at my mate, said, "Are you throwing down the gauntlet?" He said, "Yeah, we are." I said, "All right then, we'll have it." We went back to their house and it was, "Right, an E each, a drink each, a nose up each. Let's go." We all had one E, one nose up ... within an hour, the main promoter was prostrate in his front garden in the flowerbed and the other was lying on his face in the toilet with his fingertips touching the bowl where he hadn't made it, in his own puke.'
Andy

'Myself and Sasha got on like a house on fire. But we suffered a lot of drug abuse. I remember there were times when we took so many drugs we forgot when the last time was we had taken anything. And that was most weekends. I started getting electric shock feelings in my spine when I slept. Sasha went through exactly the same thing. It wasn't rushes any more, it was psychotropic. It was a bit shamanic. Mad synchronisity things started happening every day and it started getting a bit deep.
'The last time I had an E they were green Ninja Turtles. Every time I went to sleep I was dreaming I was trying to get back into life like cutting through bushes or climbing out of holes to wake up. I realised I had to get my shit together.'
Gary MacLarnan

'The first time I DJed at Wobble I blacked out after fifteen minutes into my set. The decks were suspended from the ceiling on chains. I hung onto the first thing I could grab hold of and ended up swinging on the chains. I finally let go and grabbed hold of Mark's record box before pulling it onto the floor with me.
LUVDUP

'I got the plane with Colin Hudd and he was in such a state he kept trying to put his feet up on the seat in front. We were in business class and everyone else was in suits. The stewardess brings our lunch – by this time the bloke next to us had asked to be moved – and Colin can't eat, instead he asks for a glass of water. Then he's passed out and knocked the glass of water in his lap. It's soaked a huge patch all down his trousers. When he woke up he said, "What happened?" I refused to tell him, I said "I'm not talking to you."'
Paul Oakenfold

Colin Hudd: 'He left me with this story for two years. I only found out the other day.'

'In 91-92, a couple of guys followed me home one night while I was with me girlfriend. They tried attacking me outside my house ... I defended myself with a baseball bat, but unfortunately I defended myself really fucking well. One of them ended up snoring for four days and the other got a broken collar bone and a done-in kneecap. It didn't help my career though...'
MC Tunes

'I was working as a hairdresser and I had one Saturday morning nine o'clock cut – not a good time – where I was still tripping and this man's hair was growing through my fingers as I tried to cut it. I was chopping away with the scissors but I had no idea if any was falling on the floor or not.'
Heather

BEASTLY DJs
'They're always turning up for work completely off it. I remember having to put records on for one DJ because he turned up too trolleyed to play.'
Janet

DEATH OF RAVE AND BIRTH OF GLAMOUR
February 1993: first tiny rucksack spotted. Holds just one cigarette, the only explanation of why girls ponce fags all night.

In 1993 gay fashion took its baggy-arsed straight mate by the hand and led him into Top Man to see what it could do with so little to work with. Clubland ripped the voluminous linen shirt off its back and poked its lovehandles into a bootleg T-shirt with D&G printed slightly wonky. It was springtime for club photographers everywhere as female clubbers decided that baby doll nighties and fluffy bras couldn't possibly make them look like bimbos because they were *ironic*. Photographers respected this girl power and took lots of ironic crotch shots for lonely readers to have an ironic wank over.

Rubbing their happy sticks with disbelief, promoters made the kitless bird their new emblem. Fliers featured cheaper and cheaper looking pictures of ladies in the virtual raw, with language that seemed to say, 'Crikey! Look at her! Five pounds before eleven! You can nearly see her bosoms!' Take a cross section of any twenty girls, and there'll only be five of them that actively enjoy running round in bras, while the other fifteen had happy childhoods. But the naked model became the visual representative of nineties club culture. It was the mid-seventies with better fonts. Luckily big beat clubs were just around the corner, a place where girls could get away from girl power.

LIKE HOUSE NEVER HAPPENED?
You can trace a big fat line from acid house to glamour, it was a very logical progression. But by some sick irony, the result is Mecca ballrooms full of girls in white stilettos and blokes in bad shirts. The only difference is that they're dancing to handbag, not around it.

Clattering along behind glamour came its dissolute cousin, porn, which decided that if they were going to be standing around in bondage underwear with their legs spread, it might as well go the whole hog and promote compilations too.

FASHION

STYLE BLUNDERS

Little black sweaters over big white shirts. Björk still refusing to pay for a service wash.

Trainer sandals. Mother trainer knocked up by Jesus boot.

I AM A VIKING

Pierced navels, pierced eyebrows, Celtic tatts – ouch! Tattoos were destined to follow shirtlessness sure as straight follows gay. By 1993, tattoo parlours were awash with blood and ink, and bottom lips trembled as a nation wished it had chosen a smaller design.

I AM A DRUG DEALER

Ralph shirts done up and untucked.

I AM A TOSSER

Silver and gold Chipie trainers for exhibitionist idiot girls.

OCTOBER 1993: LEGGINGS OFFICIALLY REPLACE TOO-TIGHT STONEWASH JEANS AS NATIONAL FEMALE LEGWEAR

Now we know what old ladies will look like in the future – they'll wear black leggings, the crimplene summer dress of the ecstasy generation. Instead of those perms you don't wash, they'll have their hair back in elastic bands. Old men will look like Ricky Butcher, only really rough. No one will have teeth like Mike Reid.

HIGH COLOUR

Having seen the kind of thing the British punter was prepared to wear in the name of rave, high street fashion loosened up, with an alarming range of colour and wackiness. Sit in McDonalds on a Saturday these days and it's completely normal to see a mum in orange loafers arguing with her five-year-old son in a fluorescent pink bubble jacket.

Everybody quite likes dressing up really, and blokes started ironing while girls remembered what tights were. Soon even white indie dance festivals were full of slip dresses, while dancehall and ragga scenes reached heights of glamour previously unknown outside Dalston. No inch of denim was exposed unless it had something glamorous done to it and basements clanked to the sound of a thousand gold earrings and gold hair accessories jostling for place with gold puffa jackets and gold trainers. There was a rumour that Buju Banton had had his entire head gold-plated.

The sportswear boom continued as blokes got bored with ironing and girls remembered why tights were rubbish.

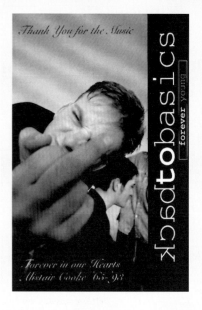

backtobasics
forever young

Thank You for the Music

Forever in our Hearts
Alistair Cooke '65–'93

'Cults equal freedom. Cults of drugs, cults of sex. Even cults of aggression like skinheads are freedom, but a different kind.'
Philip Sallon

DRUGS

THEORIES ON THE LONG TERM EFFECTS

Normal EEG & EEG Of Ecstasy User

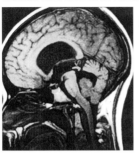

Fig. 1: brain of normal adult

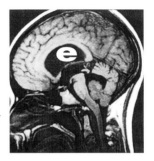

Fig. 2: brain of long-term ecstasy user

For information about the results of our selfless years of service to pharmaceutical research, look no further than the tabloids. We trust that if government scientists can't find anything they'll waste no time in making it available on prescription.

Latest Information
possible long term effects of ecstasy

altruism
hedonism
teaching yoga
going back to college
working for the *Big Issue*

proven long-term effects of ecstasy

FOOT-EYE CO-ORDINATION
You can dance better than your parents
INTER-PERSONAL SKILLS
You have more friends
EXTRA-SENSORY PERCEPTION
You swear blind you got 'a glimpse of something special'
IMPAIRED MOTOR SKILLS
While travelling by car, every so often you will pass a certain turn-off and do a double take
AMNESIA
Certain Spanish soft drinks will make you hopelessly sentimental

DRUG OF THE YEAR (INDIA)
Really weird green pliable E

'Everyone seemed more 3D; people always used to have really big boggly eyes, massive eyes popping out the front, when they were coming towards you we'd be saying, "Headlamps ahoy!" They seemed so ugly, it was partly them because of their condition and partly your condition, but the result was that they seemed over-featured. Then sometimes if they opened their mouths and they had fluorescent things in their mouths – brr!'
Raver, Hertfordshire

MUSIC

TECHNO TECHNO TECHNO TECHNO!

LEIGH MARLING, BLUE SOURCE

Blue Source started out printing their own fanzine, *The Chortler*.

'We're now one of the leading music design companies in the country and that's come out of our passion for music. The permutations of the dance scene are massive. We did the *Leftism* sleeve for Leftfield. It was big on a national scale, the whole dance scene had moved from being underground to overground. The sleeve ultimately became an icon, and that was a noticeable manifestation of what was happening in the dance scene.'

IT HAD TO HAPPEN

Take That cover the Balearic classic 'Relight My Fire' with Lulu. Andy Weatherall sets fire to himself in protest. The soapy one, Howard or Jason or Biffo, wears a Johnson's Babe Powder top in the video and prompts Pablo Escobar to halt cocaine exports for a week as punishment. London closes 'for emergency repairs'.

RRRRRAGGA!

In 1993 bass was cracking pavements everywhere – chaps were driving around with speakers pointing *out* of their cars rather than into them. Then somebody pointed out that the second bit of 'booyaka booyaka' in Buju Banton's big tune was 'and the battyman dead'. Still, this jolly ode to gay-bashing did very well nonetheless. Meanwhile, with the best bassline since Snap!'s 'The Power', Chaka Demus & Pliers' 'Murder She Wrote' was the thumping theme to the Notting Hill Carnival.

SHABBA!

The huge success of Shabba Ranks, half man half Ratners, proved that ragga was really rather popular. Within seconds every record had some twit toasting in the middle of it. Shabba himself specialised in love, as his hit 'Mr Loverman' indicated. Bored with his own subtlety, he followed it up with 'Extra Sex'. With his hilarious racey lyrics, Mr Ranks pioneered slackness, the dancehall equivalent of 'woooaar look at the mailbags on that.' The tiresome middle class Can Trainers Really Cost Seventy Pounds debate was replaced with Is Slackness Demeaning To Women.

BIG SHOUT GOING OUT – DANCE MUSIC RADIO

In 1998, Kiss FM – London's Radical Radio – took on Dani Behr as a DJ. She is on a contract of around £100,000. The DJs doing specialist shows that make it Not Capital Gold get around £40 a show. Meanwhile Gordon Mac is setting up a radio station with Andrew Lloyd Weber.

Danny Rampling, Lisa l'Anson, Trevor Nelson, Dave Pearce, Judge Jules – in a series of saucy plunderings, Radio One used the Kiss schedules as a mail order catalogue.

LIFE OF A DANCE DJ

Gets into dance music
After years of dedication to his art, gets specialist show on Kiss
Offered own specialist show on Radio One. Uncertain but agrees for the sake of the music's profile
Bites the bullet and agrees to do roadshows, helplines, rock the vote campaigns – given drivetime show
Has hit with first phone-in wet-shirt competition
Does Family Fortunes, *doesn't notice new type of music and, apparently, staggering new drug*
Launches tirade against it in the tabloids, spearheads big anti-drugs campaign. Breaks CD live on the air
Settles down with hostess off Family Fortunes, *has two kids, sends them to public school 'because the area's gone downhill'*

EVENTS
PARTIES, CLUBS, FARRAGOS

CHUFF CHUFF, VARIOUS, MIDLANDS • THE MINISTRY OF SOUND, LONDON RENAISSANCE, VENUE 44, SHEFFIELD • THE ORBIT, AFTER DARK, MORLEY BACK TO BASICS, LEEDS • CLUB UK, WANDSWORTH, LONDON • CREAM, BIRMINGHAM • MEGATRIPOLIS, HEAVEN, LONDON • MEGADOG, THE ROCKET, LONDON • LOST, VARIOUS, LONDON • THE DRUM CLUB, SOUNDSHAFT, LONDON • SPIRAL TRIBE, SOUND SYSTEM, VARIOUS LOCATIONS • VAGUE, THE WAREHOUSE, LEEDS

'We used to play Spot the Plainy... we used to skip around people who looked a bit Old Bill. You can usually tell by the shoes! Skippy, hoppy, pointy – we used to incorporate the Old Bill! Old Bill! chant. We probably used to pick out people who just didn't happen to dress the part, the one where you'd catch their eye and all you want to do is hug them but they don't smile back.'
Committed raver, Borehamwood

LIVERPOOL SPECIAL
'Here in Liverpool everyone gets on one, at any age. Even a Mother's Day or a christening can end up with sending out for half an ounce of Columbian. We were brought up with parties. In Liverpool, during the house thing, people used to drag a caravan on to the park and rig up these two eight-inch square speakers on its roof. Everyone on one after a club would go there. We even had parties in a scrap yard in Toxteth. It was £2 to get in and full of mad bastards covered in oil, we were dancing among cars piled up on each other. People used to let crow scarers off – they're as loud as fuck and the whole venue would duck. One lad blew three fingers off with one of those.'
John Kelly

The State: Inflamental
'Any one night you'd get twenty or 30 people with inflatable guitars and saxaphones, and of the 800 people, half of them would be wearing sunglasses.'
John Kelly

Quadrant Park: DJs Scared To Look At The Crowd
'John Kelly was my favourite DJ of all time. I used to just stand in one place all night and dance, I never even used to talk to anybody. There were rumours going round that girls were getting raped in the toilets because it was dead dodgy. There were no bouncers, no police and there wasn't even a bar. I loved the music mainly. You wore as little as possible because it was really hot. People used to even go in bikinis.'
Mandy, raver

'It had an atmosphere like a football ground. I was DJing with my back to the crowd and if I dropped the Quadrant Park anthem, 'Wild Times', I'd be scared to turn round – you could feel the roar, it was like someone scored a goal.'
John Kelly

'There was a woman at Quadrant Park who was about seventy called Rosie. I've got her card here. She was called Rosie, Queen Of Clubs. I've still got her rave line. 0839 700 770.'
Mandy, raver

Anarchy At The Underground: Scouse House 1988 – 1991
By Kevin Sampson, author, *Awaydays*

In 1988 the State had closed, Darren Hughes and James Barton had just opened The World Downstairs.
Fuelled by the mind-bending drug ecstasy and Colt 45, the urchins were going potty. Two whippersnappers by the names of James Barton and Darren Hughes were playing the tunes. They switched to Cindy's a dead part of town formerly known only for its porno cinema and a shop that sells terrifying knives. They christened it, aptly, The Underground. The Kelly sound made The Underground a uniquely demented, happy, stinky pit and paved the way for the brief but bleeping, belching, staggering supremacy of Quadrant Park in Bootle.

Sefton Park wasn't at all like it says in *Boy's Own* or the *Positive Energy of Madness*. In those mags everyone dances round fires, sings sea shanties and tries to chew their own ear off. Sefton Park was just cold and damp. In December 1990 Charlie Chester put together The Event On Tour. It was ostensibly a Farm tour, but Charlie asked local promoters in each city to put on a night to remember in homage to the great Ibiza clubs, whacking great productions with mystery Santa Clauses hurling tambourines and maracas into the crowd while fake snow poured down and funny little bombs exploded at the side of the stage. The Slam boys, Orde Miekle and Stuart MacMillan organised the first show at Glasgow Barrowlands. It was a riot. 'All Together Now' had just been released and the crowd went beserk when the house lights went up at 2 a.m. Orde had to hastily announce an aftershow party at the Tunnel to persuade the revolting mob to leave. Everyone ended to the Adelphi (*that* hotel from *that* BBC series) where the police staged a comedy raid. But by the time they got there an impromptu *Up Pompeii* toga party had started, and the police arrived in time to stare Terry Scottishly at a scrum of unfettered breasts and bums.

Suggs, Mick Jones from The Clash and Pete Wylie turned up for the last gig of the Spartacus tour. The aftershow party was held at The Limelight, which could safely take 200, but Keith Mullin considerately announced the location from the stage, so 1000 turned up. Mick Jones was DJing and Suggs was on the podium in a kilt. The club put beer prices up from £1.50 to £2.50 which was a misunderstood masterstroke, as the majority of the crowd left and started hurling bottles and traffic cones up at the windows. I went to reason with the police and very reasonable I must have looked too, with my beautiful dilated pupils, my washing machine-mouth complete with white spittle in each corner, and my shredded, sweat-soaked lucky Schott T-shirt. I tried to demonstrate it was a private party for relatives by showing them Peter Hooton's octogenarian Uncle George (the one from the 'All Together Now' video), and told them that the sound of debauchery coming from next door was from another club.

Unfortunately Chas Smash chose this moment to recreate the 'Nutty' Madness dance at twice the speed, with real people's heads as props. At the same time a fantastic brawl broke out in the middle of the dancefloor. Chas Smash insisted in pushing the main copper-in-charge back while he counted one of the fighters out in ten. We attempted a sit-in and a spine-tingling rendition of 'All Together Now' but the House of Balearic was falling down. It was time to go.

Wayne Anthony relaxes in Ibiza

CAFE DEL MAR, IBIZA: MARTYN PASSEY
'It's very beautiful, very art deco. There's a woman with her arms stretched up holding a ball of light. The colours in there were pink, blues, all pastel colours – it's got stained glass windows, amazing tiled floors, and lots of weird shapes, as though someone had taken a can of shaving foam and sprayed it into the corners. It would evolve into a hand holding a ball of light.

'Every time I've been in there I've seen something else I hadn't noticed before. Little hidden pictures of moons that you have to stand at a certain angle to see. At the bar there's a big fountain thing that holds glasses covered in mirrors, but when you actually stand in front of the mirrors you can't see yourself because they're set at an angle. There's this beautiful atmosphere, very calm, very serene. There's cushions upstairs on the floor with little windows you could open and have the breeze coming through. 'José's been playing there twenty years. He tells a story: he looks at the sunset and he plays what he sees. If you're looking where he's looking then you're on it too. Everybody seemed to switch off and go into their own little world watching the fishing boats, the seagulls chasing them in silhouette. José played the music and as the sun set the music stopped and people broke into spontaneous applause.'

GUARDIA

'At one time you could go to the café and sit down and smoke a joint and the police wouldn't bother you. The Guardia De Sevila are a law unto themselves – they are Carlos' bodyguards, they were Franco's bodyguards. They treat all British people the same – they don't like them. One night they came down to the café in loads of vans, and there was a group of about seventeen kids sitting on the beach and they just went into them like you wouldn't believe. A girl stood up and took a photo and they knocked her for six. They had one guy called Brutus, top guardia, about 6'5" – he looked like Fidel Castro only bigger. In the end he was thrown off the island for brutality. His favourite party trick was picking up English kids by their hair.'

AMNESIA

'Amnesia used to be a farm. In the days of Franco Ibiza was a Fascist-controlled island and it had no extradition treaty with the United States. When the Vietnam War was going on, a lot of the Americans and Canadians who didn't want to fight came to Ibiza and worked on the Island. Some of the guys asked the farmer if they could have a party one Sunday a month. And if you go to Amnesia now you'll see that part of the club used to be a farm. It's a really nice thing that the club grew out of non-violent people who just wanted to be left alone.'

THE CHEEKY HALF PARTIES

Mick Robinson and John Howard captured the vibe of exhausted North London with their slogan 'Cheeky Half – Just To Be Sociable.' As everyone knows, *Just A Cheeky Half* is a contradiction in terms. Their bachelor flat in insalubrious Finsbury Park became the centre of some Cheeky Half madness.

'Our lives went to bits. I was doing ten or twelve Es over the weekend. I was working at Top Shop and on Monday I used to go down and sit in the middle of this packed canteen. Everyone would be eating their terrible sausage and chips and I'd be asleep at the table. Our flat was non-stop. There was one night when my flatmate had to be up early and he made me swear blind we wouldn't have anyone back but somehow we came home from a boat party with forty people. We didn't hear a peep out of him - then suddenly at six o'clock in the morning he storms in in his horrible dressing gown, turns the stereo off, shouts, "You cunts!" and leaves. Looking back I can't believe how long we used to go on. Look at Shave Yer Tongue! I mean, do you fancy driving out to Bracknell on a Sunday night to go to a club in a car park?' *Mick*

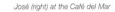

José (right) at the Café del Mar

Photo: Steve Hall

JANUARY

A Scottish judge redefines ecstasy as a soft drug as it is not addictive or a hallucinogen.

More E, Vicar? An Uxbridge church organises drug-free Christian raves. Communion is accompanied by the Orb's 'Little Fluffy Clouds'. The Rave in the Nave vibe is not all lovely as one raver tells the journalist covering the service, 'You're a witch. You're reporting about us for a coven.'

Michael Jackson reaches an out of court settlement concerning a sexual abuse case. He denies this implies guilt on his part.

FEBRUARY

Tory MP Stephen Milligan is found auto-asphyxiated with a tangerine in his mouth.

Police begin to dig up the cellar and garden of 25 Cromwell Street, Gloucester and find the bodies of nine women. Frederick and Rosemary West are charged with the murder of these and, subsequently, others.

A fund raising party for the Advance Party, a new group designed to protect ravers' rights, is broken up by police after complaints about noise.

Police begin to log travellers and their vehicle details on computers.

MARCH

32 women priests are ordained.

The crap soap opera *Eldorado* is canned.

APRIL

Kurt Cobain is found dead at his home in Seattle.

The Waco compound is bulldozed by the FBI. 86 people die.

MAY

Nelson Mandela becomes President of South Africa.

Labour leader John Smith dies of a heart attack. THE BEST PRIME MINISTER WE NEVER HAD, says the *Sun*.

Two die at a rave at Hanger 13 in Scotland.

John Major says the presence of beggars in streets is offensive and unjustified. As an example of indoor begging, it is announced that Buckingham Palace is to be opened to the public.

JUNE

Prince becomes a symbol.

George Michael loses his court case against Sony Music for unreasonable restraint of trade.

JULY

Tony Blair is elected leader of the Labour Party.

AUGUST

Nothing happens at all.

SEPTEMBER

The trial of Colin Stagg for the murder of Rachel Nickell on Wimbledon Common is halted after the judge criticises the methods used by undercover police officers which led to his arrest.

OCTOBER

Polo-playing toff wanker James Hewitt boasts in print of his affair with Princess Diana.

A demonstration against the Criminal Justice Bill in London ends in violence.

Two ministers, Tim Smith and Neil Hamilton are accused of accepting payment to ask questions in Parliament.

NOVEMBER

Australian TV reports the death of the Queen Mother. They are wrong.

Radio One chiefs are 'blasted' half-heartedly after hiring Danny Rampling, who had admitted to taking drugs and has been pretty blasted himself on occasion.

Johnny Lovemuscle organises Wilder Than Westworld, the first ever back-to-1988 one off acid house rave in Brixton Academy.

Serial killer Jeffrey Dahmer is beaten to death in jail in Wisconsin.

DECEMBER

DJ magazine claims that Andy Weatherall was thrown off the decks in Ibiza for 'playing music which sounds like a drill'.

Loved-up posho Ol Parker set out to write 'a film about ecstasy without moralising about it' but instead writes *Loved Up*, a film where a relationship between a couple who take E is doomed because, hey, E is just an illusion. Extras hired to dance during rave scenes were method acting by taking E on set, the *Guardian* reports. The giveaway appears to have been that when the music stopped, 50 people carried on dancing in silence. Brian Harvey out of East 17 decides to sample three Es at once, and is delighted to discover it simply increases the empathic mood-altering effects of the first two.

Chapter Seven
1994: WHAT'S ON TELLY

As major clubs turned back into discos full of fools in nighties, there was only one place to go – home. Fortunately there were now so many drugs around, All Back To Mine was no longer a low-key prospect.

ALL BACK TO MINE!

'We told a few people at Full Circle they could come back then we got home and saw about forty people sat waiting. We were thinking, "Oh my God, shall we turn the car back and pretend we don't live here?"'
Fiona Crawford

'A gang from Blackpool stayed at my flat for three days and nights, even inviting more mates down. We all went out to a party on the Saturday and we were in the bathroom discussing the concept of losing it when we went completely blank. Neither of us had any idea who the other was. The last thing I remembered was the postman calling on the previous Wednesday morning. A guy came into the bathroom, heard us talking and said, "Take it easy girls. Stay in control. And stay ahead of the game." And then he went and pissed in the waste bin.'
Fiona Bowker

'The cleaner would come in after the weekend and clean around Kevin asleep on the floor.'
Shelley Boswell

PERILS OF PARENTING

'We were still going one night after we'd been out. It got to about eight o'clock in the morning and the kids got up, so I got my head together and ran them to school. I got back and we thought, right, let's go. So we've got the lights off and the curtains drawn and we're dancing round the front room. Then someone said to me, "There's an old bloke at the door." I looked round and there was the school caretaker, he's brought back my kids and he's saying, "You do know they don't go back to school till next Tuesday?"'
Ann

'Terry kept going into the kitchen and coming out with Sugar Puffs stuck all over his face, saying "Mmf, I can't eat these Mmf Puffs." Then he comes out the kitchen holding a needle out in front of him. "Look," he says, "I've found a sparkler."'
Russell

NEW USES FOR A LIVING ROOM
Stair Diving
'We were introduced to stair diving by Sure Is Pure and the Golden boys years ago. Stair diving just involves throwing yourself down the stairs on your belly. We all did it. We tried to out-do each other and ended out stair tobogganing on oven trays and stair surfing on ironing boards. That's when Mark got his ribs cracked.'
Adrian Luvdup

Lovepile

Carpet Kissing – Northern Version
'This is bizarre. You lie on your belly on the floor and two people lift you up with your arms behind you and legs in the air. Somebody holds your nostril and makes you inhale poppers through each one, then you have to suck on a cigarette that was also soaked in poppers. Then they lowered you down really slowly and you basically carried on through the floor.'
Adrian Luvdup

Carpet Diving – Southern Version
'I learnt this off Brandon Block. You lay on the floor flat on your face, arms stretched out. Someone would lift your arms three feet off the floor so your back's hurting a bit, then they'd lower you down really slowly with your eyes closed. Woooorr! You felt like you were diving though the carpet. If people did it properly, you couldn't get up because you thought you were under the carpet. People would come back up saying, "Fucking hell! How mad is that!"'
Cuzzah

Temazepan Standing Contest
Take a lot of temazepan. See who can stand up the longest.

Living Room Scuba
Lying on the floor flapping your feet and your hands, looking at each other without talking, communicating in divers' sign language.

Divvy Disco
Low rent performance dancing.

LIFESTYLE

THE PERKS OF LIVING SOCIETY

'This saying originated when we was sat in a Jacuzzi in our villa in Ibiza. We decided to have a debate of who was worse off – us, or the Bosnians. We worked out that all the Bosnians have got to do is get up in the morning, decide whether to go out their door and get shot, or stay in. Whereas we have got to decide whether to do another E, do another half an E, to chew it up or swallow it, have a drink, not have a drink, have a smoke, all that. We was adamant that we was worse off.'
Andy

Talk of the Year: **Jimmy Corkhill's spectacular snorting technique**. Look ma, no tenner. His face-down-in-the-wrap habit amazed the nation – how come he never got coke on his nose?

FIRST PERSON
SUDDENLY I WAS IN PRISON

'When I got moved from Brixton into Wandsworth, I was walking along the landing and one of the cell doors was open. I looked in and inside someone had painted a fucking great big yellow smiley from the top to the bottom of the wall. Underneath they'd written "SPECTRUM 88 – GET RIGHT ON ONE MATEY"'
Anon

'I was running the Sunrise mailing list and there was a long gap between a couple of the parties. When I went to phone the people on the list up to tell them it was on again, everyone was saying, "Oh sorry, he's in prison..."'
Vicky

Class flyers from Phillip Sallon.
'I prefer to call them invitations'

DOING AN E IN PRISON

'There was an Indian bloke inside with us who an E dealer. He's said, "My mate's brought some Es in – do you want one?" I hadn't had one for twelve months. We were all walking around outside off our nuts. I lay down with me headphones on and me stereo playing house really loud and my shirt off in the sun on the grass verge, and until one of the screws said "Oi! What do you think you're doing?" I'd forgotten I was in prison. We all went back into one of the dorms, someone's put a mad acid tape on and we've given an E to this loony-looking thick bloke from Brighton with mad curly hair and a limp. We gave him an E. Shortly afterwards he was up on the table, inventing a whole dance, having a laugh with us and dragging his leg.'
Anon

TALL CHRIS AND GINGER STEVE

'You would never have clocked Crisis Chris for a dealer, he looked like some rich guy from Chelsea. He brought over a kilo of MDMA powder from India. The problem we had was we couldn't get any capsules small enough – my mate had been up to Neal's Yard and got some enormous things. They were so big we ended up cutting them down and stuffing them together until they were almost little balls, with the powder sloshing about inside them. No one wanted to touch them! It was taking ages and this guy still had a kilo, it was all there for me to get through.

A TRIBUTE TO TRADE, THE GAY CLUB SO HARD IT DOESN'T OPEN TILL 4 A.M.

For a club not to bother opening its doors 'till the God-less hour of 4 a.m., it has to be offering something more intense than the average Saturday night. Like Space in Ibiza, Trade is special.

Trade is deep in the heart of London, on a site buzzing with ley lines, supernatural wavebands and seediness. For centuries, people have slipped up rainy alleys in Clerkenwell in search of darker pleasures.

'Turnmills was a cruising zone,' says Patrick Lilley, enthusiastically. 'Sir Walter Raleigh could wander round looking for scruffy urchins and unemployed sailors. Laurence Malice is probably dancing on some queen's grave ... there was a place called Mother Clap's Molly House that used to hold mock gay weddings.' Society has lost its Molly Houses and gained a gateway to a strange new level.

On Sunday lunchtime, when a country's married population is sitting down to roast beef and constipation, somewhere under the streets of Clerkenwell hundreds of gay man are stripped to the waist, tattoos rippling and nipple rings flashing in the lasers.

'Walking into Trade, you are squeezed by all the Muscle Marys in the entrance like a roller bar, propelled forward by their sweat.'
Trade regular

A new kind of music evolved to keep the pace up: trancier, faster, bouncier techno. Leaving the dance-floor to sit down at Trade is like being thrown off the edge of a merry-go-round. Trade deals in those piquant moments where you can't remember what you do for a living or even what your own face looks like, feeling your sanity slipping through your fingers.

'There's a saying that on Saturday night all the rent boys in London are in Trade, so what does someone do if they want sex? There must be the same fifty pound note going round Trade all night.'
Trade regular

Soundtrack: *Trade 1-3*
Purchase, press play, wake up on Tuesday with a tattoo

'Meanwhile everyone who was working for me was getting off their heads too much to sell them. Everyone was getting really thin and spotty and no one was paying me back. Then Ginger's come up to me and said, "I've met this kid called Alex who says he's found this bloke wants a hundred Es, give us them." I'm like, absolutely no way. Ginger's begging me – "All I need to do is take the Es to meet this man, get the money and come back. How can I knock you?" So I've given him the Es. Ginger Steve's gone with Alex to the pub and suddenly people have run in from all over the place.

'I got a really bad solicitor, he was saying tell them everything. So I signed three pieces of paper that put me away. Came out the cell, went straight out and spent four days off my head. Got sentenced eight months later. I couldn't believe it – it sounds really clichéd now but I shouted in court, "You bastards! Are you happy now?" In the cell afterwards, I was so naive – this bloke I was in with said, "Can I have a cigarette? Can I have one for later?" I gave him all my fags and I didn't know that would be the last tobacco I'd see for about a week. They took me to this disgusting cell five-foot wide, and on the top bunk there's some lunatic staring at me with the sheet pulled up to his nose, all I can see is some little locks and some crazy eyes. I thought, "Oh my Good God". And on that first night I didn't have any knives and forks so I went up to a prison warder and said, "Scuse me mate – where can I get some knives and forks?" He looked at me and said, "Don't fucking call me mate, you cunt – piss off."'

'I can remember walking down the Antrim Road in Belfast at half nine in the morning singing 'Heroes' by David Bowie. I'd lost complete vision on one side and I was going, how am I going to get across this road? I can only see the lane coming down, I couldn't see the lane coming up. It was like I'm to have to run for it. The mescalin was started to kick in – Woh! this is a completely different type of tripping altogether, I'm in trouble. When I got in a taxi, I felt I was getting pushed in the back and there was no one in the back seat, it was just unbelievable. I must admit that after that I was like "Yeah, that's enough." But two weeks later I was completely off my face again.'
David Holmes

SHADY PEOPLE
'We knew plenty of villains who were nice people, it was the snidey little toerags who were the problem. People say there was honour amongst thieves but there was also just thieves with no honour. One day this friend had hired a car on our credit card and done off with it, and we got taken to court by Avis for the money. He had the cheek to come round and ask us to mind his car, a Honda Civic. That night we came back from Enter the Dragon pissed, and we danced on the bonnet of this Honda, poured petrol over it and tried to set fire to it. Next day I pulled back the curtains and saw it and thought, Fucking hell, who did that? It was his mum's car too.'
Ann

NIGHTMARE! Es IN THE WENDY HOUSE
'These lads we knew came round, saying, "It's all on top round our place, can you look after these for us?" and gave us a hundred Es and some sheets of trips. I hid them at the bottom of the garden in a Mickey Mouse bucket tucked behind a fence. It was a blinding hot day and I'd been out all night, so I dozed off in the back garden.

'I woke up to see a sheet of trips blow past. I got up and panicked. I looked in to the wendy house and the kids were pretending to cook on the stove. In the pans was water from the paddling pool and all the Es. I was jumping up and down in my bikini, screaming. I grabbed the pan and rang up my friend and made her come over. It wasn't just my kids, we had the neighbours' over as well.

The kids were fine but the Es had all got wet and some of them had puffed up like two pence pieces. I was panicking, trying to pat them dry with a tea towel. I felt terrible about the kids, and because some of the tablets had dissolved and my mates would never believe we hadn't taken them ourselves. The kids had taken their clothes off and they were all stroking each other and giggling, but apart from that they were OK.

My friend got there and I said, "Shall we take the kids to the hospital?" She said, "What are we going to say? That they're all a bit friendly?" The worst bit was that that's how we started drug dealing, to pay them back for the pills. There was nothing else we could do. I'd never sold a drug in my life, and when we got the bag of ten to sell I remember saying to her, "That's it now. This time next year we'll be international arms dealers."
Note: the children in question grew up to be extremely well balanced and sensible

MC TUNES

'I remember robbing a coach, out of our minds on mushrooms. We robbed a colour TV and a briefcase which we thought would be full of all sorts of money, gold and riches. We were running through Platt Fields park, I've got the telly on me shoulder and me mate's got this very elegant attaché brief case. We sits down tripping out of our heads and then we opened this brief case.

'Inside there was a twelve-inch plastic strap on cock. My mind just exploded. It took us ages to get the nerve to pick it up to see if it was real. When we did, three and a half quid fell out of the end of it. From that point I lost my mind and strapped it to my head and ran out onto Wilmslow road trying to stop a taxi with a TV on my shoulder. We get the TV back to the flat and my mate plugged it in. The silly twat forgot that you had to change the voltage and put 240 volts through a twelve-volt TV and blew it to bits. He was laying on his back with black smoke marks on his nose and forehead.'

'We were putting on an early Sign Of The Times at a brasserie, and the guy that owned it was really quite highly strung, saying "It won't be too loud, will it?" He kept insisting it shouldn't go above 90 decibels, so we, of course, said it definitely won't. But what we didn't know was that the environmental health had loaned him a decibel monitor. So we waited for him to nip out went in his office and tried it out. Even a fairly quiet record was 100 decibels, so I stuffed the microphone with loads of tissues. On the night he was having kittens, but the decibel monitor was showing below 90. We were saying, "Ah, but you see when the place is full of people, it *sounds* louder..." We nearly had to lock him in a cupboard that night.'
Paulo

'...the number of times I stood waiting for my kids in the playground in my sunglasses, in the rain and snow..."
Ann

VILLAINS

Most people have yet to battle through walls of fourteen year olds with Uzis to get into a club, nor do they spend the night having their feet hacked off by evil gangs. Clubs may well be owned by villains, but what's new?

'I came across lots of villains, and started to get concerned when I was hanging around people who were breaking people's fingers with spanners if you didn't pay them money. These people were paying us to play at their clubs. They were some of the biggest club owners in the country. We would end up sitting around with these people, thinking, "I don't fucking belong here."'
Anon

MUSHROOMS AND LAUNDRY

'We went picking mushrooms with these girls. One of us said out the blue, "I've got freshly laundered socks in the back of the car." We sat in the car sniffing these incredible socks. Meanwhile the two girls were getting really, really frightened.'
Anon

'A man handed in a carrier bag full of cannabis with a street value of half a million pounds he had found washed up on a beach. "I had no idea it was worth so much," said the man, "it's been in the family for years."'
David Quantick, On The Hour

NUISANCE CALLS

'One day back at our flat we got out the phone book and looked up some company. We rang up and said, "Hello, can I leave a message for Mr Dullip?" and the receptionist said, "We don't have a Mr Dullip here." We started ringing in the morning and carried on all day doing different voices – "Is Mr Dullip in yet? Can I leave a message for him?" – she really lost it, "I'm telling you we don't have anyone of that name!" Then at the end of the day my friend phoned back and said, "Hello, it's Mr Dullip, are there any messages for me?"'
Jono

CONFUSION!

'Sitting talking, my mate's gone to grab a guy's head. He thought he was a pint of beer.'

129

HELP! I'M FAT AGAIN: FAREWELL TO THE E-PLAN DIET

Before rave

During rave

After rave

'I collapsed at Shoom because I'd forgotten to eat for two weeks. I ended up in hospital with pleurisy.'
Anon
So? You were *thin*.

Once More Unto The Fridge, Dear Friends

By 1994 some of us were so fat we had to get undressed by Caesarean. This was not always the case. *Once you were fat.* Then you spent several years on the house front line, dancing for your country and doing battle with every narcotic known to man. One morning you got up, or rather finally stopped gurning enough to go to work, put on your trousers and it suddenly struck you – standing in front of the window no longer caused a total eclipse of the arse. You were thin. You could be one of those people that gets up early on holiday to play volleyball with Danish girls. Fucking hell!

Then, some years later, as you were getting ready for work, not bothering to check your pupils because you didn't need to any more, it suddenly struck you - you were fat again. What's more, you were fat in new and exotic ways. Parts of your body that used to contain bones now had a smooth fleshy carapace. Before acid house you had a bum like a bag of frozen peas, now a bag of oven chips seems to be following you round. Your face felt closer to your shoulders than ever before. Holiday photos confirmed this – the person in the photos seems to have grown a light beard of fat. Bollocks, you're a bloater.

But never mind! You'll live longer. You won't want to, but that's not the point. Console yourself in the knowledge that everybody else is girthy too these days. The bloke that looked like Rutger Hauer only with a girly bob now looks like Gary Barlow. The first remark everyone makes as they go through their old photos isn't *'look at our expressions of expanded consciousness and optimism for the future of mankind. One day on the red hills of Alabama etc. etc.'* it's *'Christ! We were thin.'* In the meantime, here are some corpulent heroes of dance who don't give a damn.

Fat Folk Of House

Ce Ce Rodgers: Woo! He's a wobbler. If music be the food of love, Ce Ce ate all the pies
Byron Stingily: Come on give me a hand up everybody. Ouch
PM Dawn bloke: Set adrift on memory bliss you'd sink, mate. Nino porco!
Farley Jackmaster Funk: uses the service entrance at High & Mighty
Graham Gold: Kiss FM's monstrously fat trance DJ can't get in the studio until they've buttered the doors, and then he only sucks them clean. Employs a full-time thin man to go round doing his gigs

FASHION

In the beginning it was different: 'People didn't give a shit what clothes you wore. You could walk in wearing a Bugs Bunny outfit and no one'd look at you twice. They'd just go "Oh, there's a bloke in a Bugs Bunny outfit." It changed around 94, when clubs started to be Mecca instead of mega.'
Andrew Barker, 808 State

WHEREFORE ALL THESE BIRDS IN BRAS?
And not just the thin ones either. Their cups runneth over as they jiggle on the stage. Glam and ecstasy is a risky combination, since gurning in a feather boa makes you look like Nancy after one of Sid's hilarious heroin/brick dust stunts. The ladies' toilet, however, was greatly improved by the arrival of birds-in-bras. Where previously there was nothing but conversation and focused drug abuse, suddenly there were hordes of twits to laugh at. Every mirror had five wannabe Claudia Schiffers who, come the inevitable four o'clock mong, could pass for an electric Pekinese.

I AM BIANCA JAGGER
Narrow belts, pencil skirts, pencil eyebrows

I AM AN ATHLETE, HONEST
Nike, and probably some Nike as well

I AM A FLY
Bug face sunglasses

Arrest this man. DJ Pants. Obviously

'I turned up to DJ in a dressing gown and satin pants. My nan chose them and my mum sewed a twelve foot dong on the front. It had wire inside so I could bend it out the way when I was DJing.'
DJ Pants

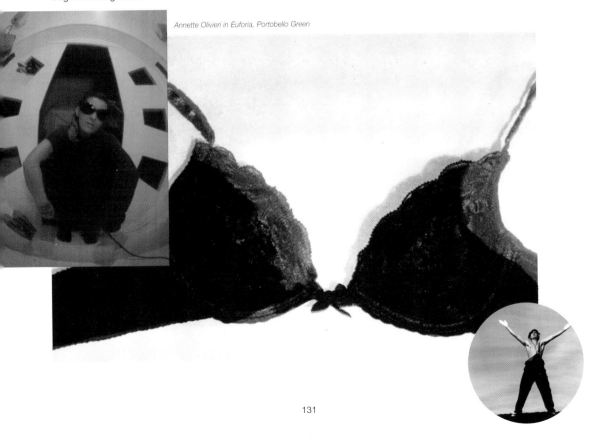

Annette Olivieri in Euforia, Portobello Green

DRUGS

REVOLTING NEW DRUG PRACTICES
GHB

'It was New Year's and we'd got back to someone's flat after this shit party. We're all lying around bored when this bloke I didn't know turned up with a crate, a whole *crate,* of GHB. Stacks and stacks of little bottles. How do you get a crate of it? We pounced on it. Each bottle had a little marker on it saying, do not drink below this line, but we were knocking them back. Fuck knows what's in that filth but you'd try to stand up and go, "Whoops! I'm down again!" and flop over. We were taking it in turns to fall down the stairs. One of us left the room to go to the bog and when we found her she was lying upside down on the stairs going, "Fu – king – hell!" People were stepping over her all night and she just lay there with her eyes open saying, "What is this stuff?"'
Amy

Ketamine

What a vet will use to get a horse stupid enough to meddle with. Exciting prospects of muddling the senses so you can smell sounds and hear colours, or brain damage and the conversational skills of a turnip? Who can say?

I WALKED THROUGH MYSELF AND FELL OVER – TOP NIGHTS OUT ON KETAMINE

'We're back at someone's house having taken a vast amount of Ketamine – we thought it was coke – and Karen is trying to get my tits out with a ladle. Later I fell off the toilet, someone came in to help me and she just fell on top of me. Then I was sick through my fingers, spraying everywhere.'
Janet

Not Recommended

'There was a phone box outside the club. We used to leave a line racked out in it and hide, waiting to see who'd do it. Only it wasn't coke, it was ketamine. We'd watch and see who'd do it and get the big fur boots.'
Perv

Bodies Everywhere

'Ketamine's a bit of a heavy duty drug. I'd say don't take it unless you've got a wide and varied drug history. I love it personally. If you have quite a lot, it affects dimensions and you don't know what the fuck's going on. It becomes pure energy. You lose all contact with normal sensation and go into a completely different world. It lasts about 45 minutes to an hour. Once we played at a college near Exeter and went to this farmhouse after. This guy turned up from Bristol with these green and yellow pills. We still don't know what it was to this day. It was some bizarre form of ketamine but it lasted six hours ... There was loads of people everywhere who thought they were dying. They were stumbling out the door, in the garden. Bodies everywhere. That was an unfortunate drug experience really. A few of us liked it but quite a lot of people couldn't stand it and never touched ketamine ever again. But I loved it. I love drugs, to be totally honest. I've had a couple of ropey times, but I'm pretty headstrong. Ketamine is quite clean and I get a sort of clarity off it. To me it's the king of drugs because you're so out there. It's revelatory. It's like talking to God.'
DiY Sound System

POINTLESS DRUGS!

'We went round to a friend's house for dinner and drugs. We had two-coloured capsules, it was like the torso of a trip with the head missing. It felt a bit pointless. I said that at the time, "That was a bit pointless."'
Darren

SMART-ARSE DRUG

'My mate gave me some kind of smart drug as a snifter after dinner before we went to see Morrissey. He got this nasal dropper out the fridge and said, "You have to put three drops up." I pushed nearly the whole bottle up my nose and suffered appallingly for the next two weeks. Physically it was an agonising condition – for two weeks I was waking up with chest pains. But mostly I suffered from massively exacerbated intelligence. The Morrissey gig was absolute agony. I think there were about ten or twelve of us in this group, and I found that I could follow all the conversations simultaneously. I was like something out of *Viz*: I didn't lose an argument during those two weeks. I became so fucking intelligent. I did the fast-track civil service entrance exam papers with questions like "1, 19, 2054 – what's the next number?" I couldn't have done them, before or since. I had super powers. My friend had some incredibly complicated slide projector that had broken and I just walked in and fixed it. As it wore off I felt myself getting thicker. You realised how comfortable it is not to be very intelligent."

Pete Burgess is an expert

AMYL NITRATE – THE BEASTLIEST OF DRUGS

'We went into a sex shop in Soho. The sex shops had started to advertise poppers heavily because they knew that club kids were after them. So we walked in and he said, "Poppers, is it?" I thought, "Oh no, we obviously look that cheap and ragged."'
Ben

Cheap, reliable, but still just about a drug,' amyl brought a new generation into the clubs. Poppers were made illegal on January 13th 1997. It was reclassified as a prescription medicine, and therefore it is now an offence to sell it without a doctor's authorisation. This means that nothing illegal happened at the Sunday Social, ever.

'I bloody love poppers. If I was sitting on top of the Post Office Tower I'd swallow the bugger. I love it.'
Anon

MUSIC

LOSING IT IN GOA: TRANCE TAKES THE EAST

'What I liked about these parties was that no matter how mad you thought you were, there'd be fifty people in there who were madder than you. Massive sound system, take drugs, go mad.'
Ozman

Midnight treks up mountains, sex on the roof of a train, total eclipses, thick black tea instead of lager, a bucket of acid punch and 500 dreadlocked loons with DAT machines and flip flops dancing like the steel guts of a blender: there's very little point in asking what trance has got that other music hasn't. Of all the acid house sub-cults, trance is the one that's taken off all over the world.

'People travel from London to Japan just for these parties, turn round and come back,' says Raja Ram, mythical figure at the centre of TIP records and the legendary TIP parties. 'We've been stamping through jungles, climbing down a cliff in the dark, searching for miles along beaches. Sometimes you can only find out about these parties from the Internet,' adds Annette Olivieri, who was once a fully-paid-up Balearic dolly with leather miniskirt and neat highlighted bob, and now walks around in eye-bleeder tie-dye with a baby called Luna. 'You can go anywhere in the world and meet friends from this scene.' Of the original Ibiza fraternity, Danny Rampling, Paul Oakenfold and Ian St. Paul have all been bitten by this strange fluorescent bug.

Trance has almost religious roots. It kicked off in the late eighties in Goa with a man known simply as Goa Gill.

'When I first saw Goa Gill play, I thought he was a Sadhu [Indian mystical figure]. He's a big fat man with locks down to his bum – when he plays, he puts a Shiva picture in front of him and incense sticks. He really was a religious leader.'
Trance fan

TIP Party: photo John Hopkins

RAJA RAM AND TIP

People talk about TIP, the record label and party organisation, the way they talk about magic kingdoms. 'Raja Ram is the most inspiring person I ever met. You see him dancing with his white beard, fluorescent clothes – he's fifty years old and dancing full power for eight hours,' said one starry-eyed trance fan. Along with Youth and Mike Maguire, Raja Ram was pioneering trance when it was seen as weird, not weird and fashionable. Instead of a terrifying Buddha arriving by cloud, you get an effervescent Australian who used to be in Quintessence, a Sixties psychedelic band. Raja Ram has just got in from a party. In Australia. Any fifty year old who travels 10,000 miles for a knees-up deserves to be called a guru.

ESSENTIAL TRANCE LISTENING

TIP – the 3D album
TIP – green and orange
Blue Room – *Juno Reactor*
Total Eclipse – *Violent Relaxation*

ESSENTIAL TECHNO ACCOUTREMENTS: BLUE ROOM SPEAKERS

The Masonic handshake of the electronica scene: spot a pair of Blue Room speakers in someone's house and you'll know he's got a bit of the techno nutter in him.

BLUE ROOM

Blue Room are a record label with something up their sleeve: a few years ago, Simon of Blue Room found a pair of strange speakers in a skip. He took them home, disembowelled them and, like a techno Doctor Frankenstein, put them back together specially adapted for large beats. Soon after, the police raided his house, and in an effort to charge him with handling stolen goods, called the speaker manufacturers to report him. But it backfired: it turned out that the speakers were a trial prototype, and the manufacturers were so impressed Simon had managed to get them working at all they told the police to say good luck to him. Blue Room now market Simon's design and sell bundles of the weird blue chaps.

TRANCE LOOK: HERDERS OF THE MOON GOAT

To make a pointless generalisation for easy reference, hardcore trance fans have a half state-of-the-art future technology, half ethnic hippie look. Indian bindi (little forehead decorations) with space-age footwear, avant-garde poncho-jackets in some strange rubbery textile left unclaimed in a cloakroom on Sirius B – some trance fans you won't spot in a crowd, others you will because they look like herders of the moon goat.

TRANCE DRUGS

'I once tried to get hold of some E at a Goa party, to their abject horror. They said, "That stuff's filth," and tried to get me some acid instead. I thought, "Yeah, that's all very well for you, you bunch of loonies," and stuck with the E. The capsule looked like it was filled with soil, and come Tuesday, of course, I could hardly speak from 'flu.'
Ruth

'I know of people who can only take acid if they've got trance to go with it. Not the other way round.'
Trance DJ Lars Andersson

FREE LOVE: THE ORIGINAL TRANCE DANCERS?

When the average house fan was still a Chianti-sodden glance across a crowded social club, one group of people had already discovered the startling power of the trance dance. Since the sixties the Sanjasin, followers of Osho, the Bhagwan Rajneesh, have been dancing their way to an expanded consciousness from their bases in California, Ibiza and India. The Sanjasin still have strong links with the trance scene.

RAJA RAM

'Sanjasin? I'm not Sanjasin. Sanjasin men are a pain in the arse and you can quote me. Mind you, Sanjasin women are the loveliest people in the world.'

SHANTI

DJ Riktam is the eldest of a psychedelic techno dynasty. His brother Shanti is just sixteen years old and also DJing. They are both Sanjasin.

1994: House/Garage/Horrible pop music
Juliet Roberts 'I Want You'
Loveland Let 'The Music (Lift You Up)'
Sister Bliss 'Can't Get A Job'
Doop 'Doop'
Juliet Roberts 'Caught In The Middle'
Baby D 'Let Me Be Your Fantasy'
Judy Cheeks 'Reach'
Pamela Fernandez 'Kickin' In The Beat'
Crystal Waters '100% Pure Love'
Reel 2 Reel 'I Like To Move It'
Atlantic Ocean 'Waterfall'
Junior Vasquez 'Get Your Hands Off My Man'

Techno
Dave Clarke 'Red 2'
Galaxy 2 Galaxy
69 'Jam The Box/Lite Music'
Paperclip People 'Throw'
DBX 'Losing Control'
Various (ART)
LFO 'Tied Up'
Jeff Mills – Anything
Relief Records – Anything

Drum'n'Bass/Downtempo/Breaks
Demolition Man 'Fire'
Peshay 'Singin' To You'
M Beat 'Style'
Roni Size 'It's A Jazz Thing'
The Prodigy 'Voodoo People'
Tranquility Bass 'Cantamilia'
Heights Of Abraham 'Sportif'
Metalheadz 'Inner City Life'

Like most DJs, you can only reach Shanti after four o'clock in the afternoon. Unlike most DJs, that's because Shanti is still at school.

'I was going to Ibiza every summer since I was twelve,' says the prodigiously young techno star, casually. 'I've played in Greece, Japan, America, Spain, Germany and Holland. What do my friends think? They're fucking jealous. I've smoked a bong in the Malaysian Embassy in Tokyo with the son of a diplomat.'

'Shanti was conceived in Goa. Riktam and Shanti are incredible, real star children. When their little brother was born he was covered in hair and had pointed ears. I said, turn him over – if he's got a tail that's it, he's the spirit of the forest.'
Yatra, psychedelic pioneer and Shanti's mum

SUNWORSHIPPERS: IT'S A MAD, MAD, MAD, MAD WORLD

Full Moons, Eclipses, North Star looking a bit bright one evening but it could have been a police helicopter - for trance fans, any bloody cosmological happening is an excuse for a knees-up. Simon Macara travels the world following eclipses – and putting on parties.

SIMON MACARA

'Lunacy is the perfect word for this scene because it revolves around the lunar cycle. People keep having parties on Saturday nights and New Year's Eve – these are just arbitrary dates in the Juno calendar, the worst time for a party.

'In 1994 we knew there was going to be a lunar eclipse – 300 people had been travelling to find this particular mountain for this eclipse. It was a snow-capped volcano with smoke coming out of the top and a lake full of pink flamingos below, in the Lauca National Park on the border of Chili and Bolivia. We all climbed up the mountain into the snow – there were people from South America, Scandinavia, all the European countries. We were almost like a sun-worshipping cult, going anywhere to see a solar eclipse – and more importantly to do a party when you get there. The air was so thin we wanted to put signs up saying "Don't forget to breathe" – you'd be dancing for three tracks, then you'd have to stop and eat handfuls of coca leaves to get your heart going again.

'Everything started to gel between us. The energy that gets generated by people when they're having the most cosmic experience you can have raises this physical potential. We were near Matepucho, the ancient city of the Incas – the Yurebamba valley there is the epicentre of all things extraterrestrial. The night of eclipse, the moon turned pink and there was an orange meteor shower and the most convincing UFO I've ever seen appeared, hovering over the lake, one minute there, then not there. This sounds weird but a sort of telepathy happened. Everybody went into an impromptu circle, a huge circle of three hundred people holding hands, then we all ran into the middle. It was synchronicity.

'It made such an impression on us all we formed a bond and all 300 of us started travelling together. We arranged a meeting place in Brazil and then we all set off in hired cars and drove right through the middle of the jungle. Others went on boats through the Amazon and the people who were skint went hitchhiking – it was like the *Wacky Races*. We went across Chili, Bolivia, Peru and all the way to Brazil.

'I hired a cargo train that the locals called El Train Del Meurte, the train of death. They were scared of this train, it went to the real back end of the Bolivian jungle, to the last frontier. We had our own carriage, hung hammocks in it and then we made an acid punch. It was an unforgettable journey. We were fire-juggling and making love on the roof of the train as it flew through the jungle. Then out of the blue, the death train broke down in a swamp in Bolivia. There were enormous mosquitoes and we ran out of food and water, we were melting. We decided to jump off the train – and straightaway, it stared moving again. It was like they were trying to get rid of us.

'We all met for a party on Christmas Day. I can't tell you where it is, that would blow it – it was a secret tropical paradise beach with palm trees. Brazil was just waiting for us. The police came, and they said "No one's allowed to leave until we get a tape of this music," and let us carry on. They had never heard trance before and they loved it.'

The next big event in the trance calendar is South Africa 2000. One huge Free Nelson Mandela Hang On A Minute tranceathon

EVENTS

NAUGHTY BUT NICE, THE ROOMS, HEREFORD • HARD TIMES, BEL AIR, MIRFIELD • AWOL, SW1, LONDON • PARADISE FACTORY, MANCHESTER BACK TO BASICS, LEEDS • HEAVENLY SUNDAY SOCIAL, LONDON WOBBLE, BIRMINGHAM • FULL CIRCLE, SLOUGH • CULTURAL VIBES, PLYMOUTH • OPEN ALL HOURS, MINISTRY, LONDON • STRUTT, THE CROSS, LONDON • CHECKPOINT • CHARLIE, READING • VOODOO, LIVERPOOL GOLDEN, THE ACADEMY, STOKE • UP YER RONSON, THE PLEASURE ROOMS, LEEDS • LOVE TO BE, MUSIC FACTORY, SHEFFIELD SLAM, ARCHES, GLASGOW • PURE, THE VENUE, GLASGOW

IBIZA: STILL 'AVIN IT

'When I went to Ibiza I danced so manically the hotel doctor would have to bandage my feet every night but I'd go out and do it again.

'The Spanish police were mad out there – if you got caught in someone else's hotel room that was enough for them to get the truncheons out. One time, to get away from them I jumped out a friend's balcony and landed on my good foot – so now I had both ankles strapped up. I was last seen going down the beach on all fours.

'Then on the last night we were there all the E dealers got busted so there was a shortage. I bought a Batman trip and a pill and whatever it was, I had to go and sit down. Eventually I couldn't even lift my little finger. I had to be carried back to the hotel. The next day it got to time to go to the airport but still no one could wake me and finally they had to choose between taking me to hospital or carrying me onto the plane. They took me on the plane and when got back my mum took one look at me staggering up the path with two bandaged feet and called the doctor. I had two weeks off work with exhaustion.'
Gemma Walker, raver

HEAVENLY SOCIAL, THE CHEMICAL BROTHERS AND JEFF BARRETT

Jeff Barrett

'I knew the Chemical Brothers from going to Manchester – they were just really, really nice lads. The idea for Heavenly Social came from one night when we all came back to mine, and Tom and Ed were going through my record collection, which is rather large as I've been collecting records for 25 years. We were having a fantastic time playing things like The Clash, and we kept saying, "This is great! We've got to do a club!"

'We started in the basement of a pub, The Albany at Great Portland Street – and the first week there were about seventy people. The manager said, "Are there going to be any more?" I said, "Oh yeah. Er. Probably..." Sure enough, that old Flowered Up mania coughed and spluttered to life and vast queues appeared on a bleak main road at seven o'clock on Sunday night. The Chemical Brothers' reputation was sealed. Listening to people's record collections – David Holmes brought his old mod singles – was liberating enough for people to go very silly indeed. And then...

'...one night someone introduced amyl, and it all went off.'

Deep under Great Portland Street, people were pogoing. 'The manager was seen taking photos to send to his management about this little club he was doing on a Sunday night,' Jeff laughs. 'Three years later and it's still going up at Turnmills.'

Big beat – student disco or fine tunes? The Social gave its name to Jo Whiley's Radio One show and a whole new strain of extremely loud music emerged: 'The Heavenly Social was about musical freedom, coming from the Balearic influence. I don't think we started big beat, which spawned a lot of terrible records too – I suppose you'd call it not wanting to take responsibility for those terrible records!'

Full Circle

JANUARY

The eighties officially end when Steve Wright leaves Radio One.

Animal riots demonstrations begin over veal exports in Sussex and Essex. The newspapers are shocked when lots of posh women join in.

FEBRUARY

Stephen Fry bottles a West End show and runs away to Belgium.

MARCH

A bizarre Japanese cult left twelve people dead and 5,500 ill after its followers released nerve gas on the Tokyo underground.

APRIL

Tom Parker Bowles is arrested outside a nightclub for possession of E. Tom, who also had some cannabis on him, was said to be suffering from stress after taunts from fellow students about the future king of England's alleged desire to become his mother's sanitary protection.

Scientist Dr James Edgar is cleared after he persuaded a jury that he had made £400,000 pounds worth of ecstasy by mistake. He said he was trying to make an anti-pollution spray to mask sewer smells. That's one smelly sewer.

MAY

The first Tribal Gathering takes place.

Convoys headed for Cornwall to protest the Criminal Justice Act by mounting illegal festivals are, unpredictably, turned back by police.

JUNE

Hugh Grant's Blow Job: Suckers! Wake up and smell the rat. Hugh 'Little Me' Grant did it with a known hooker in a place where they know hookers do it. You can't catch me... Oops, you can.

Riots occur in Bradford.

JULY

The Word, the most influential TV show of the twentieth century, is axed for being not as gut-wrenchingly crap as it used to be.

AUGUST

The Nine O' Clock Service, run by Reverend Christopher Brain, is exposed as an opportunity for Brain to use his position to sexually abuse his followers. Apparently, Brain used 'modern music and flashing lights'.

SEPTEMBER

Daniel Ashton becomes the 51st person to die after taking ecstasy.

OCTOBER

The *Mirror* says that 'rogue members of either the IRA or the UVF' are involved in making ectsasy tablets 'spiked' with ketamine and flying them into Britain.

Anxious to ply the muse with the artist's fruits of contemplation, Brian Harvey out of East 17 necks four in one go. Banging, he notes.

NOVEMBER

Leah Betts goes into a coma and later dies after drinking a great deal of water to counter the effects of an ecstasy tablet.

Israeli Prime Minister Yitzhak Rabin is assassinated.

Di goes on *Panorama* and says she would like to be a queen in people's hearts. Monstrous bloater MP Nicholas Soames calls her mental.

DECEMBER

A poster campaign showing a picture of a smiling Leah Betts next to the word 'Sorted' begins.

Chrissie Hynde is criticised after she calls ecstasy 'a fine drug'.

Ecstasy use doubles in a year among Oxbridge students.

Chapter Seven

1995: I DON'T TOUCH THEM ANY MORE OH ALL RIGHT JUST A CHEEKY HALF

1995 TREND OF THE YEAR: HANGING AROUND IN BARS

Smartly providing what everybody wanted, a place to get hammered that didn't smell, club bars started a new wave of after-work socialising. By 1995 every city centre had a gleaming modernist bar playing the Leftfield album where the Salmonella & Sawdust used to be.

1995 HOAX OF THE YEAR: THE LAD-ESS

Spice Girls, *Minx* Magazine, the *Girlie Show* – 1995 was full of girls proving how much they weren't boy toys by dressing like murder victims in Dennis Potter plays. So cynically were the Spice Girls manufactured that they started out with a sixth member as a spare, a change of knickers to be discarded along the way; and a different girl for every sexual fantasy including, rather alarmingly, Baby Spice. Still, it's nice to know Girl Power caters to every section of the community.

RAVE IN ADVERTISING AND HOUSE MUSIC MEDIA
Great lost confectionery of the late twentieth century
The hole from Polos – perfect for dealers who can run fast
The enigmatic white Smartie
Special Edition Yorkie: The Nutter

On the skids, Radio One – originally the proud scourge of dance music - hired Danny Rampling in the belief that he was Danny Baker (or Charlotte Rampling). He saved their liver-spotted skins, and the name of this ex-scooter boy from Streatham is in the *Radio Times* and on posters all over the country. Pirelli has ditched Malcolm Maclaren, Coco the bouffant punk clown, in favour of techno jester the Aphex Twin. The *Star* renamed its pop page Rave. *EastEnders* has its two DJs and features storylines about getting caught selling trippy Es. The Post Office slogan is *Sorted.* The *Daily Telegraph* has an ad by Underworld. Habitat and the Pier are full of fluorescent yellow things, and *The O-Zone* is presented by a giant E. What's going on?

ACID HOUSE TELEVISION
Long before the Teletubbies necked tubbytoast, the Soup Dragon was caning whole cauldrons of so-called 'soup', The Banana Splits were hewn from solid LSD and *The Herbs* spoke for itself. As network executives wised up to a whole E generation gurning at the cathode ray nipple in the small hours, they dug out *The Clangers* from under Alan Yentob's private *Best of Blue Peter's X-Rated Bloomers* collection and suddenly the media was catching up. Sociologists saying that the breweries are trying to lure children into drinking with cartoon characters like Hooch and Two Dogs have missed the point completely: these days cartoons are to attract adults. Cartoons are more likely to attract house fans than programmes *about* clubbing, as the exhausting *BPM* proved: people who'd just spent the night surrounded by sweaty gurners didn't want to come home and watch them on television.

The only truly classy club TV was the haunting, unforgettable *Hitman And Her,*
presented by old con-artist Pete Waterman, a black dancer in a blonde fright wig and an increasingly suicidal-looking Michaela Strachan, who was so damaged by the experience she can now only work with owls. Pete took this cavalcade of horrors round the nation's Mecca Ballrooms, gyrating from our TV screens like your drunk uncle at a wedding – the one who starts off grabbing the girls' bums, and by midnight is going for nadgers.

ACID HOUSE LITERATURE
The fucking awful *Disco Biscuits* is a perfect illustration of literature trying to catch up with the turbocharged acid house bandwagon. When *Disco Biscuits* isn't standing around pretending it had an E once, it's down the Arsenal with *Fever Pitch* pretending it's got a season ticket. Old man Nicholas Blincoe calls his crime thriller *Acid Casuals* – what's next? Jeffrey Archer's *Acid Teds*? Irvine Welsh takes E now. So does everybody in publishing. It's rumoured Rupert Murdoch won't hold a meeting until he's poked a cheeky half up his bottom 'just for the visuals'.

ACID HOUSE ADS
Advertising has been dominated by rave culture since Lucozade was saved from extinction as a cellophane-wrapped sickbed tonic and reborn as the techno rave narcotic that it is today. The Halifax used an Ibiza club anthem to sell mortgages. Now that rave culture is leading the media, analysts are looking for it everywhere in a belated rave convoy:

Stop Now While You Still Can
'The latest ad for BT rival Ionica blatantly makes visual drug references to those "in the know" as white doves (the Ecstasy connoisseur's brand name) fly, the viewer is told, "You can feel it"...'
Sociologist Sheila Henderson in Ecstasy: Case Unsolved*, possibly having taken one too many*

A WETWIPE DOTH NOT A BATH MAKE:
THE NEW FESTIVAL CALENDAR

May
UNIVERSE, formerly TRIBAL GATHERING

Reckless crazy man Paul Shurey runs Universe, Glastonbury for the twenty-first century, but with one significant modification – it's dedicated to dance music not rock.

CREAM FIELDS

Cream. With fields. Superpromoter Vince Power's biggest do yet.

June
GLASTONBURY

Every year it's the last-ever Glastonbury. The original hippies' beano on Worthy Farm, owned by Michael Eavis, owner of the strangest beard outside Amish Handstand Week. Glastonbury dance tent is the site of last reported sighting of Acid House Vibe.

July
THE BERLIN LOVE PARADE

A million shirtless Krauts converge for a 24-hour hands-in-the-air techno mindmelter. Go 24 hours without sleep to avoid paying for a hotel and accidentally supporting the German Tourist Industry. To bring people together, take a ball of string and link all the men with nipple rings in a giant love crochet. If they don't find this hilarious, remind them who started the war – the E generation forgets but it never forgives.

THE BRIGHTON LOVE PARADE

Brighton is a forward-thinking town with a large youth population and many of its older residents as gay as a French trombone. That's just as well, as this brand new festival now brings several thousand shirtless Brits down in their seaside tribute to the Berlin big fella. Floats from all the techno sound systems descend, all doing the crustie bop.

T IN THE PARK

The T stands for Tennants, and won't you know it by the end of the day.

PHOENIX

On that most mystical of sites, an airfield, now disused. Obviously.

NEWQUAY SURF FESTIVAL

Get a job. And shave that ridiculous goatee.

August
READING

Former beer lake now beer lake with dance music.

THE NOTTING HILL CARNIVAL

Mature police commissioner, NGSH, desperately seeking fat black lady to dance with for photo opportunity.

LIFESTYLE

'I was pulled over with an E in my mouth. No officer, I can't think why you've pulled me over, I'm too busy trying to swallow an E dry. I was really tripping and the policemen looked exactly the same as the ones outside the do. I thought, "Oh God, they've followed me all the way home and seen all the shit driving I've done." The policeman was talking to me and all I could think about was trying to look directly into the sun in the hope it would shrink my pupils. This is the weird thing – they breathalysed me and I'd had about two bottles of wine that evening, but I passed. I decided it was a yellow card from God and I've never driven drunk again.'

Anon

'It was the early weeks of Shoom and me and Craig were totally off our trolley on E. Obviously. The room was completely full of smoke so all you saw was just white light flashing. I had to sit down, and there was this coffee table next to the stage and I plonked down on it. I was so off my head it started moving under me. I started pushing down harder and then I've felt an arm. I was sitting on a bald man and he's sat there looking up at me. Half an hour later Craig's come up to me. He said, "You'll never guess what – I've gone to put this fag out, and I've looked round and there was a coffee table with an ashtray on it. I've stubbed it out on this bald bloke's head."'

Chris

A TRIBUTE TO THE CLUBLAND NUTTER:
THE BARRY MOONCULT LIFETIME ACHIEVEMENT AWARD

When the platoon is faint of heart, he is unwavering; when the spirit weakens, he breathes fire; when the end is near, he is still completely off his nut. Named after a man who always put valour before reason, The Barry Mooncult Lifetime Achievement Award honours those brigadier generals of the good time.

BARRY MOONCULT

Barry Mooncult (centre)

Barry Mooncult Plays Boy's Own, East Grinstead
'I was with Terry Farley, really monged, and we were watching the cows. I said, "Terry, look at that cow." There was this one cow that was eating grass, dancing a bit and eating some more grass. It started getting nearer and walked straight onto the dancefloor. Barry Mooncult had turned up at the coolest party of the year as a pantomine cow.'

Barry Mooncult Plays The Africa Centre
'Flowered Up didn't have a dancer – Barry just turned up on the night wearing a four-foot purple flower round his neck with the paint still wet.'

Barry Mooncult Plays The Deja Vu Magical Mystery Tour
'We were having an enormous fruit fight in a ruined castle, when I looked up and saw Barry Mooncult wearing some kind of bear suit. He'd climbed up a rock and he was clubbing a rubber chicken on the rock and blowing fire out of his mouth with lighter fuel.'

Barry Mooncult Plays The Boy's Own Karma Collective
'Barry comes walking across the lawn with a big frilly lampshade on his head. Pushing a hoover. He hoovered the whole fucking lawn.'

Barry Mooncult Plays The Happy Mondays Doo At The Zoo

'Barry Mooncult threw a bench in a koi carp pool full of these thousand pound fish. This photographer from the *Star* said, "Brilliant, now if we take it out the water you can throw it in again and I'll get a picture," – Barry picked *him* up and threw him in the pool.'

Barry was last seen using an out-of-date press pass with a woman's name on it to get into the Director's Box at Chelsea.

Nutter rating – stark staring mad

PETE WYLIE

Cut his wacko teeth going to clubs with a toilet seat round his head. Leant on an open gate and fell down a hole in Toxteth *Only Fools And Horses*-style and broke his back, but when the ambulance men arrived, still demanded, 'Do you know who I am? I'm Pete Wylie.'

Nutter rating – not right in the head

NICKY HOLLOWAY

Nicky once posed for photographers naked for no other reason than he found himself 'sat in a bar with a load of northern promoters banging on about how outrageous they were. I thought, "Sod this..." and I went to the loo, and came out with nothing but my socks and a pint. I went down to the magazine to check out the photos, I'm looking at the contact sheets with a viewing lens, and it occurred to me - I'm looking for my own dick with a magnifying glass. People saw the photos and said to me, "I didn't realise you were so fat." I said, "that's because every time I fuck your mum she gives me a biscuit."'

Nutter rating – up the pole

DAVE MAHONEY

A seasoned nutter, there was some difficulty tracking down Dave Mahoney since all his details were with his uncle, Mad Dog McGlinchy. Nonetheless, Dave's Nutty Achievements, involving a stay in an Arab jail, a party that left a house stripped of its kitchen and even its doors and a highly notorious New Year's Eve bash make him a frontrunner for the Order of the Purple Ohm.

Wanted: Dave Mahoney

'...the list of disasters that night is endless ... the DJs and the bouncers say they have not been paid and cannot find Dave Mahoney ... widely rumoured to be sunning himself in Tenerife.'
London Evening Standard

'Dave was dancing away near the pool at Ku in red T-shirt, baseball cap and boots. In his semi-comatose state he could see loads of people rushing towards him. He thought there must be free drinks at the bar but he carried on dancing. He said, "I thought I'd be clever so I span round. And as I span round I saw there was a bull behind me." He was chased round the pool by the bull...'

Nutter rating – cuckoo

You naughty man! Mahoney's party that never was

143

NUTTER OF THE DECADE: RUNNER UP: DAVE BEER

'When I first met Dave Beer he was walking round a narrow ledge that ran round our hotel in Rimini looking in people's windows, saying, "Morning!" By the end of the trip Dave Beer was naked trying to climb on the decks while Ralph Lawson was playing, while Barry out of Deja Vu was hanging from the ceiling tangled up in a rope.'

'Dave had these red cards and he was going round the dancefloor finding people who were dancing badly, saying "You – off!" showing them the red card and sending them off the dancefloor.'

'Dave Beer used to sweep up the dancefloor while people were dancing, shouting, "Keep it tidy, you lot!"'

'Dave Beer and Alex were dancing round the beach in old-style swimming costumes down to their knees, then they bought flowery dresses off these old women to wear. Meanwhile Ali Cooke was buying breakfast for Rod, his inflatable seahorse.'

Nutter rating – demented

NUTTER OF THE DECADE: WINNER BY A NOSE – BRANDON BLOCK

'When we first met Brandon, he was a clean living boy. The next time we met him one of his friends had just done a trip in their eye. It went all "Let's shave the cat."'

Brandon Block, Charlie Chester, Lisa Horan and Dave Dorrell

'A couple of times I ended on my knees in the Spanish police statio begging for forgiveness. They just said, "Get him out, he's pissed again."'

'Someone came up to me and said, "Does anybody know someone called Brandon Block? Because he' having a bit of trouble down in the square." I went down there and there was Brandon, arguing with his suitcase. Because his case didn't want to go, you see. He said, "Well, if you don't want to go you can stay there." So he walked off and just left it sitting there. I think he was two days in bed with sunstroke after that.'

'It was the morning after and I was in bed with a girl I'd met. Brandon poked his head round the door and said, "Pants, can I have a word? That's Rosa." I said, "Yeah, and?" and he said, "That's my girlfriend." We had a football match over her.'

In 1989, a brilliant comedy about a life dedicated to alcohol abuse, *Jeffrey Bernard Is Unwell,* opened in London's West End. *The Times* described Jeffrey Bernard as 'a national institution in the same way as Falstaff or Mr Micawber.' Overwhelmed, Jeffrey Bernard accidentally set fire to himself. Britain's best loved nutter, Brandon is Jeffrey's natural successor, although it will be a couple of years until *The Times* can accept *Brandon Block Feels Fucking Terrible,* a comedy about a less acceptable social habit. Brandon has suffered for his art. 'Clubmare!' says Brandon, unbowed. Like most nutters, Brandon had a fairly intense relationship with nosebag. After a lungtastic medical incident that got his death posted on the internet, Brandon has recovered and to prove it wears his shirt open with a fat gold chain nesting in his chest hair, smoking a cigar. He has been reborn as the Aristotle Onassis of acid house.

Nutter rating – national March hare

WORST BEHAVIOUR

'Worst behaviour? Me! I was at Swoon in Stafford. They've got a small glass window up by the DJ box and people kept coming up and waving. A girl accidentally put her hand through it and there was glass all over the decks. I hit her over the head with a record.'
Boy George

THE PERILS OF E: ROMANCE

'I hardly do Es now. That gear can do for you. I went to New York and had one in a club and when I got back to England I was shopping in Harrods and one of the women sprayed me with perfume. It was only after smelling it that I remembered I'd had sex in New York that night.'
Dave

CALAMITOUS MOTORING TALES 1: MY MUM, SHE'S LOVELY SHE IS

'We were coming back from Shoom in the cow shed in Chris' van. It was that kind of atmosphere where everyone was half mad, not knowing what was going on. Chris was going on and on about his mum, "My mum ... she's lovely she is. I'd really like to give her one." There was this insane silence in the van... And Chris has gone – "An E! An E! I'd like to give her an E!" And suddenly we've hit the side of a car and the car's spinning round...'
Anon

CALAMITOUS MOTORING TALES 2: HOME NOW

'We're driving along the motorway and he's suddenly just stopped right in the middle of the fast lane and gone, "Oh good. Camden Town." We're thinking –he's got our lives in his hands and it's another thirty miles to go!'
Ozman

CALAMITOUS MOTORING TALES 3: MAN AND MACHINE

'People used to say to you "I've drive loads better on E" – you'd have music playing and if the tape ended there'd be a few seconds panic where you couldn't do anything, then you'd turn it over and it would be all right again.'
Jayne

I'M GOING OUT, I MAY BE SOME TIME

DJ Terry Farley reflects on an ill-fated evening

'We were going over for the opening night of Amnesia but we didn't get the plane from Gatwick 'till ten o'clock that night, which left things a bit tight. On the plane was a group of girls with T-shirts saying the Wheatsheaf Pussy Posse – they must have been some soul girl gang from a club in Ilford – and the bloke with them decided it would be amusing to open the emergency door as the plane was taking off. So we spent three hours sat on the tarmac while everything got checked, getting rather stressed out.

'We finally got to Amnesia at 3 a.m., we had these things with us and we'd taken them already, so we had one of those nights where everything was heightened, being acutely stressed but also excited. I took six reels of film – these were the definitive pictures, I thought, "Brilliant". Then because I didn't want to lose the camera I went to put it in the car. But when I got back to the club they said to me, "Where've you been? You've been gone three hours." I worked out that what had happened was the cars were all white Pandas that looked the same, and I'd found the wrong car, somehow broken in and left everything in there and someone had just thought, I'll have this. So we were out-side the club with no jacket, no keys, no camera, no film...'

NEIGHBOURS STRANGER THAN US

'We had this neighbour, Geoff, who was weird. He wanted to play. He had about two teeth top and bottom, and he used to burst through our backdoor wearing some pair of flares he'd found, stick our bottle of amyl up his nose and walk around with it actually hanging from his nostril saying, "Now can I join in the sixties revival?" You'd be thinking, "Who the fuck's this trog?" It wasn't what you wanted when you were tripping.'
Ann

'Then one day we were in a car and we had a load of Phantasias. For some reason we thought the police were following us so we swallowed them all.'
Janet

'We got all of them out, divided by four and had the lot. I felt like I was in a goldfish bowl trying to talk, but just going "Blubblub!"'
Ann

'So were back at Ann's house in pieces in front of the telly, playing music, when suddenly the neighbour bursts in.'
Janet

We were playing music quite loud and Geoff bursts in and says, "Do you think I'm some kind of cunt or what?" Alex says, "We're just having a laugh, Geoff," and he says, "Laugh? Laugh? I'll show you who's having a fucking laugh!" And get a sock full of rocks out his pockets and smashes the stereo to pieces. We were so off it we sat there for an hour smiling at each other then one of us went to turn the stereo on. We completely forgot it had just been smashed with a sock full of rocks.'
Ann

COUNTRY TALES: ARISTOPRAT UP A TREE
'We were at a party in the country and one of us had gone missing. He was quite a posh Indian guy that no one really knew, and he'd taken acid. I was walking around looking for him and it occurred to me to look up – and there he was in a tree, not just lying in the branches but right up where it was virtually twigs. It scared the pants off me. I tried to get him to come down, but he sounded completely normal and kept saying, "I'm fine, I'll be down in a minute." I thought, fair enough, and walked off. Then for some reason I went back and asked him, "What are you actually doing?" And he said, "Making a cup of tea." We got him down after that.'
Stacey

COUNTRY TALES 2: I LOVE YOU
'Our friends crashed their car in a ditch on the way to the party. We were already a bit the worse for E but we went to see if they were all right. Our friends were OK but I had to be taken away from the scene because I kept hugging the ambulance men and telling them they were lovely, lovely people.'
Alan

TAKE ME TO YOUR DEALER – ALIENS AND THE NEW SPIRITUALISM IN DANCE CULTURE

Having the doors in their minds opened wasn't enough for some people: they wanted the back wall knocked out and a psychic patio built. Just like John Lennon, Peter Sellers and London's happening scene of the sixties, people are finding themselves cross-legged on the floor all over again. Shamanism, yoga, Sanjasin, paganism, Special Brew ... now there are all kinds of ways to get on a spiritual one matey.

Aliens: Better Than God

The type of aliens most popular in clubland are perfect E-babies – wide-eyed, affectionate and always coming in peace. The oval-eyed face became the symbol on the chest of optimistic clubbers in 1995, representing a nice world of love where everyone communicates without language. Ironically, the aliens of trance and techno were less alienating than the Jesus images of acid house. Even those closest to polygamous Jesus, his Brides of Christ, are proof he was no party animal living like, well, nuns. Everyone who spends the night with aliens, however, is likely to get, at the very least, shown the bright lights, taken for a spin and interfered with.

Take Me To Your Dealer

The space age hit the high street and now space cadets can be abducted in a variety of fashionable ways, from silver wraparound bug shades to silver skirts. Cosmic satirists the *Fortean Times* continue to market an extremely funny range of Schwa merchandise inviting the intergalactic tourist to take the wearer home with them.

*What are **you**?*

The Quest For Enlightenment – Shamanism In A Back Alley

'I turned up to what I thought was a religious ritual at a *very* discreet address in a London sidestreet familiar to clubbers, and was hastily ushered in by a man who looked like a docker, only dressed all in white. Inside were about thirty people standing in a queue, all dressed in white and barefoot, with an unusually high percentage of doe-eyed beautiful girls. The floor was covered in mattresses, blankets – and buckets. The atmosphere was reverential and I did what I always do in reverential atmospheres and fell over noisily, getting my foot stuck in a bucket. So far so good.

'Considering I'd careered in off the street and done nothing but take their buckets for shoes, these people were extremely personable. Someone asked me if I was drinking. What the hell, I thought, mine's a lager. Instead I was given a form to fill in warning me I might vomit, have diarrhoea or drop dead if taking Prozac. What a berk. It wasn't a religious ceremony, it was something much more diverting – they were drinking *ayahuasca,* a hallucinogenic rainforest plant. Sure enough, at the other end of the queue small measures of a dark tea was being handed out. Bummer! A once-in-a-lifetime chance to take part in a group psychedelic experience and I had work the next day. That, and I'm a coward.

'As soon as they'd had their *ayahuasca* tea, the white-robed people snuggled up in sleeping bags while the organiser guided them through it. I have to admit I was moderately alarmed when I realised the buckets were for throwing up in, but then again we don't light candles in the toilet at the Ministry. Likewise, if it all goes psychoactively pear-shaped in a nightclub, there aren't fifty gentle folk in white robes looking out for your well-being.

The lady running this unusual event had long dark hair and the kind of serene expression only achieved by years of professional calm. According to her organisation, there is a network of people taking this substance all over the world. In the rainforest, whole families get together to do it – mothers even put a drop on newborn babies' tongues, apparently. "I'm Sanjasin," she states freely, "but there are a lot of different religions practising this ritual." I ask her if she's expecting a lot of vomiting tonight. "You can never tell with vomiting," she says ruminatively. "But it's a cleansing experience. Even having a bad trip is a cleansing experience!" She giggles, which in a back alley surrounded by strangers taking tree acid is very reassuring. "I talk them through the *ayahuasca*. We'll sing, sometimes the energies of the forest come down and sing through me." At this point, in the tradition of cowardly reporters everywhere, I made my excuses and left, stopping only to fall flat on my face once for luck. Recommended.'
Jane, raver

FASHION

The summer was fierce, eyes were boiling in their sockets, so what did people do? Wore their sunglasses on top of their heads. Sartorial classic of the year: plastic hairbands in the shape of sunglasses.

By 1995, Britain was camouflage crazy. Camouflage trousers are now the alternative jeans. As fashion victims stalked the town centres in the unlikely uniform of army trousers and Birkenstock sandals, tourists trod warily, waiting for the outbreak of a strange sand war in Soho.

In no way advocating heroin chic, *i-D* ran a fashion spread called *Coming Down: A Wasted Weekend,* in which two scrawny lovebirds with smudged eyeliner and scars fumble with each other in a mucky hotel bedroom. Nothing wrong with drug fashion if it's honest. Why not *Shooting Up,* say, or *May We Borrow your Savlon? The Ragged Bum Of Ecstasy Culture*.

SLEAZE

Sleaze can be utterly charming, but the British fashion press always take it too far. The Europeans can do it: take the French. The French are a boss-ugly, big-nosed sallow race with armpit hair down to their knees but they look *hot*. They can get away with sleaze fashion spreads like the classic *Pouting On The Toilet,* because the cute 'punk' girl will be a *French* punk (translation: fringe a bit ruffled). British magazines have to go one further: in the translation it becomes *Having A Shit On Heroin.* Naomi Campbell tried it with her album cover, the absolutely resistible *Shaving On The John.* Naomi is apparently still furious Sony turned down the follow-up, *Trouble With My Coil*.

The very facial expressions of models changed in 1995. Brain damage entered the world of high fashion: after the waif came the serious retard. OK, so even paedophiles lost interest in twentysomething girls trying to look five (see *Dragged Out In My Nightie And Kneecapped;* Kate Moss knock-kneed in various babydoll dresses). They had to grow up but they were still cute because helpfully, they grew up stupid, peering into the camera as though it had confiscated their blunt cutlery. Calvin Klein and his cavalcade of lobotomy babes ruled, but the carnival queen was Ralph Lauren's Bridget Hall, the Forrest Gump of fashion. See *Learning To Speak Again After The Accident*.

I AM YOUR MUM
Crochet tunics over flared leggings. Parents' Evening? Not like that you're not.

I AM A GEOGRAPHY TEACHER WITH THE RUNS
Sarongs and Birkenstocks on boys. Made you look like you were caught short on holiday.

I AM REALLY DEEP
CKone: Kate Moss and her divvy mates stand around talking existentialist codswallop. It sells scent.

149

DRUGS

THE WAR ON DRUGS

Straw - Grass

NEW ANTI-DRUGS SLOGANS
I don't need drugs, I'm rushing off my tits on life
Stick drugs up your bum

International enemies may come and go, but one thing that will always be our enemy is the drug. Teddy boys, mods and rockers, acid housers, they all danced to the same beat – the beat of the drug. Announcing a war on drugs is the first job of any government, after killing and eating any under-secretaries left behind by the out-going administration. Jack Straw wasted no time declaring that the families of drug dealers would be kicked out of council housing, thus explaining why the Home Secretary decided not to take up his official state-owned residence. A responsible man, Straw didn't hesitate in shopping his own son for a ten pound draw. But, unable to take on Britain's huge drug traffic – not without a fence anyway – Straw was forced to appoint a drug czar. The drug czar appointed a drug Rasputin, who unbeknown to him was having an affair with the drug czarina. With the new drug czar comes a new, harshly realistic anti-drugs campaign.

NICE MUSIC (DULUX AD STYLE)

A MAN IS PUTTING UP SHELVES, WATCHED BY A CUTE DOG

MAN
There we go, Rover. Shelves!

DOG
Arf!

REASSURING NORTHERN VOICE (ALAN TITCHMARSH)
Your mind is like a house. Over the years, you've got it just the way you want it. You've put in things that you like and *[laugh in voice]* you've got rid of a few things that you don't.

MAN THROWS SPANDAU BALLET POSTER IN THE BIN

MAN
That's better!

DOG
Arf!

CUT TO –

EXT. HOUSE, NIGHT

MAN GETS IN CAR

V/O
But when you take a drug –

CAR DRIVES OFF

DOG
Arf!

V/O
It's like you're going away for the weekend and leaving the window open. And do you know what can happen then?

BATHROOM WINDOW SMASHES. A PUNK, A SKINHEAD AND A RASTA CLIMB IN

V/O
Because when you take a drug you're leaving your mind – wide open.

SMASHING. SPLINTERING

RASTA
Disturb his underwear drawer!

PUNK
Soil his bed!

SKINHEAD
Smash his piggy bank!

PUNK
(sexual)
Hello, doggy...

THE DOG WHIMPERS

CUT TO -

EXT. HOUSE. MAN ARRIVES HOME, UNLOCKS DOOR

V/O
Because when you take a drug – you can never go home again.

DOG
Whimper.

MAN
Rover...!

THE DOG IS WEARING LIPSTICK

Anti-drugs campaigns weren't always this subtle. In the US Marines, drug taking was controlled by scenes of brutal medical testimony.

US ARMY MEDICAL FILM

CRACKLE

AMERICAN MILITARY VOICE
Marine Medical Movie Unit Film Number Six: *Don't Shoot Up In Your Beef Vein, Sailor*

OLD NAVY MUSIC. TWO SAILORS WATCH AS A NAVY DOCTOR PUTS SOMETHING IN
A BAG

SAILOR
What you doin' doc?

DOC
I'm putting this man's shitter in a sack, sailor, it's broken.

SAILOR
That's a man's butt, Doc? Jeez, I thought it was a sack of lettuce.

DOC
Well – that's marijuana for you, son.

SAILOR 2
What's that graph, doc?

DOC
That graph shows how amphetamines like charlie and whizz inflame the genitals,
sailor.

SAILOR
You mean the John Thomas, Doc?

SAILOR 2
Say! I'd like an inflamed John Thomas!

SAILOR
Who wouldn't! Boy oh boy!

DOC
Yeah, sailor? Would you like it if it blew up? Would you like it if it went bang in front
of your sister's face?

SAILOR
Guess not, doc!

V/O
Also showing in this programme – *Junkie: Hot For Momma!*

Drugs may be that nameless evil whose name is drugs nowadays, but once upon a time, they were just a part of daily life. Drugs gave society many things, like the dome tent and the elastic-sided boot. Before drugs were bad, the most popular cartoon character in the history of cartoon characters was Koko The Kokaine Kat (right).

WHERE DRUG MONEY GOES

Drugs mean big money. The money from small time dealers goes to fund sinister organisations like terrorists, video pornographers, theatre groups and, of course, back to their main supplier – Prince Philip.

HOW DRUGS ENTER BRITAIN

So how do drugs enter Britain? Number one: they enter illegally, then their case is assessed by a tribunal.

This wrap of cocaine was lucky. It got a council house.

Number two: they go through the quarantine procedure.

```
INT. QUARANTINE

WOMAN
When will we be able to pick up our drugs?

MAN
Another six months.
```

Number three: they are smuggled. Drugs can be smuggled in many ways: false body parts – one man wore a false head; bribery – the French pay off sniffer dogs; or commonest of all, hidden inside other drugs. In 1994 an eighth of marijuana was concealed inside sixteen kilos of heroin.

KOKO THE KAT

'Koko was the animated toast of Europe. Millions thrilled to Koko's cocaine-fuelled antics as he played the piano and watched the keys turn to huge lines of cocaine which he snorted until his nose bled and the veins in his eyes cracked like ice. Sadly, fame and beakfood took their toll until one day, dancing wildly and talking nineteen to the dozen, Koko went on a killing spree in the nightclubs of Berlin, fatally wounding Liza Minnelli.'
David Quantick

DRUG INVENTIONS
SHOWER ATTATCHMENTS
PAINT-SPLASH CAR STICKERS
THE COLOUR GREEN

THINGS THAT HAVE THE SAME EFFECT AS DRUGS
Licking Melvyn Bragg
Sitting on your hands for an hour
Driving over certain textures of tarmac

LITTLE KNOWN DRUGS FACT
The first twenty-pence piece was discontinued because the shape was narcotic and frightening

PARANOIA

'I drove round a roundabout ten times because I thought my legs had grown grass.'
Sasha

'I've sat in silence for hours because I don't know what words would come out if I tried to speak. Sitting there with an inch of ash hanging off your fag because you don't trust yourself to say "Has anyone got an ashtray?"'
Dale

GET BACK YOU ACID BASTARD 2: WINDOWPANES

'A mate of mine wanted to go to a club. I only went with him so he could meet his girlfriend, I had to go and pick up a lorry of bananas at three a.m. He bought a windowpane but he didn't realise he'd had two stuck together. He came up to me and said, "I'm tripping my brains out." Two of us took him up the road to give him a puff to calm him down but it didn't work, so we went to the garage to get orange juice for the vitamin C to bring him down. He was in the back pulling on the handbrake and shouting at us, "This is my car! Why are you driving my car?"

'He told us after that because he was drinking Mister Juicy and me and my friend were drinking Ribena, which had bigger cartons, he thought we were two aliens trying to kidnap him. We got out the car and he chased us up the road – he was really unfit but he didn't stop and all the time we could hear this uh-huh, uh-huh coming up behind us.

We jumped over a fence and when we looked back he'd run into the garage and was barking at the man in there. He took off his belt because he thought it was melting him. The police came and it took two of them to hold him down, he wasn't that strong a bloke but he lifted them both off him and was shouting "cunt!" at them. Crown court!'

THINGS TO BE KEPT AWAY FROM WHEN YOU'RE ON ACID

1. Roofs
2. Mopeds
3. Anyone you fancy. The emotional equivalent of eating spaghetti
4. Cars
5. Blenders
6. The concept of the futility of man's existence
7. Scratchy toilet roll
8. Straight neighbours
9. Dry toast
10. More acid
NB: DO NOT, EVER, SMELL YOUR SHOES

MUSIC

MUSIC: INTELLIGENT DRUM'N'BASS V STUPID DRUM'N'BASS

'I was getting really worried for a bit 'cos drum'n'bass was getting really trendy, but everyone says it's dead so I can carry on. He he he.'
A Guy Called Gerald

With house now a fat girl in a shiny skirt jerking on a Mecca podium, it was essential to declare yourself *underground*. Who's in the underground Who's Who? By definition no one ever knows. The underground scene is so underground that the truly underground don't even know their own names. One underground DJ refuses to make records in case someone likes them. Another immediately topped that by refusing ever to leave his house again.

THE PRODIGY

The Prodigy performed an extraordinary feat: they got more credible by going overground. Which proves two things: first-ly, that like a leathery cockroach, hardcore cannot be stamped out. And secondly, that The Prodigy were always brilliant, but the overground underground were snotty about the underground overground. As well as getting to number one in the charts, staple-faced Keith is now a successful bogeyman. So alarming was his appearance on *Top Of The Pops* that parents phoned the Beeb to complain he was scaring their children. Result!

BRIT HOP

Balearic with alcohol. If you didn't have such a stinking hangover you'd dance to the sunrise, but right now the clock ticking sounds like a saw.

A MIX TOO FAR

Apocalypse mouth Shane McGowan is rumoured to have made a house record, but the Pogues wouldn't let him release it.

EVENTS

CLUBS:
FOUNDATION, HOME, MANCHESTER • PROGRESS, THE CONSERVATORY, DERBY • MALIBU STACEY, HANOVER GRAND, LONDON • SPACE, IBIZA • MISS MONEYPENNY'S, BONDS, BIRMINGHAM • DESERT STORM, SOUNDSYSTEM, VARIOUS LOCATIONS • CREAM, NATION, LIVERPOOL • SABRESONIC, EC1, LONDON • FINAL FRONTIER, CLUB UK, LONDON • SLAM, ARCHES, GLASGOW • TEMPTATION, LAKOTA, BRISTOL • GARAGE CITY, BAR RHUMBA, LONDON • TRADE, TURNMILLS, LONDON • BACK TO BASICS, PLEASURE ROOMS, LEEDS • GLITTERATI, THE CROSS, LONDON • DELUXE, NOTTINGHAM • SPACE, BAR RHUMBA, LONDON • THE FULL MONTY, MIRAGE, WINDSOR • THAT'S HOW IT IS, BAR RHUMBA, LONDON

PROGRESS IN DERBY
'...folk dancers in the hallway. At the club's anniversary, they had a Gospel choir singing them happy birthday.'
Boy George

GAY PRIDE 95
Best rave of the year turns out to be in the middle of a Saturday afternoon – Gay Pride at Victoria Park. Heroes included a man in shorts sitting astride the gun barrel of a pink tank, Tony de Vit, Sister Bliss, Gloworm, Sparks, Dead Or Alive, Danni Minogue enjoying her new role as gay icon, Boy George and D:Ream (we knew this song would get annoying, but who could have predicted *how* annoying).

MANUMISSION – COOL OR SHIT?
Someone sitting on a toilet on stage, a man in the middle of dancefloor watching a broken TV, an in-house dwarf peeling potatoes and sticking name tags on punters is cool and would probably piss off the cool people, and is therefore funny. Shagging your girlfriend on stage – that isn't. Still, there's got to be a perk.

PHOENIX
Phoenix, the newest festival, was a riotous success. On a disused airfield, in the scorching heat, four hours to get in the queue to drive out. The heat sent everyone slightly simple. By day two, women were stripping off at the sinks in the portaloos with the doors open.

FIRST PERSON

IBIZA: LOST IN SPACE
'It's predominantly a gay club under a camouflage canopy – always bright sunshine because it doesn't open 'till six. There's a policeman standing on the entrance with his club, behind you a woman in a little kilt miniskirt and nothing else, a man in a blue body stocking cut to ribbons with a big Copa Cobana chorus girl feather on her head. And a girl with a vegetable strainer on her head. It's surreal because it's in daylight, you've got planes going overhead, and there's trannies behind you and armed police on the door. One morning I was in an E coma with my head in a speaker. Age of Love starts with the loudest scream ever heard on a record. I just sat up and said, "Who's for another one?"'
Andy

'We finally got back to the hotel from Space on Monday afternoon. We got to the front entrance, left our shoes outside because we thought it was the door to our room, staggered in and passed out in the lounge. The maids carried us both upstairs, locked the windows and put us to bed. The next day I convinced Colin that I'd been sober.

'I said, "You were in a right old pickle last night." He only found out when the maids said it was the other one of us they were worried about...'
Paul Oakenfold

TEN YEARS OF GLASWEGIAN HEDONISM: THE SLAM CLUB

Orde Meikle, One Half Of The Slam Duo. International DJ, Producer And Co-Runs The Soma Record Label, And Slam Club In Glasgow

'It was absolute fucking mayhem. We started in 1988, in the summer, at Tin Pan Alley. We were only given one floor, so we still had the suits coming to a club on the top floor. At one o'clock when they closed the doors, you'd have all these suit people coming down with their missus' and tarty girlfriends – the look on some of their faces when they came into our floor was a picture. It was unbelievable – there were hands in the air, and so much power. Some people would end up on our floor in their suits and plastic shoes, caught up in it. I remember seeing all these trendy shop staff and hairdressers losing it majorly, getting up on the bar and dancing, which was unheard of in Glasgow at that time.

'I think the introduction of drugs helped. I can remember some young crazy-head from the east end of Glasgow offering me what I thought was a mint imperial, and when I went to take it he pulled the matchbox away and said it'd cost me £20. I wasn't aware that E's came quite as big as that. I remember so many hugging and squeezing hands sessions, all coming up on the rush at the same time, the watery big eyes, looking at each other and smiling, and shivering with your come-up. Everyone was knocked sideways by the rush and the strength of the feeling of it.

'There was a genuinely very lovey atmosphere. Before, in Glasgow we had a real drinking mentality, which seemed to mellow out a lot. To see a lot of young crazy-heads in the clubs, totally in love with everyone, squeezing people and smiling was astonishing, because before it used to be about grimacing, drinking as much as you can and trying to start a fight. That was a real change in the atmosphere of clubs.'

The Slam lot at Es Paradis. Orde Miekle (left) and Stuart MacMillan (centre)

DANNY RAMPLING: FROM SHOOM TO 97-99FM

A tale of one man and a lot of positive energy

AN AWAKENING

'My life changed: when I was in America, the car I was in piled into barriers and I had a very lucky escape, but I was hurt and in quite a lot of pain for several days. When I came to, I knew I'd been given a second chance and my life started to change straightaway. Things weren't so positive before that, but suddenly I was just so thankful for being here on the earth. I opened Shoom because I wanted to share the feeling that I was feeling.'

THEN THERE WAS THE MUSIC

'My feelings of being alive were backed up by this new music: it was fresh, and it had a different, positive message; Frankie Knuckles, Marshall Jefferson, Ce Ce Rogers, Ten City and the other people making it are very spiritual people.'

THEN THERE WAS, ER, SOMETHING ELSE

'We went to Ibiza and things were tasted. We tasted the delicious flavours that the Europeans had to offer!'

'The most extraordinary night down Shoom? When everyone thought they'd left the planet on a spaceship. All at the same time. They said they'd travelled to Sirius B: a very strange evening! There was definitely some good acid around that night. I never took drugs while I was DJing, but I connected with the energy that was coming from everyone else that night ... there were some people that went the wrong way. A couple of times I had to take people home and look after them in my flat, because they'd lost it on acid. They weren't the same again, not for years.'

CHRIST!

Like Eric Clapton and Jesus, Danny Rampling found himself with people coming up to him and informing him with absolute certainity that he was Christ.

'Someone came up to me with a Bible, read out a passage to me and said, "This is about you, isn't it?" It's scary, because *they* really believe it, and there's this moment where you believe them. Did I get given presents at Shoom? They didn't give me enough drugs! I still don't know why.'

RADIO ONE

'I think the new DJs are a positive benefit to Radio One. I was surprised how old the studio was - we even had to order in Technics. Would I do a roadshow? For a million pounds. Who in their right mind wouldn't?'

WORST OUTFIT WORN IN THE NAME OF HOUSE

'A pair of luminous stripey pedal pushers, just below the knee, with a Stephen Sprouse jacket. I looked like a liquorice allsort. That outfit was for one night only.'

JANUARY

Take A Break officially replaces The *Sunday Sport* as paper of the drug user. Sample story: security camera captures woman giving birth in corner shop. Headline: HELP HELP THE BABY'S IN MY LEGGINGS.

FEBRUARY

Bristol University scientists claim that sixty per cent of bank notes are impregnated with cocaine.
Jarvis Cocker heals the world by invading the stage during Michael Jackson's wankathon at the Brits.

MARCH

Gun enthusiast Thomas Hamilton murders sixteen children and their teacher and wounds fourteen others at Dunblane primary school in Scotland.

MAY

Irvine Welsh's *Ecstasy* is published, complete with a soundtrack album, *Anthems For The Chemical Generation*.
Brian Harvey out of East 17 ups his dose to eight. Despite traumatic mood swings, stomach ache and on one occasion waking up in bed with Daniella Westbrook, Harvey's commitment to his research remains unswerving.

JUNE

England get to the semi-finals of Euro 96 before Gareth Southgate paves the way for an unfunny pizza advert.
4000 ravers 'invade' Incombe Hole, a site of special scientific interest and one of the few homes of the rare pasque flower. Mobile sound system Exodus – who point out they would rather organise raves with land owners' permission but would be prosecuted if they did – tidied up and left the place undamaged. The pasque flower was unharmed.

JULY

Tennis boy Tim Henman becomes first British man to reach quarter-finals at Wimbledon for 23 years. Still doesn't win, though.

AUGUST

The Tories are told to withdraw the 'scary demon eyes' poster of Tony Blair.

SEPTEMBER

Headmaster Philip Lawrence is knifed to death outside his school in London.
Jailbird rapper Tupac Shakur is killed.

OCTOBER

The *Sun* is tricked into printing stills from a naughty – and fake – video of Di and James Hewitt.
MP Neil Hamilton drops his cash for questions libel suit against the *Guardian* because the smug fucker is guilty.
Liam Gallagher is arrested by police for looking like a tramp.

NOVEMBER

Nightclubs could lose their licences if they play too fast music, to avoid dancers becoming 'over excited or exhausted'.
New drugs heading your way, according to *Time Out*, are Bliss, DMT, 2CB, Cathinone and P-funk.

DECEMBER

Over seven years since the tragedy, compensation was paid to John McCarthy, who saw his brother die at Hillsborough and suffered post-traumatic stress. Although police had already received damages, McCarthy was the first fan to be compensated.

Chapter Eight

1996: WE'RE GOING TO GET A WINNEBAGO AND GO TO GLASTONBURY – THE SPIRIT LIVES ON

IS THE VIBE STILL ALIVE?

'We got stuck at the airport going home, we were all sat on the steps feeling miserable, when a mate of a mate of ours turned up with twenty Es. He was on his way back so he gave them all to us. We bought a couple of bottles of champagne, we couldn't find any ice so we put them in a bucket with frozen brussel sprouts, and two hours later we were having a party on the steps. We were just playing Roughneck – 'Everybody Wants To Be Somebody' – when a Greek policeman pulls up his car. He gets out, walks up to us and goes, "I like this one! Good beats!" and leaves.'
Anon, promoter

The love and peace bit might be keeping its head down, but the beastliness and the piss-taking aren't.

A GENERATION OF PISS-TAKERS

Never mind irreverent youth, it's a generation of total piss-takers. Banks and building societies tell you there are two kinds of mortgage, endowment or repayment. As every blagger knows, these days there's a third - dodgy. Gone are the outlaw's days of living undercover: now he gets a mortgage through his equally cynical broker. Unless he's a drug dealer, in which case he pays cash.

Efforts failed to raise people in a Ladybird Book world, where 'shoplifters raise prices for the rest of us', as though if we'd only put that Bounty Bar back, supermarkets would instantly drop their sixty per cent mark-up and hand us our groceries neatly wrapped in wax paper. These days Big Brother comes back from work with an Adidas bag of stuff he's half-inched. Blagging is the ultimate home shopping service, the tupperware party of the nineties.

With a Last Days of the Roman Empire spirit, people miss no opportunity for disgraceful behaviour. The more serious everything gets, the less seriously they take it. Take ecstasy. Everyone else does. It started out with simple nicknames like 'Calis', 'burgers' and 'drugs', but now the *News Of The World* has the gall to report a new one: '*Leahs'*. Roll on the Straw Draw. Meanwhile, a wag in a London record shop blithely fiddles with the CD racks so that 'East 17' now reads '17 Es'.

Today, more than anything else, people want to get drunk. Blatantly. They do not nonce about in the appreciation of fine wine or the contemplation of real ale. They want to get slashed, now. Alcoholic lemonade is a very modern invention essential to counter the effects of low-alcohol lager. In recent years alcohol has been marketed in solid vodka jellies, test tubes and giant syringes. It's time to do away with the time-consuming bottle/can format: for two pounds, let people suck the barman's sponge.

Sport is full of blaggers. Henry Cooper used to bravely pugil away until his face looked like a Francis Bacon portrait and his spit bucket was full of eyes. Prince Naseem just pouts and blows raspberries. Nowadays anyone that can get off their arse for long enough to be called a sportsman has got an easy ride. Modern steroids will virtually do the running for you. Steroids might give you heart problems but only being caught gets you barred. Which would you rather – train all day for a bronze, the runt of medals, or take a magic pill and end up paid thousands of pounds to say you owe it all to a nasty breakfast cereal?

But if you're a true blagger, money will mean nothing to you, because you'll never spend any. Instead you'll flirt with old people and make them pay for everything. Then you'll do a runner, to hang out with people of your own age whose sexual organs do not clunk around their torsos like carrier bags from the greengrocers.

POSH BLAGGERS: GRASS THEM UP

'I'm thoroughly sick of meeting people called Jez who sign on. There should be a rule that if you went to private school, you shouldn't be allowed to get the dole. That would halve the money going out.'
Sara

PISSTAKING: A MISSION

'We were on a mission to find the most dangerous place to do it. I've done it in most nightclubs and bars. In a bubble car. We ended up doing charlie off a railway line. Rather silly. The best way to take coke is off a record player – rack it out on the deck in a circle and press play. You don't even have to move your head.'
Perv

PISSTAKING: THE LONGEST SESSION WE EVER WENT ON

DAVE:
'Our local pub was our base for all the madness. The landlord was one of those who done what he was told; he let you do tooting and all sorts. No one went in there except those who knew what to expect: strangers would walk in, take one look at what was going on and walk straight out again. We used to get brasses we knew in and hold "board meetings" in the back room. These ordinary women came in once and found me stripping on the table. I held a pint glass out and said to them, "You ain't seen nothing like this and I don't even want no money for it."

'I did a week on the session in there. We only went out to go to a house music night at the local country club. The session finally ended on a Monday with the landlord having to put me to bed. "This is my own bed," he said, "and I'm letting you sleep in it." He was a really nice old feller. And when I woke up, I've properly parnied the bed right through. I was soaked right through to my jacket; it looked like someone had thrown a bucket of water over me in the night.

'Then what happened was some people came by when the pub was closed, tried to knock him up, and when they found no one in they broke in and helped themselves to the taps. That was the final straw: the landlord was only the licensee and the brewery took the pub off him and knocked it down. We felt a bit bad about that.'

ACID HOUSE POLITICOS
In the eighties, political protest meant wearing a T-shirt saying 'Frankie Says Relax'. In 1998 you dig a thirty-foot tunnel.

Techno has its own alternative army. House changed the face of counter culture, scooping up thousands of disenchanted rock fans, because it had more energy, more sense of community, and much, much better drugs. In the Middle Ages, these techno warriors/travellers/crusties would have been the ragged wood tribe that dropped from the trees onto the wicked baron and stole his testicles. Today, looking pretty much the same, they are environmental warriors, part of an army of direct action groups ready to descend in a flurry of dreadlocks wherever an evil bypass threatens to deflower a verge. The result of the techno warrior movement was front page headlines like 'Animal Is Right'.

Call them dole scroungers if you like, but most travellers live in poverty conditions, huddled in damp squats or on the road in windy old buses. This does not apply to Upper Crusties, who live in damp squats during the week and enormous mansions in Berkshire at the weekends and deserve every excellent insult *Boy's Own* ever threw at them, being worthless 'soap dodgers' and 'dog-on-a-string' types.

When real techno loons aren't up a tree, under the ground, or more likely having the chick peas kicked out of them by police and DoT mercenaries, they are putting on the only really underground parties left.

FOREWARNED IS FOREARMED: HOW THE POLICE DETECT LOCATION OF RAVES
The classified ads in the *Sunday Telegraph*
The side of cereal packets
Patterns in the traffic
The shape of raindrops on a window
The colour of the officers' faeces
Reading the guts of a fat man

'I taught my cat to dance to techno'
Steve Friend

RECLAIM THE STREETS

To you, it's a motorway, to them it's a dancefloor – it's 1989 all over again. Direct action group Reclaim The Streets regularly attract thousands to their 'dance against the car' rallies, blocking the road by *dancing* in it. Surely the nineties version of putting a flower down the barrel of a gun.

'Lots of smelly people in Trafalgar Square waving their arms about. The one in Hyde Park was surreal, because on one side people were dancing peacefully to a sound system, really blissed out, and on the other was a full-scale riot. People would stop dancing for a bit, go and chuck a few things at the police and then go back and have a dance. Some of the dancers were unrecruitable because they were too E'd up. Then there were the ciderheads, in their element...'
Ozman

LIFESTYLE

JUST GIVE US THE DRUGS

'It was Christmas and me and all my staff were dressed as Santa Claus. I wanted to buy a couple of grammes but my dealer wouldn't come to the club, so I jumped in a cab in my Santa suit and went round to his. But his two little kids answered the door – "Dad! Dad! It's Father Christmas!" – and I ended up stuck at his house with two kids on my lap for ages explaining how I *tried* to get down the chimney but I had to ring the doorbell.'
Anon, promoter

THE STRANGEST FLAT I EVER WENT BACK TO: THE SNAKE MAN

'At the peak of my drugs madness, I decided to go back with this bloke I didn't know from Adam and his mates, leaving my friend behind all by herself in this warehouse. I look back and I think I was mad. He lived in this crusty council flat, and at seven o'clock the next day I was sitting in his front room surrounded by poisonous snakes. He had one that was green with red eyes and he was wrapping it round his face. We were lying on the sofa with snakes up my legs. I went to have a bath and all he had to wash with was Fairy Liquid. It tells you a lot about the times that we ended up getting engaged after a week.'
Janet

I WAS THE WORLD'S WORST DRUG DEALER PT. 1
Ginger Steve And Tall Chris From London

'Ginger Steve went into partnership with Mick and they were hopeless. The day everyone remembers is both of them are standing in the hall, E'd up senseless with their mouths touching their ears. And all we can hear is "But Steve – we've sold two hundred Es, we've got three left, and we're four hundred quid down." "Yeah but Mick – you had the pills!" "Yeah but Steve – you had the money!"

'And they were literally gurning away and fighting each other. How Ginger Steve got into it was, this big blonde shaggy traveller geezer comes up to him in the club and says, "Here - look at these Es. You can have as many as you want for a tenner, you can sell them for twenties." Steve sold a hundred Es that night. Steve had never earned any money in his life, and he there he was with a grand from a night's work.

'Suddenly Steve went into the designer mode, giving me twenty pound notes and saying, "Here you go, Chris, treat yourself." He's walking round like he's the king of the pub saying, "Who wants Es?" Finally I saw him outside the pub with white tracksuit bottoms, white trainers, white polo shirt, long ginger hair – he turned into a Marbella gangster overnight. He was spending bundles of money, then it all started to go backwards and he started to owe proper horrible people money. Steve's knocked this guy, that guy, anyone that could be knocked he'd knocked. People were pulling up in Mercs saying, "Have you seen Ginger Steve? Tell him when you see him, he's going to get this [cutting throat]."

'One Monday night, these blokes from Notting Hill came round Ginger Steve's house to buy a load of E, and said, "Show us them." So Ginger Steve showed them his bag and they punched him, knocked him out and took his Es. Later that night he went to Spectrum and there were the blokes, E'd off their heads on his Es – and they come running up to him, hugging him and saying, "Oh, mate, we're sorry, we didn't want to do that...'''

I WAS THE WORLD'S WORST DRUG DEALER PT. 2
Stuart From Portsmouth

'I really don't know how I ever made any money. People would give you a fiver, say it was a twenty and you give them ten quid, a pill and tell them you loved them. On my worst night, I had forty Es and was so desperate to get rid of them I went down to some party in Brighton with my friend. But they didn't tell me their car had no tax, no insurance and no front numberplate, and that they were really bad at driving – all the way there they kept bumping the kerb.

'When we got to Brighton there was a police roadblock diverting all the cars straight to the police station. By this time I was so paranoid, I jumped out the car and ran round the block, but my friend drove so slowly the convoy just left her behind. I eventually got to the party and didn't manage to sell one pill, they hadn't been out my pants once. The car was towed and I paid for the train back so I'd even lost money. On the train I was convinced everyone was plain clothes, I nearly threw the Es out the window. When we got to Victoria Station I just sprinted off the train and ran all the way to Hyde Park, and hid behind a tree for three hours.'

'Acid house was plebs on acid. It was a first person thing. People say acid house made everyone talk to each other, but they weren't talking to you, they were talking at you. It was just heavily sedated soulboys. You didn't care about people any more than you cared about the people you met on your summer holiday in Bournemouth.'
Philip Sallon

VERY NAUGHTICAL LANGUAGE WITH ANTON LE PIRATE

'The whole language was about how silly can we make it and still be understood. It was amazing how quickly phrases would spread. "All right mateys! All aboard for the skylark!" We had this gentlemanly thing going. You'd be rolling around an illegal warehouse party in a total state, mashed, going, "I find this gear absolutely pukka! What a tippy tip top buzz!" Everybody had a term of endearment. The scene allowed free expression. The days of being confined by being Steve Jones were gone. You could be Mad Stevie Jones! My biggest problem was that for about the first three years I called everyone matey so I never learnt anyone's name.'

'Anton the Pirate – didn't he end up in prison? Oh no, hang on, that was Roger the Dodger.'
Tall Chris

I WAS THE WORLD'S WORST DRUG DEALER PT. 3
An Anonymous Journalist And His Bag Of 38 Es

'There was a party at Linford Film Studios and we bought an ounce of MDMA powder to sell. We had to cap it up really last minute and the only capsules we could find were vitamin B12 in a late-night chemist. Vitamin B12 stinks. It was a bit like being covered in Marmite. It was disgusting – for days we stank. I capped up 250 and sold most of them but I had 38 left at the end of the night – that's where the trouble started. That period I was living with a balearic pop star and I'm sure he noticed the smell of marmite, but I think he was more concerned that in the brief snatches of sleep I'd been having I'd wake up and rush into their bedroom and babble on to him and his wife about this parallel universe I'd discovered, where everyone we knew lived with biomechanical wings and had the freedom to fly and communicate by telepathy. I had the bag of capsules with me all week, taking them every day and still going to work at the [PAPER]. One afternoon I'd already had three or four Es and I thought the editor was giving [STAFF MEMBER] a hard time. So I went up to him and said, "I resign."'

MY DAY WITH HIM AND HIS BAG OF ES
Another Journalist Writes:

'I bumped into him at work when the bag of 38 Es was down to twenty.

'"I resign," he'd declared, adding "You cunt," as an explanation, and began the long symbolic walk to the door – but then went back to his desk because he'd forgotten to finish his article. An E later, he'd finished the piece and I walked him out of the building to make sure he didn't fall down a lift shaft and went for what was supposed to be a quick drink. "Have an E!" He chirped, generously. "No!" I said, for probably the first time in three years. My very anti-drugs, anti-scene boyfriend was due round later and the old hamster face didn't seem like a good idea.

'We took the bag of nineteen Es to a horrible office pub full of suits where in front of all of them, he got out the bag out and tried to wrestle one into my gob. No one batted an eyelid. He asked me to walk him to Euston Square station, and there at the exit was the dodgiest looking man ever – I hadn't twigged he was meeting a dealer. The dealer looked like a proper football hardcase, a ginger skinhead with ginger stubble. My friend popped another E and mentioned that he hadn't actually got any money to buy the drugs yet, so while he was on the payphone calling everyone he knows to see if they'd lend him £800, right away, and bring it to Euston, I ended up trying to make soothing smalltalk to this ginger psycho. I swear to God I said, "Brown's a nice colour for a floor." By now the bag of E was down to seventeen, had a hole in it and was leaving a faint trail of MDMA up the street because my friend was swinging it as he walked. It was a very fine moment. My boyfriend was due any minute. You've got to go, I said, but the bag of Es came out. "Have an E!" He cautioned. I refused and he said, "It's OK, I'll hide," and lay down on the carpet, where an idea struck him: "Have an E!" he suggested. My boyfriend arrived to find my friend curled up in the foetal position in the middle of the landing – "hiding".'

HE WAS THE WORLD'S WORST DRUG DEALER:
Pete

'I last saw Pete lining up Es on the stage at Shoom because he could no longer see to count them so he had to do it by touch.'
Anon

FASHION

FASHION: JESUS BOOTS AND BLUE HAIR – WHAT DOES IT ALL MEAN?

Call the police! Paul Oakenfold has dyed his hair blue and Keith out The Prodigy is the new Morrissey. The nation's campuses are shimmering with navel rings and pink highlights. Who said this was allowed?

In the old days if you were alternative you had to wear an overcoat and black jeans like a cross between a child molester and an ant. Now its perfectly possible to dress like a pinwheel and sulk at the same time. New indie is a bird of paradise compared to the days before acid. Even young William Straw, Kula Shaker fan that he is, broke out the Crazy Colour.

CALVIN KLEIN BOXER SHORTS HOLD IT ALL IN

'Everyone got more and more paranoid. One bloke told me the secret of Calvin Kleins – they've got a pocket underneath which you could only get to from behind, and if you were smart you could get about fifty Es in there. I bought no clothes that year but I did get about ten pairs of Calvin Kleins. I said, "A secret pocket?" And he got really angry with me for saying it out loud because "then it would get out" and the police would know.'
Naz

I AM A TREE FROG

Fat soled shoes

I AM AL GORE

Tommy Hilfiger

I AM GANGRENOUS

Yukky coloured nail varnish

DRUGS

'Nowadays it's fucking hard work finding friends who don't do gear when you want some time out.'
Anon, promoter

REVOLTING DRUGS: SNOWBALLS
Latvia: exports include local wine, Vodka and, apparently, snowballs. Nicholas Saunders was told the following by Dr King of the forensic laboratory at Aldermaston. A particularly strong brand of 'ecstasy' known as Snowballs and actually containing very strong pure MDA was available in the early 1980s. It came from a government laboratory in Latvia. Latvia needed Western currency and, taking advantage of its non-existent drug laws, teamed up with a German businessman and for a couple of years produced MDA for export as ecstasy. It all ended at Frankfurt airport when a consignment of ten million tablets was found by the authorities.

WHAT ARE *YOU?* WEIRD PILLS
'We had these pre-med pills – they were so horrible we used to call them Jacob's Ladder after the film about the bloke that's been experimented on. Ten, nine, eight, seven and you're on the floor. I was in a corridor talking to my mate and he suddenly says, "Fuck me, Ann!" and puts both arms out like Jesus and slides down the wall. Another of our friends broke into the car of a woman he didn't know and fell asleep on the back seat. Another of our friends went to visit his seventy-year-old Nan and she said, "Oh, I've been so worried about you!" and he had no idea why. She told him he'd gone round her house the week before and lain on the couch for two days with her nursing him and he didn't remember at all.'
Ann

1996 – despite a huge media campaign, *sensible ways of dealing with recreational drug use* start to emerge.
More outdoor events helped prevent overheating
Spray Men appeared, safety chaps with water canisters on their backs spraying people trapped at the front
Practical advice for dealing with people having a bad time emerged, finally promoting a culture where they are not ignored, even if they are hard work

The tabloids still pursued *Not sensible ways of dealing with recreational drug use*
Non-Satanists take drugs too. Scare tactics are still being used, despite the fact that everytime a drug doesn't leave you dead/blind/sexually molested/divorced/violently insane, your faith in this anti-drugs lobby diminishes

IT TOOK EIGHT YEARS FOR THE AUTHORITIES TO COME UP WITH THIS
1. Don't get too hot
2. Drink water, but not too much water
3. Drink salty stuff too

To which could be added,

4. Wait a couple of hours and see what happens to everyone else
5. Don't take drugs in a room full of wankers

MUSIC

WHO GETS TO BE LED ZEP? THE NEW STADIUM DANCE BANDS

'But it's all done on computers,' people thought. 'What are they going to do in front of an audience?' Well, Aerosmith could come on stage, put on a CD and leave, but invariably when the record-buying public are curious to see what the band look like. The rather large success of The Prodigy, The Chemical Brothers, Orbital, Underworld and Leftfield proved that playing music in front of an audience doesn't make it 'Kumbaya' round the campfire. What's more, dance musicians becoming accepted as stadium stars has brought hope to the boss-ugly everywhere.

Even at the height of E, when in theory everyone was equal, people still found DJs to worship. As Patrick Lilley succinctly puts it, 'When the lights in clubs started pointing at the DJ, that was the end. I was tempted to take DJs' names off my flyers to make a point ... But I didn't. Most DJs have no friends, they can't even get anyone to go in the car with them. Who wants to hear another story about how great they are?'

In 1989 Steve Hall wrote a very funny article in *Boy's Own* about not giving up your day job over house. Since then he gave up his day job to become boss of Junior Boy's Own, the label that gave us the Chemical Brothers and Underworld.

'I was one of the people that were staunchly against it. The mere thought of a PA was enough to send me into nightmares. We never had any at our parties. Never! We thought the DJ would take over, that live bands were finished. I can't remember when it started turning that way. We just thought you were in a band or a shit PA. When *dubnobasswithmyheadman* came out, I didn't take that much notice of the response from the inkies. You thought "*NME* – Fuck 'em. What do they know?" It was one of the first dance albums to be accepted by the *NME*.'
Steve Hall

EVENTS

TRIBAL GATHERING • ATOMIC JAM, QUE CLUB, BIRMINGHAM • BUGGED OUT, SANKEYS SOAP, MANCHESTER • RETURN TO THE SOURCE, THE FRIDGE, LONDON • MANUMISSION, PRIVILEGE, IBIZA • LOGICAL PROGRESSION, THE MINISTRY, LONDON • MALIBU STACEY, HANOVER GRAND, LONDON • REPUBLICA, BAKERS, BIRMINGHAM • GATECRASHER, ADELPHI, SHEFFIELD • LUSH, PORTRUSH • METALHEADZ, LEISURE LOUNGE & BLUE NOTE, LONDON • STEALTH, BLUE NOTE, LONDON RHUMBA CLUB, ICE FACTORY, PERTH • SCREAM, THE WAREHOUSE, PLYMOUTH • CREAM, NATION, LIVERPOOL • THE GALLERY, TURNMILLS, LONDON • THE END, LONDON • BIG KAHUNA BURGER, SMITHFIELDS, LONDON • THE LOFT, HQS, LONDON • MEGADOG, VARIOUS, NATIONWIDE LOVE TO BE, MUSIC FACTORY, LONDON

THE MARDI GRAS E
'At the 1996 Mardi Gras (gay and lesbian) parade in Australia, a giant ecstasy tablet is carried through the streets.'
Nicholas Saunders

1996 House/Techno/Garage/Toss

Tori Amos 'Professional Widow'
Underworld 'Born Slippy'
Way Out West 'The Gift'
Lisa Marie Experience 'Keep On Jumping'
CJ Bolland 'Sugar Is Sweeter'
Kadoc 'Night Train'
Chicane 'Offshore'
Faze Action 'In The Trees'
BBE 'Seven Days And One Week'
Blueboy 'Remember Me'
Boris D'lugosch 'Keep Pushin'
Ian Pooley 'Chord Memory'
Robert Miles 'Children'
Stretch & Vern 'I'm Alive'
I Cube Disco 'Cubism'
L'Homme Qui Valait Trois Milliards 'Foxy Lady'
Kelou IV 'What A Sensation'
Faithless 'Insomnia'
Funky Green Dogs 'Fired Up'
Total Eclipse 'Violent Relaxation'

Drum'n'Bass/Breakbeat/Big Beat/Hip Hop

Fugees 'Killing Me Softly (Remix)'
DJ Zinc 'Super Sharp Shooter'
Unknown 'Or Not (Remix)'
Busta Rhymes 'Woo Hah (Got You All In Check)'
Adam F 'Metropolis'
The Prodigy 'Firestarter'
Chemical Brothers 'Setting Sun'
DJ Trace 'Mutant Revisited'
Goldie 'Inner City Life (Remixes)'
David Holmes 'My Mate Paul'
Crystal Method 'Keep Hope Alive'
Jeru The Damaja 'Ya Playin' Yaself'
Squarepusher 'Squarepusher Theme'
Ed Rush 'Kilimanjaro'
Ruffage Crew 'T3'
Roni Size 'Share The Fall'
Jonny L '2 Of Us'
Arcon 2 'Liquid Earth'
Dead Calm 'State Of Grace'
Aphrodite & Mickey Finn 'Bud Ass'

JANUARY

London's Camden Council becomes the first council to stipulate that any club seeking to renew its licence must guarantee free water behind the bar. One club is reported as saying this is a 'stupid idea'.

His research complete, Brian Harvey out of East 17 decides to announce his discovery to the world.

FEBRUARY

Michael Jackson has a little boy and isn't prosecuted.

Sophie Dahl becomes the world's first giant supermodel.

MARCH

39 members of a Californian cult commit Hale-Bopp related suicide.

Channel Five brings boredom to hundreds.

Fat rapper Biggie Smalls is murdered.

APRIL

Boy George wins a libel case brought by his former lover Kirk Brandon who opens his prosecution with the immortal line, 'So, Mister O'Dowd, we meet again.'

MAY

It's a Labour landslide in the General Election – 419 seats to the Tories' 165. Michael Portillo losing is the funniest TV for years.

The ravosaurus that is Kraftwerk plays Tribal Gathering.

JUNE

Camilla Parker-Bowles flees the scene of car crash in case it is a kidnap attempt. Yeah, right.

Jeremy Beadle has to beg ambulancemen to take him to hospital because they think it's a prank.

The Hacienda closes.

JULY

A man is found with the face of Simon Mayo. He asks doctors to remove his head so he can lead a normal life.

AUGUST

A surgeon who refused to treat a girl because she had taken ecstasy is told they acted correctly.

Diana Princess of Wales and her lover Dodi Fayed are killed in a car crash in Paris.

ten per cent of sheep are gay.

SEPTEMBER

Scotland votes for devolution. Wales votes narrowly for devolution

Two million people attend Princess Diana's funeral. At a cost to the taxpayer of £50 million a year, the Queen now learns to smile for it.

OCTOBER

Pocket lasers on football pitches and in clubs – temporarily blinding visuals.

NOVEMBER

Louise Woodward's murder charge is reduced to manslaughter as village idiots sing Louise Is Coming Home to tune of *Three Lions*.

DECEMBER

Michael Hutchence hangs himself.

The Prodigy tell Chris Evans to fuck off at awards ceremony.

1997: I'VE BEEN INTO DRUM'N'BASS FOR YEARS

The drugs don't work　　　　　　*The drugs don't work*
I'm going to kill that dealer　　　*Better take some more then*

The drugs don't work
But I know I'll pull that face again

Andrew Currie, Rocky, Phil Perry and Otis with classic T shirts

Fiona Crawford 10 years later

HOW THE ACID GENERATION HAVE TAKEN OVER

By 1997 Chumbawamba were at number one singing about pissing the night away, Mrs Merton announced that everyone backstage at an awards was looking for Charlie and record companies' Christmas party were serviced by portaloos with built-in cameras at snorting level. The fabric of society had collapsed.

You knew the real significance of acid house when the Conservative Party, whilst declaring it a national disgrace, changing the law and spending millions stamping it out, approached its musicians on the sly to do the theme to a Party Political Broadcast.

Liverpool University credited Cream – a nightclub! – for its record number of applications. The Ministry of Sound – a nightclub! – produced a very good cinema advert urging young people to register to vote – just because they felt like it.

There is an argument that this grass-roots upsurgence had more significance than the sixties, by weight of numbers: if the sixties was a party had by some-one else, acid house and the culture that came out of it was a party had by everyone you ever knew that lasted till your brain was smeared up the wall. Whatever else it achieved, at least acid made the style generation irrelevant: petulant, lonely little Tony Parsons, in his time employed by the *NME*, the *Mirror* and the concept of mysogyny; preposterous Sloaney boy Peter York; pointless Magenta De Vine. The decade of looking good and feeling lonely was over.

BRITAIN'S MOST ROMANTIC COUPLE

WINNERS: SUE AND PAT

Britain's most romantic couple - during acid house

How they met

'He came round at Christmas and I was so off it I'd forgotten to cook a turkey. He saved me.'
Sue

Their first date

'We went to Ibiza and by the end of the holiday, we tried to get married there, but you had to have been on the island three weeks, and we'd only booked a two-week break.'
Pat

'His clothes had holes from spliff burns, so I threw them down the rubbish chute. Then I realised he didn't have any other clothes.'
Sue

'We didn't leave our hotel room for a week, so even though we were in Ibiza all we had was beer and spliff. It was like house never happened.'
Pat

Britain's most romantic couple - eight years later and still loved up

LIFESTYLE

HAIRY MOTORWAY MOMENTS
When the man who's driving turns round with the accelerator pedal in this hand.

NOW WE ARE OLDER: ECOLOGICAL FUNERALS FOR THE LOVE GENERATION
1. The cardboard coffin. Unsuitable for those that met a violent end. In such cases Friends of the Earth sell the Funeral Pipe, below.
2. Funeral pipe – conveys your remains from the hearse straight into the grave. Washable.
3. The only truly green funeral is to rub yourself with cat food and lie down in an alley.

THE COVERED IN POO STORY
'We were staying in a villa in Ibiza and we'd all taken acid. One of us went to the loo and disappeared for eight hours. Finally we went upstairs and found him on the bed. He's lying there stiff out like a board with his hands out by his sides. We said, "Are you coming down?" He said, "I can't." We said, "Come on, don't be silly." He says, *[SMALL VOICE]* "I can't. I'm covered in poo..." The loo downstairs had no light and was called the black hole of Calcutta. He'd gone in there for a shit, tripping, and convinced himself he's covered himself in poo and lain there for eight hours too embarassed to come down.'
Phil Perry

THE 'HAISMAN GOES FISHING' STORY
The famous acid house chant 'Aciieeed' was started by the young blade Gary Haisman at Future and Spectrum. Music producer Dancing Danny D heard Gary and got together with him to record the extremely light-hearted anthem 'We Call it Acieed', the one that got the word banned from *Top Of The Pops*. In other words, he started it.

'Gary said "I'm getting out of this," so he took up the relaxing sport of fishing. He drove into this country lane, sporting his fishing hat, and drives straight into a convoy of cars. The country lane is jam-packed with ravers all dancing on their bonnets and shouting "Acceeeiiid!"'
Dave Little

WHAT HAPPENS WHEN IRVINE WELSH MEETS HOWARD MARKS
'I bumped into Howard Marks – he said, "Want a bite of this?" and gave me a lump of dope the size of a hand grenade. I went into the toilets and chewed a piece off. That was the beginning of a session that lasted three days.'
Irvine Welsh

NO HAND LUGGAGE
'I lost my friends in the middle of some fields on the way back from a party. I had to get on the back of a farmer's truck, and it only took me as far as Gatwick. But I took advantage and cruised the arrivals lounge. I have a penchant for internationals arrivals.'
Patrick Lilley

FASHION

DESIGNER: THE SEQUEL

Essex girls used to wear white stillettoes. Now they wear Gucci white stillettoes. The first wave of designer was modern: Gaultier, John Richmond, Comme des Garcons – designer-worship rather than fashion houses. Now the second designer wave is straight-down-the-line bourgeois: Gucci, Prada, Hermes – clubbers dress like old rich women. In legend, Parisian girls starve to buy a two hundred pound Givenchy belt. In the suburbs, blokes are driving Audis and Saabs, while living with their mum.

I AM A FRUIT & VEG MAN

Fleeces, fleeces everywhere

I AM THE WIFE OF A GERMAN ORTHODONTIST

Gucci, Prada, Hermes

I AM A GOTH

Bonkers eyeliner. Keith out The Prodigy – right; Nadia Auermann - wrong

I AM THE MILK TRAY MAN

– only a girl. Black polo neck, tight dark jeans, navy body warmer

AAARGGH!

Contact lens with smiley faces

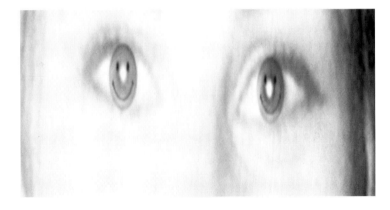

Bill Clinton spoke out against fashion making junkies look cool. Fashion magazines furiously denied this, although no word from *i-D*, who'd run that dinky spread called *Coming Down*.

DRUGS

CAKE – CHRIS MORRIS AND *BRASS EYE*

Comedy performer Chris Morris organised a hoax that perfectly illustrated the shallowness of moral outrage. He invented a fake drug and made it the most ridiculous thing imaginable – a vast pill the size of a Fray Bentos pie. He had a ludicrous yellow pill made and took it to various celebrities, who greatly relished the opportunity to join a bandwagon. They missed clues like being told people were making cake in kitchens, so blinded were they by lust for smugness. Finally he took it to an MP, whose eyes visibly lit up as he asked Chris if someone had already raised the question of cake in the House, gleeful at the thought of making himself a star with a whole new subject to moralise about.

DRUGS: NO DRUGS AT ALL

'Before ecstasy, it was like, there I wasn't, then there I was.'
Anon

'Afterwards everything seemed so dull. Everyone felt let down – that was the chemical as much as the scene. Your thinking changes. You do think differently. It takes a while for your thought processes to go back to normal.'
Kym Kennedy

Consensus seems to say that it takes a long time for your body to 'rebalance' to a life with no drugs. One thing that did last was using your brain like you were still on E: trying to 'protect the buzz', being careful not to get paranoid, and then remembering you weren't on bloody drugs at all.

'I know someone that had colonic irrigation about two years after she stopped doing Es. She said it churned up all the sediment of the Es in her colon and she was off her head for three days.'
Ella

'I remember when I braved half a trip for the first time. I was dancing and getting into it, and this person I was with kept hopping around claiming to be the Peekaboo Bunny. He did it on purpose, because he knew what would happen – since then I still get those black bunny rabbits and black cats, just slipping out of sight. I was working for a really straight American company and I used to be reading my e-mail and see the Peekaboo bunnies. It used to make me chuckle. If only they knew...'
Raver, Hertfordshire

'I was going out with someone ten years older than me, and one time round my flat he made some sarcastic remark about me taking a lot of acid. I said I wasn't, there were people taking two or three trips a night, and I was only taking one at the most. He said, "Well, you seem to take it every weekend," and when he put it like that it seemed true, so I stopped. Although not because I was personally worried about the acid but because I was eighteen and he was my first boyfriend and I was really in awe of him. Then one day about two months later I was on the bus going to college and it suddenly struck me – the other people on the bus didn't have funny faces any more.'
Anon

'I don't take them because I'm older now and everyone's more self-conscious. I don't want to be the centre of attention anymore and I'm worried what they might think. In the old days everyone was the centre of attention.'
Nicky Trax

'I don't take drugs any more because I've got a bloody house now, haven't I?'
Anon

DRUGS

NICHOLAS SAUNDERS' TEN DRUG MYTHS:

1. That You Can Get The Same Effect From Herbal Ecstasy

Herbal ecstasy does not cause serotonin and dopamine release. This is where the emotional effect of ecstasy comes from. Some brands contain Ephedra, (a plant from which the drug Ephedrine is extracted) which may actually be more dangerous than MDMA. Saunders points out that poisoned darts are tipped with natural herbal extracts.

2. That MDMA Causes Loss Of Spinal Fluid

Might have come from research carried out on ecstasy users where samples of spinal fluid were removed for analysis.

3. That Ecstasy Use Leads To Parkinson's Disease

Investigated and dismissed in 1986: scientists found that a different street drug had caused symptoms similar to those of Parkinson's Disease.

4. That Tablets And Capsules Sold As Ecstasy Often Contain Heroin, Crushed Glass And Rat Poison

In 1993 an article claimed this was the case but no supporting evidence was offered and The National Poisons Unit was not aware of any recent cases of poisoning by crushed glass or rat poison. The same magazine stated three years later that heroin in ecstasy was an 'urban myth' (Medicated Followers of Fashion by M. Collin, p13, 13 November 1996). Heroin has not been found in ANY analysed samples of ecstasy. Saunders says the most convincing argument is economic. Heroin is a more expensive drug so it would not make sense to sell it as ecstasy.

5. If You Have A Bad Experience It Must Be Due To Poor Quality E

Saunders says: 'Although users nearly always blame the quality of the drug, bad experiences can also occur with pure ecstasy.' He does say that bad reactions are rare and that a more common problem is resisting the effect of the drug which can lead to headaches and nausea.

6. The Way In Which The Media Deals With Drug Issues Reflects The Real Level Of Risk

100,000 people die each year out of 12,000,000 smokers, i.e. 8,300 per million

25,000 people die each year out of 40 million alcohol drinkers, i.e. 625 per million

120 people die each year out of 500,000 solvent sniffers, i.e. 240 per million

Seven people die each year out of 1,000,000 ecstasy users, i.e. 7 per million (Saunders 1997, p139)

It could be argued that these figures simply reflect a higher level of use of other substances. Therefore, to calculate the actual risk, one would need to take the number of times ecstasy is consumed and divide it by the number of deaths. Not easy.

7. Es Just Aren't As Good As They Used To Be

Saunders says: '… the average quality of ecstasy has improved in Britain over the years.' But that's if you get it at all: 'The chance of getting pure MDMA in

Britain or Holland is about two out of three, and the chance of getting a pill containing a similar type of drug (MDA or MDEA) is about three out of four.'

(i) Tolerance – a first dose of MDMA produces more open and loving feelings. This reduces with each subsequent experience and the feeling becomes more speedy. Although taking a break of several weeks may bring the effect back to normal, it's unlikely to be the same as your first time (although this might be due to familiarity with the effect).

(ii) Your state of mind – Saunders says this applies less with MDMA than with other drugs such as LSD, but is still important.

(iii) Expectations – people tend to get what they expect, i.e. the placebo effect.

However, the quality of ecstasy did drop at one time:

'Since ecstasy first arrived in Britain, the quality has varied widely. At first it was almost entirely pure MDMA, but as it became more popular the quality declined, reaching a low ebb in the winter of 1992. Since then quality has generally improved, with a higher proportion of pills containing MDMA, and average doses ten per cent higher.'

8. LSD Might Be Contaminated With Strychnine (Rat Poison) Or Other Drugs
Part of folk wisdom for ages, people blamed it for neck aches when tripping. Saunders says: 'The very low dose of LSD used (a thousand trips contain less drug than a single E) has the result that purity can be pretty well guaranteed simply because active amounts of other drugs would not fit on a blotter. Psychological dangers do exist, but medically it is harmless.'

9. The Experience On Acid Depends On The Type Used – A Windowpane Will Give A Different Effect To A Microdot
This is not the case, Saunders says: 'It is a myth that different varieties of acid having different effects.'

10. Those Blue Ones, They Were The Best: Speckled Ecstasy Pills Contain Several Active Ingredients
A speckled effect is produced to convey this impression but is actually achieved by mixing different colours of filler.

All of the above taken from: Saunders, N. (1997) *Ecstasy Reconsidered*, self published, London.

EVENTS
CLUBS:
TWICE AS NICE, COLOSSEUM, LONDON • WIGGLE, VARIOUS, LONDON • BIG BEAT BOUTIQUE, CONCORDE, BRIGHTON • CREAM, NATION, LIVERPOOL • BUGGED OUT, SANKEY'S SOAP, MANCHESTER SUNDISSENTIAL, PULSE, BIRMINGHAM • GATECRASHER, REPUBLIC, SHEFFIELD • ATOMIC JAM, QUE CLUB, BIRMINGHAM • FRUIT CLUB, BRUNEL ROOMS, SWINDON • HARD TIMES, NATION, LEEDS • SUB CLUB, SUB CLUB, GLASGOW • CAMOUFLAGE, COMPLEX, LONDON • PROGRESS, THE ECLIPSE, DERBY THE GALLERY, TURNMILLS, LONDON • OUTER LIMITS, RIVALS, BOURNEMOUTH • THE POD, THE POD, DUBLIN • RISE, THE LEADMILL, SHEFFIELD • DTPM, THE END, LONDON • THE ORBIT, AFTER DARK, MORLEY • SCARAMANGA, VARIOUS, LONDON

MUSIC

SPEED GARAGE: CLASS!

'Exclusive, classiest, no caps, quality, Pure Silk, luxurious' – speed garage clubs sound like an escort service. You expect the next words to be Unhurried Service and Genuine New In Town.

Turn on a radio, and the stuff on the dial between *Woman's Hour* and Simon Mayo is what the young people are calling Speed Garage.

'Party into the new year in London's most exclusive and luxurious venue. Adults only! Elaborate decor. Champagne bar. Glamorous dress code: Suits & Designer.'
And what is this Babylonian palace? Crystal Palace Football Club.

'So? We work all week! We want to dress up! That's what the whole underground garage scene is about. So you can tell it's a weekend!
TImmi Magic

Champagne, cocaine, Suits and Designer... it sounds rather uptight, but...

'People think we're really quite straight, but we stayed out for days on end! I am an acid housarian! Even speed garage and jungle is classed as acid house to me. Before acid house it was all about going out to drink and meet the opposite sex. I even used to go out on my own. I had the shiny ball, the luminous toothpicks, those fly glasses where you can see nine people out the side – the whole outfit, everything that you needed...'
Timmi Magic

You can take the man out of the acid house, but you'll never take the acid house out of the man.

MERRY PRANKSTER 97

Wry fellow Jeremy Deller put together a project that earned him exclusive rights to the word whimsy: *Acid Brass,* a compilation of house classics perfectly orchestrated for a brass band. Neither 'Strings of Life', 'Voodoo Ray' nor even 'What Time Is Love?' were safe. In 1997 Jeremy took the whole brass band on tour, playing everywhere from Glastonbury to *This Morning* with Richard And Judy: it was an intensely silly but strangely effective performance. The inside sleeve features a photo of the disconcerted audience, no less than twelve of whom are scratching their chins.

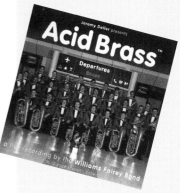

CALENDAR

1999 Whitbread launch their new alcopop, Drug. Sold in tablet form, under the slogan *Do You Swallow?* it doesn't actually contain any alcohol but is described as 'a blend of hops and stuff, look, don't hold us to this one'

2000 Sharing – water bottlers invent new highly-contagious disease to stamp out this unprofitable trend. Trials with green coldsores in the Mersey region go largely unnoticed

2005 Archbishop of Canterbury consecrates garages to officially replace churches as focus of community
2006 Prozac manufacturers buy France as a holiday home

2007 A senile Margaret Thatcher is put on display in a glass class for the amusement of the nation

2010 Years of unrestrictive footwear sees bunions and corns become extinct. Footbinding returns as feet mutate into circular flippers.

2015 *News At Ten* local news dropped, replaced by *Vibe Zone sponsored by Two Dogs,* featuring all the latest local muggings and house fires over live mixing by a hairy old man.

2030 The last woman who can still remember how to assemble Wonderbras dies at age of 102. Good.

2040 Brian Eno, who still can't believe his luck, finally dies laughing

2049 Palace announce that due to backlog of royalty, Prince William will never become king

2052 A mosquito that bit Nicky Holloway is found trapped in amber: his DNA is used for Juracid house revival

2055 Senile Margaret Thatcher finds old nuclear button briefcase and destroys the world

2060 Hacienda re-opens on the moon. Clubbers complain there's no atmosphere

Chapter Nine

1998: THEY CALLED IT ACCEEEEIID

Following decriminalisation, the match of drugs and advertising agencies is an explosive love affair waiting to happen. They are rumoured to have already had a few secret trysts.

The Marijuana Cowboy

The wind blowing through his goatee, THE MARIJUANA COWBOY herds cattle across the rugged landscape on his trusty BMX, although he never actually gets anywhere because he keeps stopping for a smoke…

Here in Marijuana country, we use only the freshest, youngest marijuana leaves...

THE DRUGS DON'T WORK? TAKE THEM TO OFFHEAD THE DRUG OMBUDSMAN

Acid Lite

The Acid You Can Take All Day Without Ruining Your Career!

TV HITS, Bumper Xmas New Year edition 2002
Cindy Beale on Why She Looks So Rough:
'It's the coke,' she sighs, 'I just can't knock it on the head.'

I MAY HUG MY FRIENDS OCCASIONALLY: THE ACID HOUSE LEGACY

Perhaps the deepest changes from acid house are its trickle-down social effects. Previously, if you hugged someone, it gave them a basic claim to marriage or a punch in the face. Simple behaviour changes like sharing water, checking strangers are OK and feeling safe to smile are par for the course. And everybody has a chance to let go and dance, washing away years of conditioning.

WAS IT ALL WORTH IT?

'Before acid house, clubland was spiritually void. It was a whole new feeling, a massive release. It was like a train - get on board, come with us. It gave a lot of people a chance, people who'd been on the scrapheap, signing on for years. It opened doors. People started their own independent record labels, shops, making their own music; sharing the positive energy. A lot of the people who started out then are doing very well now, running their own companies among other things and having success in other areas of their careers ... What we achieved completely changed the face of youth culture in this country. I played a major role in its change, and I'm proud of that.'
Danny Rampling, DJ

'Not in obvious ways, but then I may be a nostalgic old fool. Certainly no one thinks twice about wearing a tracksuit and trainers all the time. Maybe it's made some people a bit younger at heart: I'm a parent but I still feel people turned into big kids overnight. I still don't feel like ninety five per cent of the parents at the kids' school – God! They look like mums!'
Former raver, Hertfordshire

'Did acid house empower us? Oh yes. It opened up your consciousness to the possibility of your own potential ... It was like an explosion of energy – it squashed some people, but other people harnessed it and did really well out of it. The bad side of it was the drugs. Most of the people who have made it are the people who were able to stand back and say, "Hang on a sec..." You've got to be careful. I have to say that ecstasy changed my life, it opened me up, but I did too much and I suffered a lot for a while, ups and downs, depression and so on. If you wanted me to wind back the clock, I'd do it all again. It was a catalyst.'
Leigh Marling, Blue Source

LIFESTYLE

'[FAMOUS DJ] went to get a record out of this cupboard under the stairs where he kept his records and got too paranoid to come back out, so he climbed in the cupboard and stayed there. The gas man arrived and we let him in and he had to climb over these bodies and when he looked in the cupboard there was [FAMOUS DJ], curled up looking at him.'

EXTRACT FROM INCONTINENT BEATS – FIONA BOWKER
Imagine a time when me and my elderly friends
We'll be intent on embarrassing our own grandchildren
As we practise our own form of 'Old Time Dancing'
Pretending, we're on the stage, at the Hacienda, again.

You'll come crashing in on your artificial limb
With your 88 remix of Mel & Kim
Holding it aloft and declaring that 'Everything
Went downhill after Tribal Gathering.'

By half past two we'll be chilling out
She'll have the rusty 'Rovers' biscuit tin out
And the geriatric silence will be broken be senile shouts
As we pour over photos of us lot at Bugged Out!

And when we are dead and six feet under
Our families will find our address books and wonder
'Who're all these people with Blackburn phone numbers?'
Well don't fucking ask us, 'cos we can't remember.

Fiona Bowker has supported Murray Lachlan Young and is much better.

Rocky before acid house

Rocky during acid house

FASHION

FASHION PHOTOSPREADS OF THE PAST TEN YEARS
10. Walking The Novelty Dog
Big in women's mags, along with…

9. Me, My Boyfriend And Our Chunky Sweaters
Sod off the four of you.

8. Looking Stern For Charity
So you'd rather go naked than wear fur. I'm *so* scared.

7. A Baby! Can We Keep Him?
Christy Turlington gets dewy-eyed over this strange person-thing she's found on a beach.

6. Still No Sign Of Land, We'll Have To Drink Our Own Piss
Broad on the bridge of a boat.

5. Caught By The Papparrazi Not Being Gay
Charmingly natural shots of models with men. Cindy and Richard, Claudia and David Copperfield, George and Lynne.

4. Standing In Front Of Some Poor People
Linda and some ugly old women. It's ironic or something. See also, Standing In Front Of Some Soldiers – Sam Fox without the morale boosters.

3. Bad Sandals Girl Gets Lost With Mr No-Maps
Tarantino white trash outlaws – yawn – in the best desert they could afford. Probably Bournemouth.

2. Oh My Quirky Purchases!
More real-life fun against the background of a contemporary supermarket. Model shares a joke with some cereal.

1. Whoops! Lost My Kit In The Sea Again
Kate Moss for *The Face*, Kate Moss for Obsession, Kate Moss for her butch games mistress on a school journey...

FASHION SPREADS THEY'VE YET TO USE
On A Drip
Chemical Spill
Consenting Adults: Stapling My Knob To A Poodle

FASHION PREDICTIONS FOR YEAR 3000:
1. being pretty
2. combat trousers
3. T-shirts so fashionable they change designer while you're wearing them

DJ John Kelly - National Hero

Aisle Gazing. The first ten minutes of a shopping trip, spent trying to remember what you came to the shop for.

Soul Searching. Having remembered what it was, realised you don't fancy that anymore, trying to think what on earth you *do* want.

Checkout Dumping. Surreptitiously trying to offload this pile of stupid crap you seem to have acquired before the cashier rings it up.

Bollocks! Realisation, as you leave the shop with two tins of pineapple chunks, of what you *really* came out for.

DRUGS

NON-DANCE USES OF ECSTASY

Saunders described various non-dance uses ranging from creative activities such as painting or poetry, problem solving, treating addiction to other substances, making friends and taking a 'mini-vacation'.

THE MINI ECSTASY VACATION – GOING AWAY FOR THE WEEKEND JUST TO TAKE E

A voyage to a favourite holiday destination of old, with a cerebral wash'n'blow dry into the bargain. Ideal solution to the problem of having a proper job and/or responsibilities of a sudden. Pharmaceutical awaydays for the former raver.

CRAZY NEW DRUGS: DMT

Heaven only knows what's in this stuff. DMT fans recommend you don't do it more than once a year and you have to get exactly the right dose or it doesn't work. Apparently it's a crap, instant coffee version of psychedelic drugs: you put some crystal in a pipe and smoke it. On the third puff 'lightning bolts shoot through the sides of your eyes and you crash into a vortex. You fly through this black space incredibly fast, staggered by the speed. Then you're usually met by a goddess who takes you by the hand and leads you on a journey.' Other figures of mystical authority are also reported, including mermaids, aliens and woodnymphs. If you are the unlucky type, expect your maths teacher to take you back to school for double fractions. It's all over in fifteen minutes when you come to and carry on with the washing up.

Two young men in Shepherds Bush tried it; one of them was taken off by aliens. As he was on the last stages of his drug express, he shouted, 'No, not South Kensington! Shepherds Bush!' convinced they weren't going to take him all the way home.

IF YOU KNOW ANYONE WHO HAS AN E THAT THEY HID AWAY IN 1988

According to Alexander Shulgin, the beardy king of pills, 'If MDMA had been hidden away in the pyramids by the Pharaohs of ancient Egypt, it would still be active today.' LSD, on the other hand, will decompose in warmth, light and air. This book is impregnated with acid – by now, you will be off your head.

MUSIC

A RETROSPECTIVE OF DANCES – FROM PICKING APPLES TO GATHERING THE HAY

1. HELP! FIRE! *(also Washing the Windows)*
Emergency! Which service do we require? Why, fire! Where's the fire? It's over here. It's over there. Fuck me, the whole place has gone up.

2. PICKING APPLES
Hands up, farmer's boys and girls. Reach for that first apple. Look – there's another one. And another, shinier than the first. Where have all these apples come from? Quickly, wrest them from the bough, before the wasps come!

3. GATHERING THE HAY
The first, the classic, the dance that set us all free – raise your hands in the air, reach out and wrap them round that hay. Embrace the grain crops of all nations. Reap the bounty of nature to a four four beat.

4. THE HITCH HIKER
Thumbs out, in, out, in, out, whoops, now my feet are going. Now my head's wobbling too. A lift, quickly. Where am I going? Er... I've forgotten.

5. FRYING PAN
One hand on hip, the other tossing a pancake that only you can see. Not cool. Looks particularly silly on a podium.

6. TALES OF THE UNEXPECTED
They have no shirt, whoever they are; their front it glistens for all to see. Their legs are spread and they vogue, vogue, vogue. Do ya think I'm sexy? Do you want an answer?

7. I – CAN'T – GET – THIS – CHEWING GUM – OFF – MY – FINGERS!
Spotted by Phil Perry all around the South West. Usually a big fella with one tooth and something very disconcerting happening to his fingers. Do not offer to help – he won't know what you are. If he's still there after the club closes Phil will get him a cab home.

8. THE BALEARIC SHUFFLE
Stamp a Patrick Cox to the left, stamp a Patrick Cox to the right, head down and flick that proud mane back for all to admire. Bamboleo. Jibaro. Jojoba. Football violence is a thing of the past. He's going to step on you again. If he wants his lights punched out.

9. RAVE 'TILL YOU COLLAPSE AND DIE
DJ Skin Condition is on the decks, MC Death is on the mic, you're on drugs – let's go – let's go – let's go – MENTAL! Dance any way you like. In the land of rave there are no rules. Try not to swallow your lightstick.

10. HAPPY HARDCORE HOP
You want to be a hippie and you want to get stoned? No you don't, you want to bounce around for eight hours like the Duracell bunny, grinning like a lunatic because you are the only remaining dance sub-cult that gets away with it.

OUTSIDER: THE RAPIST ROBOT
The slightly unacceptable dance. When the Doris hogged the dancefloor, Big Joe of Surrey knew what do. Raise those curious fingers to nipple level and twirl away. You'll be labelled a pervert 'But,' as Joe always used to say, 'it clears a space though, dunnit?'

REGIONAL VARIATIONS
1. THE MOST EXCELLENT DANCE
Shake your head, swing your hair, punch the air.

2. RIDING A HORSE
Put one arm in front of you and one arm on your hip and move backwards and forwards, while bending your knees like you were riding a horse. A bit reggae-ish.

3. ACID, MAN
'Your hands would be like those men who hold flags when a plane comes in to land, but you would have your fingers spread out wide. You didn't move much, you just criss-crossed your hands in front of your face.'
Mandy Molyneux

THE GEORDIE HOP

A huge sideways leap, like Monty Python's Northerners
'I used to do the Geordie Hop with Michael Clark [the famous modern dancer]. I bumped into him when he'd got back from Paris meeting Rudolph Nureyev before he died, and he said, "Do you know what I did? I taught him the Geordie Hop."'
Dave Little

AFTERWORD: ARE YOU ON ONE DADDY?

Yes. Now get me some Evian and go back to your homework.

ACKNOWLEDGEMENTS

Were you there? Are you still there? If you've got a story, photo, adventure or favourite memory, write to –

Jane Bussmann
P.O. Box 16 801
London W9 3SZ

Photography:
Olivia &
David Swindells: Pages 7, 10, 20, 21, 22 (colour) Large pics on pages 24 & 25, 39 (sunrise) 41 (haybales), 53, 60, 79 (large pic) 142

Design:
Andrew Savill

Contributors:
David Quantick, Rachel Condry, Kevin Sampson, Helen Walsh, Barney Greenway, Mick Robinson, Gaynor Higginson

Interviews:
Jane Bussmann, Joanne Wain, Emma Warren, Nigel Fox, Helen Walsh, John Bussmann

Additional Graphics:
Tommy Bussmann & Guy Wingate

Charts:
Rob Wood with help from Update

Acknowledgements:
Cat Ledger, Guy Wingate, Dave Angel, Anne at Button, 808 State, Ali, Wayne Anthony, Arden, James Baillie, Nicky Bailley, Andrew Barker, Jeff Barrett, Jack Barron, Ashley Beedle, Simone Beedle, John Berry, Bradley, Brandon Block, Richard Bloor, Roy Boulter, Emma Buckley, Chris Butler, Fiona Cartledge, Mandy Cavanagh, Charlie Chester, Tall Chris, Rachel Condry, Russell Coultart, Carl Cox, Fiona Crawford, Andrew Currie, Diesel, DiY, Louise Dono, Karon Dunn, Eastern Bloc, Sara Ellis, E-Mix, Terry Farley, The Farm, Andy Fife, Flowered Up, Steve Friend, Nigel Fox, Trevor Fung, Derek Furnival, Ian Gittins, Hannah Gove, Steve Hall, Dave Haslam, Nicky Holloway, David Holmes, Peter Hooton, John Hopkins, Jayne Houghton, Colin Hudd, Chris Jam, Janet, Jo, Kym Kennedy, Dave Little, Steve, John Kelly, Timmi Magic, Jon Marsh, Kris Needs, Vanessa Parker, Lance and Richard, Lu Vukovic, Patrick Lilley, Luvdup, Simon Macara, Gary Maclarnan, Ben McKnight, Leigh Marling, Steve Mayes, Orde Meikle, Mandy Molyneux, Paul Oakenfold, George O'Dowd, Olivia, Ozman, Alex P, Anton Le Pirate, Martyn Passey, Phil Perry, Des Penny, Louise Rainey, Raja Ram, Danny Rampling, Richard at TIP, Justin Robertson, Mick Robinson, Rocky, Ian Pendleton, Ian St Paul, Philip Sallon, Jarvis Sandy, Kevin Sampson, Sasha, Eileen Schembri, Shanti, Wayne Shires, Amy Simmons, Gerald Simpson, Andrew Spurgeon, David Swindells, Tank, Heather Thatcher, Dale Thompson, Nicky Trax, MC Tunes, Lu Vucovic, Wade, Gemma Walker, Johnny Walker, Sam Whittaker, Brian 'Brains' Wilson, Yatra.

Dedicated to David Quantick, the funniest man in the world, and Nicholas Saunders